The New ICT Ecosystem

The ICT sector is crucial as a driver of economic and social growth. Not only is it an important industry in its own right, it also provides the information and communication infrastructure without which modern economies could not function. How does this sector work? Why is it stronger in some countries than in others? What should companies, governments and regulators be doing to enhance its contribution? In *The New ICT Ecosystem*, Martin Fransman answers these and other questions by developing the idea of the ICT sector as an evolving ecosystem. He shows that some components of the ICT ecosystem, particularly the innovation process, work better in some countries and regions (e.g. the USA) than in others (e.g. Europe and the developing world). This enables policy-makers and regulators to understand why some parts of the ICT ecosystem are underperforming and what can be done to enhance their performance.

MARTIN FRANSMAN is Professor of Economics and Founder-Director of the Institute for Japanese–European Technology Studies in the School of Economics at the University of Edinburgh. He has published widely in the fields of innovation and competitiveness. His books include *Global Broadband Battles: Why the US and Europe Lag While Asia Leads* (2006), *Telecoms in the Internet Age: From Boom to Bust to . . . ?* (2002), *Visions of Innovation: The Firm and Japan* (1999), *Japan's Computer and Communications Industry: The Evolution of Industrial Giants and Global Competitiveness* (1995) and *The Market and Beyond: Information Technology in Japan* (1990).

The New ICT Ecosystem

Implications for Policy and Regulation

MARTIN FRANSMAN

CAMBRIDGE
UNIVERSITY PRESS

CAMBRIDGE
UNIVERSITY PRESS

University Printing House, Cambridge CB2 8BS, United Kingdom

One Liberty Plaza, 20th Floor, New York, NY 10006, USA

477 Williamstown Road, Port Melbourne, VIC 3207, Australia

314-321, 3rd Floor, Plot 3, Splendor Forum, Jasola District Centre, New Delhi - 110025, India

103 Penang Road, #05-06/07, Visioncrest Commercial, Singapore 238467

Cambridge University Press is part of the University of Cambridge.

It furthers the University's mission by disseminating knowledge in the pursuit of education, learning and research at the highest international levels of excellence.

www.cambridge.org
Information on this title: www.cambridge.org/9780521191319

First published 2010

A catalogue record for this publication is available from the British Library

Library of Congress Cataloging in Publication data
Fransman, Martin.
The new ICT ecosystem : implications for policy and regulation / Martin Fransman.
   p. cm.
  ISBN 978-0-521-19131-9 (hardback) – ISBN 978-0-521-17120-5 (pbk.)
  1. Information technology. 2. Communication–Technological innovations.
3. Internet. I. Title.
  T58.5.F73 2010
  004–dc22

                   2009048588

ISBN 978-0-521-19131-9 Hardback
ISBN 978-0-521-17120-5 Paperback

Contents

Exhibits

Preface

The importance of the ICT ecosystem*

Contribution of the ICT sector

The ICT (information and communications technologies) sector plays a crucial role in the modern economy and society. The ICT sector includes computer hardware and software, telecommunications, consumer electronics, and Internet-based contents, applications and services.

From a long-run historical perspective, it is clusters of new technologies that have driven economic and social growth and change. New technologies drive growth and change by creating new opportunities for consumption and investment. The ICT cluster of technologies emerged around the time of the Second World War and since then they have been the most important driver of global economic and social growth and change. Earlier clusters were based on textile machinery in the late 1700s, the steam engine (including railways and steam ships) in the early 1800s; electricity and steel in the late 1800s; and the internal combustion engine, oil and petrochemicals in the early 1900s.

In most industrialised countries the ICT sector is one of the largest in the economy, accounting for around 10 per cent of GDP. However, its contribution to economic growth is even more important than this. According to the OECD up to some 20 per cent of all economic growth is attributable to the ICT sector. The same source reports that about one-third of all business research and development (R&D) is done by the sector (Fransman 2009).

Significantly, the ICT sector provides one of the most important and ubiquitous infrastructures of the modern economy and society,

* This section draws on the author's paper for the OECD's Innovation Strategy (Fransman 2009).

the infrastructure that facilitates information processing and storage and communications. Together with electricity and transportation networks the ICT sector provides the infrastructural basis on which all human activity depends.

The role of the ICT sector in the global crisis of 2007 –

The ICT sector has a key role to play in dealing with the global crisis of 2007 – This crisis has two components. The first is the *global downturn in economic activity*, the proximate cause of which was the global financial crisis sparked off by the sub-prime crisis. The second is the *global environmental crisis* caused by global warming. The ICT sector will be important in dealing with both of these.

The ICT sector will contribute to the reversal of the global downturn in two related ways. The first is by creating the innovations – both incremental and radical – that motivate and incentivise consumption and investment. It is consumption and investment that are the most important components of gross domestic product (GDP). By incentivising consumption and investment, ICT innovations complement Keynesian countercyclical policies. The second is through creating an improved ICT infrastructure that will stimulate the economic and social activities that depend on it. An example is high-speed fixed and mobile communications networks and the improved computing facilities that facilitate related economic activity. It is this same ICT infrastructure that will contribute to the global environmental crisis by making possible more environmentally efficient ways of working that will help to reduce global warming.

However, in order to play this constructive role the ICT sector will need to both *innovate* and *invest*. Innovation and its related investment must, therefore, be the central objective of the players who make up this sector and benefit from its output – corporate players, private consumer-users, government policy-makers and regulators.

But this raises three key questions:

- What do we mean by the ICT sector and how does it work?
- How does innovation happen in the ICT sector?
- What should be done by government policy-makers and regulators?

It is these three questions that are analysed in this book.

Ecosystems thinking

Catastrophic collapse versus reasonable performance

The contrast between the performance of two sectors of the economy in the global crisis of 2007 has been remarkable. While the financial services sector catastrophically collapsed, the ICT sector on the whole performed well. Clearly, very different things have been happening in these two sectors, but how should these differences be explained? More specifically, how should we think about the dynamics of sectors?[1]

The ecosystem metaphor and the creation of knowledge

Marshall and Darwin

Change has long been on the agenda of economics, although not all economists have gone as far as the nineteenth-century Cambridge economist, Alfred Marshall, who insisted that economics be 'concerned throughout with the forces that cause movement' and the corollary that 'its keynote [must be] that of dynamics, rather than statics'.[2]

How should we think of the forces that cause movement in the socio-economy? Marshall had little hesitation in answering this question. 'The Mecca of the economist', he said, 'lies in economic biology... the central idea of economics . . . must be that of living force and movement.'[3] However, while this was Marshall's meaning, he was forced to compromise when it came to choosing his method. The reason, Marshall reluctantly accepted, was that 'biological conceptions are more complex than those of mechanics'. He therefore decided to accept that 'a volume on Foundations [of economics] must therefore give a relatively large place to mechanical analogies; and frequent use is made of the term "equilibrium", which suggests something of [a] statical analogy'. The question is whether this method corrupted Marshall's meaning.

---

[1] This book provides a detailed analysis of the dynamics of the ICT ecosystem. Although reference is made in various places to the financial services ecosystem it is not discussed in detail here. However, the general conceptualisation here of sectoral ecosystems is relevant for all sectors, including the financial services sector. For a similar approach to the financial services ecosystem to that taken here to the ICT ecosystem, see Lo, (2004: 15–29).

[2] This statement comes in the preface to the 8th edition of Marshall's *Principles of Economics* originally published in 1890 (1962: xiii).

[3] *Ibid.*: xii–xiii.

For Darwin, change was evolutionary, and the force behind evolutionary change was the interaction between the generation of variety and selection from that variety. Darwin's understanding of variety was considerably enriched by the subsequent development of genetics, including the understanding of mutation. Populations of organisms, or species, interacting in a natural environment constituted Darwin's evolving ecosystem. This Darwinian conception, we now know, has yielded rich insights in the natural sciences.

But is the ecosystem metaphor helpful in understanding the forces that cause movement in the socio-economy? Certainly, the idea of interacting organisms in a constant process of change is more appealing than that of a mechanical system settling into equilibrium, if the aim is to understand living force and movement. But before deciding whether or not to employ the ecosystem metaphor, some basic questions must be answered. The first of these is: What are the 'organisms' that are interacting in a socio-economic ecosystem?

The interacting organisms in the socio-economic ecosystem

The first set of organisms in the socio-economy consists of *firms*. But 'the firm' is a strange organism in that it is made up of other organisms, namely people. Nevertheless, we tend to think of a firm as a single organism, internally united in its goal under a single hierarchical chain of command. However, for some purposes this abstraction is inappropriate. 'Firms' seldom have one view of the world, since different leaders of the firm may have different understandings. Furthermore, there is a fragmentation of knowledge within the firm as a result of the intra-firm division of labour (which co-evolves with the inter-firm division of labour). It cannot be assumed that all those within the firm are fully dedicated to achieving its stated purposes, raising issues of *motivation* and *incentive* as well as the *forms of organisation* that might facilitate them. Nevertheless, for most social scientists the firm remains a necessary analytical unit of analysis since it is a key locus of ownership, decision-making, resource allocation and innovation – knowledge creation.

However, firms have to be disaggregated if their interactions are to be understood. Two disaggregations in particular are important:

- The first disaggregation is into *competing firms*. Firms compete not only in product markets but also in factor markets. Competitive rivalry is one form of inter-firm interaction. (In the Darwinian schema, the metaphorical parallel is the struggle for survival between species, Darwin drawing on Thomas Malthus' *An Essay on the Principle of Population* (1798) in his elaboration of this theme.)

- But also important, and interacting with competitive rivalry, are cooperative symbiotic interactions between *interdependent firms*. The word 'symbiosis' comes from the Greek meaning living together. Firms always live with other firms and the effectiveness with which they do so is an important determinant of their ability to survive and thrive in the socio-economic ecosystem. On this basis, two primary symbiotic relationships may be identified – namely that between a firm and its suppliers and a firm and its partners. A third relationship is between a firm and its competitors. Although at one level not a collaborative relationship, at another level firms often learn from and imitate their competitors, benefiting from the rivalry relationship. However, from the perspective of the firm which loses its ability to appropriate returns from its knowledge, the flow of knowledge to competitors appears as an externality, a spill-over from which it is unable to reap a reward.

There is another crucial set of symbiotically interacting organisms that needs to be added to the ecosystem picture. These are *final* consumer-users. They must be distinguished from *intermediate* consumer-users – firms that use the output of other firms (such as a producing firm that uses equipment made by a supplying firm). Both final and intermediate consumer-users interact symbiotically with their suppliers, acquiring knowledge through using the products and services they have bought and, in various ways, feeding this knowledge back to the suppliers. They constitute the fourth primary symbiotic relationship.

One group of supplying firms is particularly important – the financial firms that provide their customers with financial services. They are also part of a distinct sectoral ecosystem, the financial services ecosystem (the catastrophic failure of which since 2007 is teaching us more about how this ecosystem has worked in the past, and what happens when it fails). However, this is not the place for further discussion of the financial services ecosystem.

Symbiotic interactions and the creation of knowledge
While the first basic question asked in employing the ecosystem metaphor dealt with the organisms of the ecosystem, the second relates to

the nature of the *interactions* between the organisms. The key point
here is that these interactions are processes that are continually
ongoing, forever changing as learning, exploring and adapting take
place through the symbiotic interactions. The interactions are the
antithesis of static states of affairs where the parties involved in the
interactions have optimised their objectives and have settled into a
state of equilibrium. It is in understanding these dynamically changing
interactions that the wisdom of Marshall's insistence that we compre-
hend 'living force and movement', rather than stationary mechanical
states, becomes apparent.

So far, we have ignored one key dimension of the symbiotic interactions, a dimension that produces the most important 'forces that
cause movement'. This is the generation of *new knowledge* through
the symbiotic interactions between knowledge creators and users.
It is the creation of new knowledge that puts the final nail into the
coffin of the static mechanical analogy, rendering it inadequate as a
framework to explain change.

Not all symbiotic interactions involve the creation of knowledge.
An example is the interaction between the supplier of an unchanging
machine and the firm that uses it. The ongoing interaction – involving
initial supply, maintenance and repair – may be crucial for both firms.
And it is possible that little new knowledge is created in the process.
However, as has long been apparent, the symbiotic interactions between
the users and producers of machinery frequently result in the creation
of new knowledge. In some cases the users have also been the producers
of machinery.

Writing in 1776 at the start of the first industrial revolution Adam
Smith observed that 'A great part of the machines made use of in those
manufactures in which labour is most subdivided, were originally the
inventions of common workmen, who, being each of them employed
in some very simple operation, naturally turned their thoughts towards finding out easier and readier methods of performing it'
(1910: 9). Smith went on to note that 'All the improvements in
machinery, however, have by no means been the inventions of those
who had occasion to use the machines. Many improvements have
been made by the ingenuity of the makers of the machines, when to
make them became the business of a peculiar trade' (1910: 9). He could
have added that the specialist makers of machinery do not improve
their machinery in a vacuum. Rather, their efforts are spurred by the

feedback they get from the users of their machinery (that may include users within their own firm) through *their* symbiotic interactions.

Symbiotic interactions between the creators and users of knowledge provide the interacting parties with the knowledge and information on the basis of which further knowledge is created (by both parties). It is this knowledge that injects novelty into the ecosystem, (in the words of Joseph Schumpeter) creating the new and destroying the old. It is this creation of new knowledge that, to return to Marshall, is the main force that causes movement in the socio-economic ecosystem. In particular, as Schumpeter emphasised, it is new innovation-knowledge – that is, new knowledge embodied in new products and services, new processes and technologies, new forms of organisation and new markets – that challenges the status quo, forcing learning and adaptation on the interacting organisms in the ecosystem and making capitalism the restless system that it is.

But it is also with the creation of new knowledge that the biological conceptualisation of an ecosystem reaches its limits insofar as its applicability to the socio-economic realm is concerned. The reason is that it is the human mind – more specifically, *interacting* human minds – that is the most important cause of movement in the socio-economic ecosystem. Although new knowledge is created within the *context* of evolving symbiotic interactions, knowledge creation does not happen automatically or costlessly. Furthermore, it may not happen at all. Context does not determine in a predictable way the content of new knowledge, but by determining the conditions under which human minds may create new knowledge, context may influence content.

Ultimately it is the creative leap of the human mind – as new associations, inferences and connections are made – that constitutes a rupture from the past and causes movement in the socio-economic ecosystem. But this creative leap does not have a counterpart in the biological or physical worlds. It cannot be equated with the mutations and chaotic non-linear interactions that drive change in the natural world, even though there may be some similarities in their systemic consequences. The human act of creation is not a mutation but a regular part of the functioning of the human mind.

Other components of the socio-economic ecosystem
The ecosystem comprises more than symbiotically cooperating and competing firms and final consumer-users. Crucially, these players are

embedded in institutions. Institutions have been defined by Nobel Laureate Douglass North as the 'rules of the game'. One example, important for our later discussion, is the regulations that determine what firms can and cannot do. The legal framework defined by legal institutions is another example (including the laws of property and contract and intellectual property rights (IPRs)). A *de facto* rule of the game is the macroeconomic conditions under which players interact, including the availability of finance, and interest and exchange rates. These conditions affect interactions within the sectoral ecosystem as a whole (although direct interactions between firms and the other financial firms that provide them with financial services are treated here as an example of the symbiotic relationship between firms and their suppliers).

Other non-firm organisations also play an important role in the ecosystem. These include universities that provide research and skilled person-power and perhaps entrepreneurs. Firms may develop a symbiotic relationship with universities. However, the interface between firm and university may be quite different from that between firms as a result of the different ways of organising the production of knowledge in these two kinds of organisation. Government research institutes (such as those embedded in hospitals) and standards-setting bodies are two other examples of institutions that may also have an influence on the workings of the ecosystem.

Finally, government policy-makers may also have an important impact in many ways that will not be elaborated upon here. (Both regulation and government policy are considered in more detail in connection with the ICT ecosystem in chapters 5 and 6 of this book.)

Platforms, architectures and networks

Symbiotic interactions may also be shaped by *platforms*, and in recent years a rich stream of literature has emerged exploring the implications of this development.[4] Gawer (2009) defines a platform as 'a building block, which can be a product, a technology, or a service, that acts as a foundation upon which other firms can develop complementary products, technologies, or services.'[5] In an earlier

---

[4] For a recent contribution see Gawer (2009).
[5] *Ibid.*: 3–4.

work Gawer and Cusumano (2006) refer to 'the modern high-tech platform – an evolving system made of interdependent pieces that can each be innovated upon.'[6]

Platforms – defined here as systems that support complementary economic activity – vary greatly in terms of complexity and the level of the ecosystem at which they exist. For example, the Internet – a complex system of systems – serves as a platform at the sectoral level of the ICT ecosystem. The Internet as a platform has facilitated the rise of the Internet content and applications providers (ICAPs) who now comprise an important group of players in layer 3 of the ICT ecosystem (the content and applications layer, as shown in chapter 3 of this book). These companies include Google, Yahoo!, eBay, Amazon, Skype and Facebook.[7]

But the Internet is not only a network of networks; it is also a platform of platforms. For instance, the personal computer (PC) and smart mobile phone are platforms within the Internet platform. But platforms exist at even more disaggregated levels. Some writers have analysed platforms at the level of PC operating systems (e.g. the Linux open source operating system or Windows)[8] and microprocessors (e.g. Intel microprocessors).[9]

Platforms shape symbiotic interactions. Apple's iPhone may be taken as an illustration. The iPhone depends on the platform provided by the mobile communications network without which it would not work. But the iPhone itself serves as a platform for contents and applications. This architecture of interdependencies shapes the co-operative symbiotic relationships between four actors – the mobile network operator, Apple and its suppliers and partners, the independent creators of content and applications for the iPhone, and those who compete with the iPhone. This dynamic set of evolving symbiotic interactions is but one part of the broader set of interactions that constitutes the mobile communications industry.

---

[6] Gawer and Cusumano (2006: 2–3).

[7] Significantly, virtually all the globally dominant ICAPs are from the USA. The explanation of this fact lies at the sectoral rather than the firm level. See appendix 7 (p. 123) for an explanation of the success of the US ICAPs.

[8] See, for example, Eisenmann *et al.* (2008).

[9] Gawer and Cusumano (2006).

Globalisation and performance

Sectoral ecosystems have simultaneously both a global and a local existence. In any country the players of the ecosystem are embedded in *local* (national and/or regional) interactions with other players under the influence of local institutions. (Institutions are shaped by what North called *organisations* – consisting of groups of people with common objectives. Organisations include firms, political parties and trade unions. Organisations have the power to change institutions at the same time as they themselves are influenced by them. Institutions, therefore, are inherently political constructs and politics still largely occurs within the realm of the nation state, even though the actions of states may be influenced by global determinants.)

But many of the players also have an *international* ecosystem existence. Some players are globally dominant, with involvements in the sectoral ecosystems of many countries, and also involved in global trade and financial activities. Significantly, much of the knowledge created in national sectoral ecosystems will diffuse through many channels and in many different ways and influence other national systems. (All knowledge, however, is in the first instance created within a particular local context – that is, the place where its creators are – under a specific set of circumstances.)[10]

Important questions arise regarding the shifting positions of national sectoral ecosystems within the global ecosystem. These questions deal, for example, with the processes of catch-up or falling behind, as some national systems improve or deteriorate in terms of their relative performance. The dynamics of sectoral ecosystems are important in explaining these differential performances. (In the case of the ICT ecosystem the catch-up of East Asian countries – such as Japan, Korea, Taiwan and China, discussed in appendix 8 of this book – was a global system-changing event.)

A key problem lies in explaining inter-ecosystem performance differences. One example, discussed in appendix 7 of this book, is the Internet content and applications part of the ICT ecosystem. US companies dominate this part of the system globally – companies such as Google, Yahoo!, Amazon, eBay, Skype, Facebook and MySpace. Why is this the case? Why have European and Asian Internet

---

[10] For a detailed elaboration of this important point see Fransman (2009).

companies (Skype excepted) not featured in this space? Symbiotic ecosystem thinking is used in appendix 7 to provide an answer.

The new ICT ecosystem: implications for Europe

This book covers some of the same ground as the author's *The New ICT Ecosystem – Implications for Europe*, (Fransman 2007b) which was awarded the 2008–10 Joseph Schumpeter Prize. Although that book was written with a European audience in mind the analysis and supporting empirical evidence is relevant for all national ICT ecosystems, whether the ecosystem in question is in Britain, Brazil, or Botswana. Every country has an ICT ecosystem, although the players, their symbiotic interactions and the institutions in which they are embedded will be different. The task of national policy-makers and regulators in all countries is to understand how their ICT ecosystem works, its strengths and weaknesses, and what might be done to improve its contribution. The analytical and empirical tools provided in this book will help them in this task.

In a few places, the references to Europe in the earlier work have been removed in order to accentuate the generality of the argument. But for the most part the book addresses essentially the same questions.

A further comment is necessary regarding the division of the book into chapters and appendixes. The proportion of the book devoted to appendixes is unusual, but was intentional. The rationale was to make the argument of the book – pitched largely at corporate players, government policy-makers and regulators – succinct, leaving background material, evidence and supporting detail as far as possible to the appendixes. This does not mean that the appendixes are relatively unimportant: indeed, several of the commentators on the earlier book have stated that some of them contain important novel contributions. This applies in particular to appendix 7 (Why do US Internet companies dominate in layer 3?) and appendix 8 (How did East Asia (Japan, Korea, Taiwan and China) become so strong in layer 1?).

Abbreviations and acronyms

ADSL	asynchronous digital subscriber line
BCR	benefit-cost ratio
BIOS	basic input–output system
BT	British Telecom
capex	capital expenditure
CATV	cable modems
CDMA	code division multiple access
CEO	chief executive officer
CNC	computer numerically controlled
DB/km	decibels per kilometre
DRAMS	dynamic random access memories
DRM	digital rights management
DRPT	dominant regulatory paradigm in telecoms
DSL	digital subscriber line
DWDM	dense wave division multiplexing
ELM	ICT ecosystem layer model
EPZ	export processing zone (Taiwan)
Esprit	European Strategic Programme for R&D in Information Technology
FCC	Federal Communications Commission (USA)
FTSE	Financial Times–Stock Exchange (100 Share Index)
FTTP	optical fibre to the premises
GDP	gross domestic product
GSM	global system for mobile communication
IAP	Internet access provider
ICAP	Internet content and applications provider
ICT	information and communications
IP	intellectual property
IP	Internet Protocol (inter-network protocol)
IPO	initial public offering
IPR	intellectual property rights

IS	innovation system
ISDN	Integrated Services Digital Network
ISO	International Standards Organisation
ISP	Internet service provider
IT	information technology
ITU	International Telecommunications Union
JETRO	Japan External Trade Organisation
LAN	local area network
laser	Light Amplification by the Stimulated Emission of Radiation
LED	light-emitting diode
LLU	local loop unbundling
LRIC	long-run incremental cost
M&A	mergers and acquisitions
MIC	Ministry of Internal Affairs and Communications (ministry-regulator) (Japan)
MII	Ministry of Information Industry (China)
MITI	Ministry of International Trade and Industry (Japan)
MNC	multinational corporation
MPT	Ministry of Posts and Telecommunications (China)
MSN	Microsoft network
NGN	next-generation network
NIE	new ICT ecosystem
NIE–IS	new ICT ecosystem–innovation system
NMT	Nordic Mobile Telephony
NRA	National Regulatory Authority
OECD	Organisation for Economic Cooperation and Development
OEM	original equipment manufacture
ONP	open network provision
OSI	The Open System Interconnection Model
PAS	Personal Access System (China)
PC	personal computer
PHS	Personal Handy Phone System (China)
R&D	research and development
Race	R&D for Advanced Communications in Europe
ROE	return on equity
ROIC	return on capital invested

SEEP	Schumpeterian Evolutionary Economics Paradigm
SITC	standard industrial and trade classifications
SME	small and medium-sized enterprise
SMP	significant market power
SOE	state-owned enterprise
TCP/IP	Transmission Control Protocol/Internet Protocol (inter-network protocol)
TELRIC	Total Element Long-Run Incremental Costs
TSLRIC	Total Service Long-Run Incremental Cost
VoD	video-on-demand
VoIP	voice-over-IP
VSLI	very large-scale integrated circuit
WAP	Wireless Application Protocol
WCDMA	wideband code division multiple access
WiFi	Wireless Fidelity
WiMAX	Worldwide Interoperability for Microwave Access
WTO	World Trade Organisation
www	World Wide Web

Introduction

Telecoms and computers gave birth to the Internet, which transformed its parents, leading to what has been called *the new ICT ecosystem*. The new ecosystem is made up of equipment (computers, servers, routers, switches, phones, etc.) configured in networks and providing platforms which Internet providers use to deliver content and applications. It is a dynamic system which provides a key engine for economic and social development at both the global and national levels. However, the New ecosystem requires new ways of thinking and new modes of governance if the most is to be made of its potential.

The main argument of this present book is that at the heart of the new ecosystem is *innovation*. It is innovation that fuels the system as it transforms it. However, the innovation that occurs at national levels of the new ecosystem does not occur automatically. It cannot be assumed that the innovation process in this system will always work the way we want it to. Indeed, the comparative analysis of the new ecosystem in different countries reveals that some components of the system work better in some countries and regions than in others. This raises at a national level the policy dilemma of whether to try and catch up in an area where a country has fallen behind or to abandon it to the shifting sands of the international division of labour.

For example, in the early days of the mobile industry, mobile communications worked best in Scandinavia. Europe was able to utilise the learning process (including standards) that emerged in Scandinavia and this resulted in the global system for mobile communication (GSM) which in turn encouraged the global diffusion of mobile and in the process helped turn companies such as Nokia and Ericsson into the global success stories they have become.

However, in terms of Internet-based content and applications it is US companies such as Google, Yahoo!, eBay, Amazon and MySpace that dominate the world stage. In consumer electronics it has been Asian companies such as Samsung and Sony that have dominated, although the emergence of new products from the new ecosystem, such as the iPod and the iPhone, shows that success can rapidly shift to other parts of the global system. In optical fibre to the premises (FTTP), it is the Japanese who are way ahead.

These few but important examples have significant implications for thinking about policy and governance – more specifically, for a process of *re-thinking* in these areas. Indeed, it is the main aim of this book to contribute to this process of re-thinking. One key area in which re-thinking is required is *regulation*. The reason why re-thinking is needed in this area is that the conceptual framework within which regulation has evolved has omitted significant parts of the process of innovation. Since, as we have seen, innovation is at the heart of the new ecosystem, this state of affairs in the field of regulation is inadequate. A more appropriate conceptual framework is needed for both policy and governance purposes, one that puts innovation at the centre. This book suggests a way forward.

The book is structured in the following way. In chapter 1 a summary of the basic argument of the book is presented, including the major challenges facing Europe. Chapter 2 elaborates on the new ICT ecosystem, its various sub-sectors and how they are structured. Chapter 3 treats the new ICT ecosystem as an innovation system and asks how innovation can occur within such a system. In chapter 4 the contemporary ICT ecosystem is examined through a quantitative analysis. Chapter 5 examines the role of telecoms regulation in the new ICT ecosystem. Chapter 6 suggests how government policy-making might be formulated for the new ICT ecosystem and in chapter 7 the main conclusions of the book are presented, spelling out the message that is being sent to policy-makers. Finally, particularly for those who want more background on the ICT sector, ten appendixes provide further information.

1 | *Summary of the argument*

In this chapter, a brief summary is presented of the arguments put forward in this book. The chapter begins with a discussion of the eight key challenges facing countries in the ICT area. The conceptual framework used to analyse the ICT sector is then discussed, including the idea of this sector as an ecosystem, the layer model of the new ICT ecosystem and the key symbiotic relationships that exist among the four groups of players in the system. Finally, the role of innovation and investment and of telecommunications regulation is discussed.

The importance of the ICT sector

It is widely accepted that the ICT sector – which includes telecoms, IT, consumer electronics and Internet/media – is a key part of the economy of all countries. Not only is it an important industry in its own right (making a significant contribution to GDP, international trade and employment) but it also provides the crucial information and communications infrastructure without which economies and societies cannot function. In this book Europe is used as an example, although the argument applies, with suitable modification, to all countries.

The new ICT ecosystem

However, with the widespread global adoption of the Internet since around 1995, the ICT sector has been fundamentally transformed, so much so that it has been referred to as a *new ICT ecosystem*.[1] This raises three important questions:

---

[1] The conceptualisation of the new ICT ecosystem in a four-layer model (equipment, networks, services and content) comes from Didier Lombard, Chairman and CEO of France Télécom group.

Exhibit 1.1. *Eight key challenges facing the new ICT ecosystem in Europe*

Challenge

1 Remaining/becoming *internationally competitive producers or providers* in selected parts of the new ICT ecosystem
2 Being *internationally competitive users* in selected parts of the new ICT ecosystem
3 Ensuring that Europe has a *globally competitive communications infrastructure*
4 Overcoming the *ICT/Productivity gap* with the USA and Japan
5 Strengthening *basic and long-term research* in the new ICT ecosystem
6 Providing for the *needs of heterogeneous European countries* while furthering the European single market
7 Invigorating the *richness and diversity of European cultures*
8 Developing *appropriate conceptual tools* to understand and shape the evolving new ICT ecosystem

- What exactly does this system contain, i.e. what are its component parts?
- How does the system work and how effectively does it perform in the European context?
- What can be done – specifically in terms of policy and governance – to make the system in Europe perform better?

It soon will become apparent to anyone working in this area that there are crucial challenges confronting the new ICT ecosystem in Europe. These are discussed in the following sub-section.

Some of the challenges facing the new ICT ecosystem in Europe

The eight key challenges facing the new ICT ecosystem in Europe are shown in exhibit 1.1.

Challenge 1: remaining/becoming *internationally competitive producers or providers* in selected parts of the new ICT ecosystem
Europe needs to be clear about those parts of the new ICT ecosystem in which it wishes to remain or become internationally competitive.

Shifting international competitive advantage has meant that European competitiveness is threatened in some parts of the new ecosystem, particularly by the USA and in Asia by Japan, Korea, Taiwan and, increasingly, China. Specialisation and the international division of labour means that it is neither possible nor desirable to try and be involved and internationally competitive in all areas, the experience of Japan, Korea and now China shows that it is possible for countries to become competitive in areas in which they do not initially have a classical comparative advantage. However, this raises the difficult challenge for Europe to define those areas in which the region wants to remain or become internationally competitive and those areas which it is prepared to abandon to the shifting sands of international competitive advantage. Examples discussed in this book include high-speed telecommunications networks (e.g. optical fibre networks) and Internet content and applications.

Challenge 2: being *internationally competitive users* in selected parts of the new ICT ecosystem

In some parts of the new ICT ecosystem, it will be sufficient for Europe to be competitive users of the most globally efficient technologies without necessarily becoming producers. For example, it may not be necessary for the computers that European users (such as banks and households) use to be made in Europe. Users may be just as efficient as their counterparts in the most productive parts of the global economy by using imported computers. However, in some areas efficient use and efficient production may go together. The challenge is for Europe to choose those areas in which it is content to be only efficient users.

Challenge 3: ensuring that Europe has a *globally competitive communications infrastructure*

It is essential that Europe has a globally competitive communications infrastructure, which includes the Internet. The challenge is for Europe to ensure that its infrastructure at least keeps up with the best in the global economy. If this infrastructure falls behind it may threaten the international competitiveness of other sectors (e.g. financial services, manufacturing, etc.). This is at the same time a financial challenge in view of the high sunk cost of modernising the infrastructure (e.g. through the development of all-IP Next-Generation Networks or NGNs).

**Challenge 4: overcoming the *ICT/productivity gap*
with the USA and Japan**
There is substantial evidence to suggest that Europe has fallen behind
both the USA and Japan and that there is now an ICT/productivity gap
between Europe and these countries. This gap needs to be addressed if
European competitiveness is not to be adversely affected.

**Challenge 5: strengthening *basic and long-term research*
in the new ICT ecosystem**
Basic and long-term research in the new ICT ecosystem is important, for
at least two reasons. Before the liberalised era in telecoms a good deal
of basic and long-term research was done in the *central research
laboratories* of the monopolist telecoms network operators (such as
Bell Labs in AT&T, CNET in France Télécom and the Electrical
Communications Research Laboratories in NTT). Some of this
research generated substantial seeds that subsequently germinated to
fuel the growth of the entire ICT sector and contributed to its openness.

However, one of the fallouts from the liberalisation of telecoms was
that the resources devoted by the incumbent telecoms operators to
such research declined as a result of the competitive pressures faced by
these companies. Although telecoms equipment companies significantly increased their R&D in response to liberalisation, basic and
long-term research tended not to be a high priority. A strengthening of
basic and long-term research may boost the future prospects of the
new ICT ecosystem, in both Europe and elsewhere.

A second reason for the importance of basic and long-term research in
Europe is that it may help Europe to cope with the increasing pressures
emerging from *lower-cost countries* that are rapidly developing the more
sophisticated sectors of their economies, notably China and India. Countries such as the USA, Japan and Korea have come to the conclusion that
this kind of research must constitute an important part of their response
to this challenge. More generally, the challenge for Europe is not only to
finance and undertake more basic and long-term research but also to
ensure that it feeds productively into the *innovation process* which is
the main source of dynamic growth in the new ecosystem.

**Challenge 6: providing for the *needs of heterogeneous European
countries* while furthering the European single market**
It is obvious that the new ICT ecosystem is very different in
the different European countries. It is therefore not possible for

policy-makers to come up with one size for the new ecosystem that fits all: account must be taken of the heterogeneous needs of these countries. But this raises the question of the methodology that should be used in order to identify these needs, and devise ways of meeting them.

Challenge 7: invigorating the *richness and diversity of European cultures*

Europe's distinctive cultures are a source of social stability, pride and in some cases international competitiveness. Since the new ICT ecosystem includes the Internet and media, it plays an extremely important part in invigorating the richness and diversity of European cultures.

Challenge 8: developing *appropriate conceptual tools* to understand and shape the evolving new ICT ecosystem

The final challenge is conceptual and analytical. The identification of strengths, weaknesses and solutions for the new ecosystem in Europe requires appropriate conceptual and analytical frameworks. One of the initial assumptions motivating the present book is that a further challenge must be faced in honing the conceptual and analytical tools that we need for this purpose.

Some stylised facts

The challenges faced by Europe in the new ICT ecosystem can be concretised by the four stylised facts shown in exhibit 1.2. Each of these raises numerous complex policy-oriented questions. In order to deal

Exhibit 1.2. *Four stylised facts*

- Europe lags significantly behind the USA in Internet content and applications (c.f. Google, Yahoo!, eBay, Amazon, MySpace, YouTube, etc. are all US companies)[1]
- Europe lags significantly behind the USA and Asia in computers, semiconductors, and consumer electronics[2]
- Europe lags significantly behind Japan in areas of telecoms infrastructure such as FTTP[3]
- Europe lags significantly behind the USA and Japan in productivity[4]

Notes:
[1] See appendix 7 for a further discussion.
[2] This judgement is based on international market share data (not shown here).
[3] See chapter 6 for data.
[4] See, for example, Van Ark, Inklar and McGuckin (2002).

with these, we need an appropriate conceptualisation of what precisely the new ICT ecosystem is, what its components are and how it works.

The ICT sector as an ecosystem

It is suggested in this book that it is fruitful to understand the ICT sector as an *ecosystem*: an ecosystem refers to a number of organisms that interact within an environment. In this book, a relatively high level of aggregation has been chosen in order to analyse the ICT ecosystem as a whole.[2]

Four key groups of players can be identified:

- Networked element providers (who produce items such as PCs and their operating systems, mobile phones and telecommunications switches and transmissions systems)
- Network operators (who create and operate telecoms, cable TV and satellite networks)
- Content and applications providers
- Final consumers.

These players interact within their environment which is shaped by the institutions that define the 'rules of the game' and influence the players' behaviour. The institutions that are important in the new ICT ecosystem include financial institutions, regulators, competition authorities, standardisation bodies and universities. In turn, institutions are driven by organisations that have the power to change them. Organisations include government, political parties, corporate interests and trade unions.

The interactions of the players are influenced by the architectural structure within which they exist. This structure may be depicted by a *layer model* that is summarised in the following sub-section and analysed in more detail in chapter 2. The dynamics of change within this system – including the key role of innovation – are examined in chapter 3.

A simplified model of the new ICT ecosystem

A simplified model of the new ICT ecosystem is shown in exhibit 1.3. A more detailed explanation of this model is provided in chapter 2, but here a brief summary will be given.

---

[2] For some purposes it will be necessary to disaggregate the analysis.

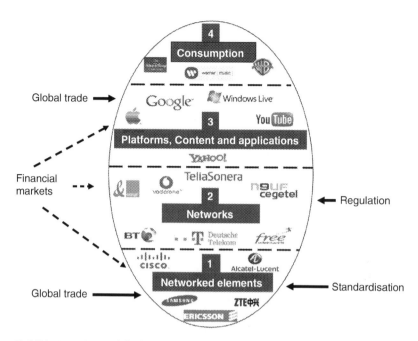

Exhibit 1.3. *A simplified model of the new ICT ecosystem*

Exhibit 1.4a. *The four layers of the new ICT ecosystem*

Layer 1: *Networked elements* (including switches, routers, servers, PCs, phones, etc.)

Layer 2: *Converged communication and content distribution networks* (including mobile, fibre, copper, cable, satellite)

Layer 3: *Platforms, content and applications* (including ICAPs)

Layer 4: *Final consumers*

The new ICT ecosystem may be conceptualised as a modularised, hierarchically layered system consisting of four layers, as shown in exhibit 1.4a. The new ICT ecosystem is structured in the following way:

- In layer 1, *networked elements* are produced (including switches, routers, servers and PCs).
- Some of these elements are strung together in layer 2 by network operators (including telecoms, cable TV and satellite operators) to form *converged networks* that are interconnected.

- In layer 3, the *platforms* are created upon which *content and applications* are provided to the *final consumers*, who sit in layer 4.

As this simple account of the new ecosystem illustrates, the four layers of the system, although hierarchically structured, are interdependent. Each layer depends on the layer (or layers) adjacent to it. For the system as a whole to operate, each layer needs to do its own functional job.

It is worth stressing that this system is at one and the same time both a technical and an economic system. Indeed, technical layer models were first developed by engineers in their attempt to understand the structure and functioning of computer and telecommunications systems. But the system is also economic. For example, the layers also define input–output relationships, where the activities within and between each layer are coordinated by firms and markets. Competition and innovation are important drivers of change in each layer, and in the system as a whole.

The layer model used by Japan's ministry-regulator, MIC

In Japan the country's ministry-regulator, the Ministry of Internal Affairs and Communications (MIC), uses a layer model very similar to that developed here. Exhibit 1.4b shows the author's representation of this model based on several MIC publications available on the Internet. MIC's Terminal Layer corresponds to our layer 1. Layer 2 in our model includes MIC's Physical Network Layer and Telecom Services Layer, while the ministry's Platform Layer and Content and Application Layer are incorporated in our layer 3.

In one of its publications MIC notes that the traditional domain of telecoms regulation pertains to the Physical Network and the Telecom Services Layers, as shown in exhibit 1.4b by the dotted square. In the present book, this traditional focus raises the question of whether changes that are occurring in one or more of the other interdependent layers (i.e. apart from the Physical Network and the Telecom Services Layers) are adequately taken into account within the limits of this focus.

Furthermore, the issue is also raised of coordination between other governance agencies that have responsibility for the other layers and the telecoms regulators. For example, it is traditionally the Ministry of Trade and Industry (MITI) (or the corresponding ministry in the

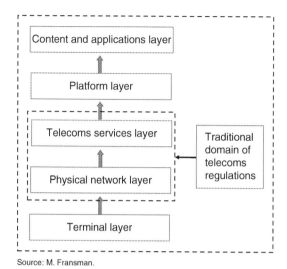

Source: M. Fransman.

Exhibit 1.4b. *Layer model used by Japan's ministry-regulator, MIC*

country concerned) and to some extent other ministries – such as the ministries of science and technology, education, etc. – that have responsibility for layer 1 (referred to as the Terminal Layer in MIC's layer model). The point is that the layer model emphasises the inter-dependence – in both a technical and economic sense – of the different layers. However, the governance of these interdependent layers is fragmented and may lack effective coordination since different ministries and agencies have responsibility for different layers.

MIC has implicitly used its layer model to begin to analyse the international competitiveness of the Japanese ICT ecosystem, an approach that is very similar to that proposed in the present book for use within the European context. This is evident in the ministry's publication, '2007 White Paper: Information and Communications in Japan, Progress of Ubiquitous Economy and Global Business Development'.[3]

This document begins with an analysis of the contribution made by the ICT sector to the growth of economic output and employment in Japan. Particularly relevant for the concerns of the present book, however, is the fact that the report goes on in its second section to examine the international competitiveness of the Japanese ICT sector.

[3] MIC (2007).

This analysis focuses primarily on layer 1 of the ICT ecosystem (referred to as the Terminal Layer in MIC's layer model). Unfortunately, little attention is paid to layer 3, apart from a part of one insightful sub-section dealing with software.

While this is not the place for a detailed summary of the 2007 White Paper, it will be useful to give a flavour of its contents. In the report, a key measure of international competitiveness is global market share and export share in specified ICT product markets. Regarding the overall international competitiveness of the Japanese ICT sector the report concludes that 'Japan's global market share and exports share declined in almost all ICT-related products between 1997 and 2005. This implies the decline of Japan's corporate competitiveness and locational competitiveness as a production base.'[4]

In the report, Japan's ICT performance is compared primarily with that in the USA, China and Korea, although there are also comparisons with countries in Europe and India. Generally, the report concludes that between 1997 and 2005 'US locational competitiveness declined, while its corporate competitiveness [was] maintained. China rapidly increased its locational competitiveness with the establishment of many production bases of foreign vendors by the development of the international division of labor. Korea increased its corporate competitiveness in some products.'[5]

Significantly, the report also draws attention to the important role played by institutions – such as universities and standardisation bodies – in shaping the international competitiveness of the Japanese ICT ecosystem. In the case of universities, for example, the report concludes that 'The number of graduates from ICT-related departments in Japan has been smaller than that in the US, China and India. It is essential for Japan to strengthen [the] professional education system after university education to keep and improve technological competitiveness in the ICT sector for the future.'[6]

In the report, specific product markets used for the purposes of benchmarking international competitiveness include: routers/switches; mobile handsets; flat screen TV/flat panel displays; semiconductors; software; and content. Attention is also paid to the use of ICT.

---

[4] *Ibid.*: 10.
[5] *Ibid.*: 10.
[6] *Ibid.*: 21.

Since communications networks (in MIC's Physical Network Layer) are to a large extent not internationally tradeable it is harder to measure international competitiveness in this layer. However, elsewhere MIC has drawn attention to Japan's superior performance in areas such as broadband (measured in terms that include broadband speed and price and the adoption of superior broadband technology such as FTTP). Broadband services are included in MIC's Telecom Services Layer.

It may be concluded, therefore, that MIC's approach to the ICT sector represents a useful attempt to analyse some of the key challenges facing Japan in this area.

Symbiotic relationships in the new ICT ecosystem

The interactions between the players in the new ICT ecosystem may be thought of as being *symbiotic*. Symbiotic interdependence between organisms may be mutually beneficial, although in some cases they may be harmful to one of the parties. In chapter 3 attention is focused on six key symbiotic relationships within the new ICT ecosystem. However, it is important to stress that there are other symbiotic relationships that, although also important in the functioning of this ecosystem, are not considered at the level of aggregation used in this book. Furthermore, it should be noted that symbiotic relationships also exist within layers of the new ICT ecosystem as well as within firms.[7] The six key symbiotic relationships in a simplified model of the new ICT ecosystem are summarised in exhibit 1.5.

The importance of innovation

The crucial characteristic of the new ICT ecosystem is that *innovation lies at its very core*. It is innovation that provides the system with its fuel and drives its relentless change. Crucially, it is the *ability to innovate* that determines how well this new ecosystem will perform in different national contexts.

---

[7] One example is the intra-layer 1 symbiosis between semiconductor providers and the makers of the systems in which the semiconductors are incorporated.

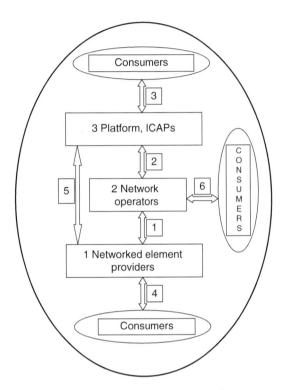

Exhibit 1.5. *Six key symbiotic relationships in a simplified model of the new ICT ecosystem*

Definition of innovation

Following Joseph Schumpeter, *innovation* in this book will refer to the creation of at least one of four different things:

1. New or improved *products or services*
2. New or improved *processes* (including technologies or materials)
3. New or improved *forms of organisation*
4. New *markets*.

It is important to note that this definition of innovation includes far more than the activities involved in conventionally measured R&D, although the definition certainly includes such research. Indeed, many of the important innovations that are made in the new ICT ecosystem – for example, service innovations – involve no R&D as usually measured. Data on R&D in the new ICT ecosystem are discussed in chapter 4.

Frequently (though not always) innovation emerges from the symbiotic relationships of the new ICT ecosystem. This is discussed in more detail in chapter 3.

Innovative capability

By *innovative capability* is meant the ability to produce internationally competitive output in one or more of our four areas. Innovative capability is embedded within firms and non-firm organisations (such as universities and government research institutes). The innovative output which draws on this ability is often difficult to measure in aggregate. As a result innovation is often measured indirectly rather than directly. The measures include R&D, patents, proportion of new products or processes and, in some cases and even more indirectly, other performance measures such as market share or profitability, where the performance itself is known to be caused by the innovation(s).

It is important to stress that the determinants of innovative capability are not only to be found within single firms (although they certainly are to be found there). Often innovative capability is the result of *cooperation* between two or more firms. Often non-firm *institutions* play a key role in shaping these capabilities, sometimes for the better and sometimes for the worse. For example, institutions relating to *intellectual property rights* (IPRs) will influence the incentives to innovate which, in turn, will shape innovative capabilities. *Financial institutions* and their ability (or lack thereof) to finance potential innovative activities under conditions of uncertainty are another determinant. *Standardisation* is a key institution. In a highly complex and modularised system such as the new ICT ecosystem, standards provide a crucial coordinating mechanism that helps economise on and develop knowledge. *Universities* are also very important as creators of knowledge, as developers of knowledgeable people and as incubators of entrepreneurs.

As this brief discussion makes clear, therefore, the system consists not only of competing firms but also of cooperating firms and the institutions that shape them and their innovative capabilities. This suggests the value of a *conceptualisation of the new ICT ecosystem which sees this system also as an innovation system*. This concept of the new ecosystem as an innovation system will be further developed in chapter 3. Given the central role that innovation plays in driving the process of incessant change in the new ICT ecosystem, it logically follows that policies and governance structures designed to influence the performance of the system should focus centrally on the *innovation process* (although, of course, they will have other foci as well).

The telecoms sector and telecoms regulation

The telecoms sector is a key component of the new ICT ecosystem, and provides an increasingly ubiquitous infrastructure for it. However, it is in the regulation of the telecoms sector that we meet a problem. The reason, simply, is that the conceptual framework within which telecoms regulation has evolved does not include endogenous innovation as part of its logical fabric.

As shown in more detail later in chapter 5, telecoms regulation has co-evolved with the telecoms sector. A key moment in this evolutionary process occurred in the mid-1980s when three countries, for different reasons, decided to allow new licensed competitors to compete with the telecoms companies that had hitherto monopolised the provision of telecoms services. Thus in the USA two new competitors, MCI and Sprint, were allowed to compete with AT&T in long-distance communications; in Japan, DDI, Japan Telecom and Teleway Japan were given permission to compete with the incumbent, NTT; and in the UK, Cable & Wireless (through its subsidiary, Mercury) began to compete with BT.

This momentous event was conceptual as much as it was pragmatic. Until then, the theoretical conventional wisdom had been that in order to be efficient telecoms services should be provided by a monopolist as a result of the economies of scale and scope and network externalities that existed in this industry. This was known as the *natural monopoly argument*. By allowing competition, these three countries were challenging this conventional wisdom.

However, in so doing they were also creating a significant problem for themselves because their actions raised a crucial question: What should be done in those cases where the former monopolist-incumbent had 'significant market power' (SMP) in a particular market? It was in order to answer this question that regulators turned to academic economists for help.

Help was quickly forthcoming. These economists already had a well-honed tool in their theoretical toolkit, namely *price theory*, with which to tackle the question. As is explained in more detail later, in appendix 3, price theory was used to determine the optimal price that a new entrant should pay an incumbent with SMP for access to its network, and therefore its customers. This price would turn out to be a key plank in the telecoms regulator's portfolio of solutions. The optimal price was particularly important because, as the economists' deductive models showed, it would enable a maximisation of *social welfare* (that is the welfare of both producers and consumers). In this way, through regulation, it was argued that the regulated price would bring about the same outcome in this market as would have occurred had there been perfect competition.

This solution has been highly influential, so much so that it has become part of what is referred to in this book as the Dominant Regulatory Paradigm in Telecoms (DRPT), although some of the limitations of the practical use of the concept have also been analysed (see appendix 3).

More generally and apart from the question of the optimal inter-connection price, regulators have been keen to try and maximise the intensity of competition in telecoms markets. Behind this objective lies the same conceptual framework as that informing the analysis of the optimal interconnection price. This framework demonstrates logically that under conditions of intense competition an *equilibrium state* is brought about such that social welfare is maximised. Indeed, intense competition *is* social welfare maximisation insofar as the former logically implies the latter.

However, there is a significant problem with the underlying conceptual framework that informs these conclusions: it does not allow the *process of innovation* to be an *endogenous* part of the production and consumption activities that are implicit in the theory. In some cases, innovation (i.e. technical change) is assumed to happen in theoretical models and the consequences are examined. However, in these models no explanation is provided regarding how the innovation came about in the first place, and why it has taken the form that it has. In short, the *process of innovation* is inadequately treated.

Starting as we have in this book with the key observation that it is innovation which is the main driver of the incessant change transforming the new ICT ecosystem, the conceptual framework underlying the DRPT is found wanting. If we are to come to grips with this new ecosystem, understand how it works – and hopefully be able to develop policies and modes of governance that will improve its performance nationally through improving its ability to innovate – a broader conceptualisation is needed, one that, like the new ecosystem, has the innovation process at its heart.

Competition and innovation

The argument of the present book is that the telecoms regulators discussed in the last sub-section are right to emphasise the importance of competition. Competition is important, not because it brings about an equilibrium state in which social welfare is maximised – in equilibrium states, there is no innovation – but because it is a key driver of the incessant innovatory change that drives the new ICT ecosystem and over time brings the important improvements that we have seen.[8] Most importantly, competition can be an important determinant of innovation because it incentivises it through the production of powerful threats and opportunities. However, significant though this statement is, it needs qualification.

To begin with, although competition and innovation are often causally related, the former does not automatically lead to the latter. (It is worth recalling here our earlier definition of innovation as the ability to produce *internationally competitive* new or improved products and services, processes and forms of organisation, and to develop new markets.) Specifically, as already noted earlier, *institutions* often play a necessary intermediating role, influencing both the quantity and the kind of innovation that takes place.

Secondly, it is worth recalling that significant innovation can occur without competitive markets. Of immediate relevance is the innovation that took place during the monopoly era in telecoms, up to about the mid-1980s. Indeed, many of the innovations that have powered the new ICT ecosystem emerged during the monopoly era in places such as Bell Labs, part of the AT&T monopoly that had a significant hand in the creation of inventions like the transistor (invented totally in Bell Labs), the laser, digital telecoms switching, cellular mobile communications, and the C software language.[9]

---

[8] A paper examining these kinds of issues within the European context is Aghion and Howitt (2006). This chapter discusses within a Schumpeterian framework the process of product–market competition among incumbents.

[9] For further details regarding these and other innovations that took place at the time, see Fransman (1995a).

Thirdly, it is also conceivable that, under some circumstances, competition may be excessive in that it reduces innovation below what otherwise might occur. For example, in some circumstances intense competition may generate uncertainty that, by increasing the risk premium on investments, may deter new entry and investment, at least for some time.

Having said this, however, it remains that competition usually is a powerful driver of innovation. The point, though, is that policies and forms of governance, insofar as they aim at the improvement of the new ecosystem, need to take into account not only competition but also innovation. The innovation cannot be taken for granted.

Innovation and investment

In discussing the relationship between innovation and investment it is necessary to distinguish between the *creation* of an innovation and the *diffusion* of it.[10] Investment may be necessary for both the creation and diffusion of an innovation. In the telecoms sector, for example, both the creation and the diffusion of a network innovation – for instance, 3G or WiFi – may require substantial amounts of investment. However, this is not always the case. For example, the creation and the initial diffusion processes of innovations in firms such as Amazon, MySpace and YouTube did not require very much investment, although larger sums were needed later. As these cases make clear, in some areas the existence of the Internet keeps down investment costs while at the same time allowing rapid global diffusion of innovations.

Nevertheless, since investment is often necessary for innovation it is important that an effective innovation system and its modes of governance provide both an adequate supply of investment funds and the incentives necessary to encourage the investment that must occur to facilitate innovation.

---

[10] Schumpeter made a further distinction between an invention and an innovation. An invention refers, essentially, to a new idea, while an innovation involves a commercialisation of an idea. Accordingly, an innovator is not necessarily an inventor. Furthermore, Schumpeter argued that an innovator is not necessarily the main risk-taker. That role is played by the provider of the capital needed to innovate, although an innovator might also be a risk-taker if he or she provides the risk capital.

Analysing innovation: the relevance of Schumpeterian evolutionary economics

Since the 1980s a new paradigm for the analysis of innovation emerged within academic economics. This paradigm may be referred to as the Schumpeterian Evolutionary Economics Paradigm (SEEP), since it was inspired by the work of Joseph Schumpeter and Charles Darwin. The broad outlines of this paradigm are discussed in more detail in appendix 4.

The main concern of SEEP is with the innovation process and the role that it plays in the dynamics of capitalist economic systems. It is no accident that the contemporary founding fathers of SEEP all began with a close interest in the innovation process. They include Richard Nelson and Sidney Winter (now at Columbia University and the Wharton Business School, respectively), Christopher Freeman (founder of the Science Policy Research Unit, SPRU, at the University of Sussex) and Nathan Rosenberg (Stanford University). (See the bibliography for some of their key writings.) A number of academic journals have been particularly important in helping to develop and refine SEEP, including the *Journal of Evolutionary Economics*, *Industrial and Corporate Change* and *Innovation Policy*.

Significantly, SEEP has also begun to have an important impact on innovation policy. In particular, the concept of *systems of innovation* (developed originally by writers such as Christopher Freeman, Bengt-Åke Lundval, Richard Nelson and Nathan Rosenberg) has led to a burgeoning policy-related literature (some of which is referred to in the bibliography).

In chapter 3 we analyse the ICT ecosystem as an innovation system.

2 | *The new ICT ecosystem: architectural structure*

In this chapter, we examine the architectural structure of the new ICT ecosystem using a layer model. In chapter 3 the innovation process in this system is analysed.

Introduction

We need to ask four key questions here:

- What are the component parts of the new ICT ecosystem?
- How do these parts interact with one another to form a coherent industrial system?
- What are the main forces that drive the new ecosystem?
- How has the system been affected by globalisation and the international division of labour?

We start by constructing a qualitative model that will provide an answer to all these kinds of questions.

The structure of the new ICT ecosystem: the ecosystem layer model (ELM)

Introduction

A Google search reveals how widespread is reference to 'ICT' and even to the 'ICT sector'. However, such a search does not readily reveal (indeed hardly reveals at all) what is meant by the 'ICT industry'. What is clear is that the letters I and C refer to information and communications, respectively, and that T refers to technology. Less clear is what we are meant to understand by the ICT *sector*, that is a sector of economic activity based on information and communication technologies: What

are the component parts of this sector? How do these parts
interact with one another? What are the forces that drive change
within each of these parts? What drives 'the system' as a whole, consisting of all the interacting parts of the sector – that is, how does this
sector work? Where are the boundaries of the ICT sector, separating it
from other sectors?

Despite the widespread reference to ICT, the answers to questions
like these are still poorly understood.

Further underlining the lack of clarity is the inadequacy of our
existing classifications. Leaving aside standard classification systems
(such as the standard industrial and trade classifications (SITC),
which are essentially product-based) it is illuminating to look at
pragmatic attempts to provide a classification of business activity in
this area. One such attempt is that made in the *Financial Times'*
online classification. Here three sectors are to be found that refer
most directly (though implicitly) to ICT: telecommunications (telecoms); IT (information technology); and Internet/media. However, a
perusal through these three separate sectors in FT.com on any day
reveals a significant degree of cross-posting, indicating that the categories are neither water-tight nor mutually exclusive. This begs
several questions concerning the relationship between these three
sub-sectors.

Furthermore, the addition of 'media' to accompany the word 'Internet'
adds further complications. While a number of organisations have
attempted to define the ICT sector their definitions have tended to
focus on telecoms (network operators and equipment suppliers) and
computing (hardware and software) and have excluded 'media' (a term
that itself is vague and becoming vaguer, as we shall see). How does
'media' fit into the new ICT ecosystem?

The Internet greatly complicates the attempt both to classify the
components of the new ecosystem and to understand its dynamics.
The Internet has rapidly become a key and ubiquitous infrastructure
(its widespread commercial diffusion only occurred from around
1995), paralleling other infrastructures such as electricity and roads
and supporting (and shaping) virtually all economic activity. But
where does it fit into the new ICT ecosystem and the dynamics of this
system?

These few words of introduction and the questions raised should
be sufficient to convince even the sceptical reader that a deeper

understanding of the new ICT ecosystem is necessary. But where should the attempt to provide such an understanding begin?

The ICT ecosystem layer model (ELM): preliminary comments

The approach taken in this book is to begin with a particular kind of layer model of the new ICT ecosystem. Such layer models (such as the OSI and TCP/IP layer models – p. 168, appendix 5 for further details) originated from the attempt of engineers to define and understand the components and structure of the computer and telecoms industries. Essentially, they conceptualised these industries in terms of a number of hierarchically defined, modularised and interdependent 'layers' of functionality. These layer models have played a crucial cognitive role in facilitating communication and coordination among engineers working in these areas.

However, a number of writers and organisations have begun to explore the use of the broad layer model conceptualisation in order to understand other issues such as industrial and market structure, industrial dynamics and regulation.[1] The present book falls within this emerging framework. Here specific interpretations and uses are made of the general layer model concept. Collectively, these are referred to as the ICT ecosystem layer model (ELM), to differentiate the present approach from the other layer models used in this area.

What is the ICT ELM?

ELM is a model of the global ICT sector developed by the present author in order to assist analyses of this sector and to help inform the development of appropriate corporate strategies and government policies. It is a qualitative model that views the entire ICT sector as a *system*. In so doing, it incorporates sub-sectors such as: semiconductors; computers; software; consumer electronics; telecoms equipment; network operators (including telecoms fixed and mobile operators, cable TV operators, satellite and other operators); broadcasting; media; newspapers; books; music; and advertising.

---

[1] For example, see Fransman (2002b) and Mindel and Sicker (2006: 136–48).

Exhibit 2.1. *Why is the ICT ELM valuable?*

1 Allows us to conceptualise the entire ICT sector *as a system* and understand *interdependencies* and *complex interactions* within the system
2 Allows us to identify the role played by *markets, firms* and other *institutions* (such as regulation and standardisation) in *coordinating* the activities undertaken within the system
3 Allows us to analyse *corporate specialisation* and *corporate strategy*
4 Allows us to analyse different *evolutionary drivers* that shape industrial structure in the different layers
5 Allows us to examine the effects of *globalisation* and the *international division of labour* (including the role of *government policy*)
6 Allows us to understand the *role that specific key companies play* in the new ICT ecosystem
7 Allows us to analyse the importance of *co-evolving demand*
8 Allows us to analyse the different *profitability* in different parts of the system

How does ELM differ from other layer models?

ELM is both an engineering–architectural and an economic–institutional model. It conceptualises the ICT ecosystem as a set of *functionalities*. The ICT system that we are conceiving in ELM has a dual existence. On the one hand it is a technical or engineering system with a set of technical (and modular) interactions defined and determined by a technical architecture. However, on the other hand it is also *at the same time* an economic–institutional system with markets and other institutions (such as regulation and standardisation) that shape how the system and its parts evolve over time. This is the feature that most strongly distinguishes the present ELM from technical or engineering layer models, such as the OSI and TCP/IP models (discussed briefly in appendix 5).

In what ways is ELM valuable?

Exhibit 2.1 indicates some of the uses to which ELM may be put, although this list is not exhaustive.

The basic ICT ELM A: a description of the structure of the ICT industry

The basic layer model, ELM A, is shown in exhibit 2.2. It provides a description of the entire ICT industry, by functional layer.

Exhibit 2.2. *The basic ICT ELM A: description of the ICT industry, by functional layer*

Layer	Function
Layer 6	Final consumption
Layer 5	Content, applications and services
Layer 4	Middleware, navigation, search and innovation platforms
Layer 3	Connectivity
	TCP/IP interface
Layer 2	Network operating
Layer 1	Networked elements

Source: M. Fransman.

Layer 1: networked elements

Layer 1 consists of *networked elements*. A fundamental characteristic of the evolution of the new ICT ecosystem is the increasing tendency over time for all the components of this sector to be integrated into networks. This tendency began with telecommunications networks from the late nineteenth century with the integration of transmissions equipment, switches and customer premises equipment. The tendency continued with the development of computer networks in the post-Second World War period. The tendency was given a significant boost from the mid-1990s with mass adoption of the Internet, which became the integrator *par excellence*. It soon became commonplace to observe that almost everything in the ICT sector was becoming integrated and networked within the Internet.

In the ICT ecosystem the networked elements in layer 1 include: telecoms equipment (including transmissions equipment, telecoms switches, routers and servers); computers; consumer electronics (including mobile phones, MP3 players, digital cameras and TVs); semiconductors and other devices embodied in these elements; and the systems software necessary to make them work.

Layer 2: network operating

The elements produced in layer 1 are integrated in layer 2 into *information and communications networks* and run by *network operators*. These network operators include telecoms operators (fixed and mobile), cable TV operators, satellite operators and broadcasting operators.

While these networks and their operators were initially separate from one another – and were incorporated into distinct markets – from the 1990s they became increasingly interconnected. As a result their services have become increasingly substitutable (although in some cases they have also become complementary). The term 'convergence' is often used to capture this phenomenon. Thus, for example, films and television programmes can be provided to households by telecoms companies using DSL or FTTP connections, by cable companies using coaxial cables, by satellite companies and by mobile phone companies.

TCP/IP interface

The advent of the Internet had the most profound impact on the structure and dynamics of the new ICT ecosystem, the effects of which are still to be resolved. In ELM this is partially represented by the Transmission Control Protocol/Internet Protocol (TCP/IP) interface. As noted earlier, TCP/IP refers to the suite of communications protocols used to connect hosts on the Internet.

An analogy is useful in order to understand the significant implications of TCP/IP for the dynamics of the new ecosystem: containerisation in the field of transport. The advent of the container had a major impact on the cost of transport and therefore on international trade and the growth of the world economy. As a result of being able to move containers (as opposed to products) across different transport networks these networks (which include air, sea, road and rail networks) became increasingly interoperable and substitutable. The result was increasing competition between the different networks that contributed to a substantial fall in transport costs. (It is worth noting, however, that it took a significant amount of time and resource for containerisation to be fully implemented. The reason was that big changes in capital goods and infrastructure were needed in order to facilitate the movement and storage of the standard-sized containers.)

In analogous fashion TCP/IP facilitates the movement of packets of information across different information and communications networks, also allowing them to become interoperable and to some extent substitutable. This has facilitated the emergence of the process of convergence and the Internet as a network of networks.

However, TCP/IP has had another equally profound effect. As shown in ELM (exhibit 2.2), it has facilitated the emergence of new layers consisting of new functionalities – layers 3–5. Furthermore, it has allowed a technical separation of layers 1 and 2 from these upper layers which has made possible the entry of new players into the new ICT ecosystem providing new functionalities.

Layer 3: connectivity

With the diffusion of TCP/IP new firms were able to enter layer 3 and provide Internet connectivity. These firms were Internet access and service providers (IAPs and ISPs). Significantly, although the incumbent telecoms operators who dominated layer 2 also entered layer 3 to provide Internet connectivity, some of the most successful layer 3 players were new entrants.[2]

For example, in the USA, AOL – which had previously been an online provider of content – adapted its operations to the Internet and quickly became the dominant ISP. In the UK, Freeserve soon came to dominate a host of smaller new entrants after it developed the then novel business model of providing free dial-up Internet access. It was able to do this because, due to a business tie-up with the retail electronics company, Dixons, and the new entrant telecoms operator, Energis (the telecoms subsidiary of the main English electricity company), it was able to share in the revenue generated by this new Internet traffic. Although British Telecom (BT) also entered this market, BT Openworld was only the third player. However, in France and Germany the incumbent telecoms operators, France Télécom and Deutsche Telekom, dominated the connectivity market through Wanadoo (now Orange) and T-Online, respectively.

However, from the point of view of the market structure of layer 3, the key feature was the entry of new players into this new competitive market. Later we shall see how the advent of local loop unbundling (LLU) (i.e. the regulatory requirement that the incumbent telecoms operators open the local switches in their local access networks to the equipment of competitors) was to further boost competition in the Internet access market.

Layer 4: middleware, navigation, search and innovation platforms

The addition of layer 3 to the new ICT ecosystem following the diffusion of TCP/IP meant that the function of Internet connectivity

---

[2] Over time, however, IAPs and ISPs were increasingly displaced by telecoms operators.

was provided. However, although necessary, this was not sufficient for people to make use of the growing number of hosts connected in the World Wide Web (www, based on an innovation made by Tim Berners Lee at the CERN particle-accelerator in Switzerland). Other functionalities had to be provided.

For example, in order to locate information it was necessary to be able to navigate through the 'cloud' of hosts that made up the rapidly growing World Wide Web. This required *browsers*. Further necessary functionalities included things such as security software that would safeguard Internet interactions. These functionalities are referred to generically in ELM as 'Middleware'. Furthermore, there still remained the need to be able to *search* for specific information from the huge and rapidly growing number of servers holding it.

Significantly, it was on the whole new entrants rather than incumbents from other parts of the ICT ecosystem that came to dominate in the provision of these new functionalities. The partial exception was the area of browsers.[3] Here a brief battle ensued between two contenders. The first was a start-up called Netscape, founded by Marc Andreeson and based on the ideas of Tim Berners Lee. Netscape had its initial public offering (IPO) in 1995. However, it was the second, Internet Explorer, championed by Microsoft – which with Intel dominated personal computing – that eventually came to triumph. In 1999 Netscape was bought by AOL.[4]

Many medium-sized software companies established niches for themselves in the area of middleware. For example, a number of Israeli software companies were able to become strong in niche markets for security software such as firewalls.

However, most significant from the point of view of the future evolution of the new ICT ecosystem, as we shall see later, was the area of *search*. The demand for a search function followed naturally from the rapid commercial diffusion of the Internet and the World Wide Web from around 1995. Users needed to search for what they wanted. One of the start-ups that responded to this need was a small firm called Google started by two Stanford University students. It focused narrowly on the search function, developing the mathematical

[3] Technically, a web browser is a software application used to locate and display Web pages.
[4] For a brief history of Netscape and Andreesen and the browser wars, see http://en.wikipedia.org/wiki/Marc_Andreesen.

algorithms that would facilitate search while constructing a minimalist website that would help users search quickly and efficiently.

It is crucial to note in analysing the new ICT ecosystem that the functionalities provided in layers 3 and 4 together constitute *innovation platforms* for the content, applications and services providers in layer 5. Examples of such providers include Amazon, eBay, MySpace, YouTube and Skype, who were able to build their content and applications on the platforms provided by layer 3 and 4 players and also on the networks provided by layer 2 network operators.

Significantly, the companies that dominated layers 1 and 2 – that is, the networked elements companies and the telecoms operators – had little to do with the events shaping the evolution of layer 4. Why? Why did they not see the new opportunities opening up in layer 4 and take steps to enter and take advantage of these new markets?

The answer is that although, as ELM clearly shows, the functionalities of layer 4 were closely connected to those in layers 1–3, the competencies and focuses required were quite different. For example, telecoms operators, providing voice and data services and even Internet access, had neither the competencies nor the focus necessary for the development of browsers or search engines. Although with their substantial R&D capabilities they probably could, in theory, have developed browsers and search engines, their existing competencies and priority business activities meant that in practice they were precluded from doing so. (France Télécom is something of an exception. Until 2001–2 France Télécom, through its Wanadoo Internet subsidiary, was number one in the French search market with its search engine 'Voilà' which was invented by France Télécom's R&D division.)

Layer 5: content, applications and services

With connectivity and Internet access provided, and with the navigation, search and middleware functionalities in place and acting as an innovation platform, it was possible to generate the content, applications and services that consumers would use. These functionalities are provided by the activities undertaken in layer 5. The terms 'content, applications and services', although in widespread use, refer to complex economic outputs and various uses of the terms in different contexts can cause confusion. Accordingly, it is useful to spend a little time clarifying their meaning.

Content is a commonly used term with regard to the Internet and other electronic media (e.g. television and DVDs). In its broadest sense, it refers to material which is of interest to users, such as textual information, images, music and movies.[5]

An *application* may be defined as a program or group of programs designed for end-users. It often refers to software programs (as in the case of applications software). However, in this book the term 'application' will also be used to include functionalities such as electronic commerce provided by new Internet companies such as eBay (electronic auctions and trading) and Amazon.com (the electronic selling of books and other commodities).

The best definition of a *service* – that provided by IBM Research – is that of a provider/client interaction that creates and captures value. An elaboration of this definition is provided in appendix 6.

It is important to note that intermediate demand and supply relationships (and therefore markets) exist both *within* and *between* layers. For example, in layer 1 systems producers (such as the producers of PCs or mobile phones) demand semiconductors and other devices from component producers; telecoms operators in layer 2 demand telecoms equipment from telecoms equipment suppliers located in layer 1; and so on.

Furthermore, it should be noted that conceptually the services referred to in layer 5 refer to services for *final* consumers/users. These should be distinguished from services for intermediate consumers/users. For example, new entrant telecoms companies purchasing local loop access services from incumbent telecoms operators under LLU regulations are conceived of as making an intra-layer 2 transaction in the access market located in layer 2. However, in using the local loop access to provide Internet access to final users (such as households) they are conceived of as making a market transaction involving layers 2 and 6.

While this distinction may seem arbitrary it has the advantage of distinguishing between services and markets according to the kind of customer involved. The importance of distinguishing between different kinds of customers and their tastes, preferences and demands is emphasised by adding a sixth layer to ELM, namely layer 6, final consumption.

---

[5] www.bellevuelinux.org/linmo/content.html.

Exhibit 2.3. *Some services and corresponding layers*

Service	Layer
Electronic mail	Layer 5 (application)
(e-mail distributed content)	Layer 5 (content)
Voice-over-IP (VoIP)	Layer 5 (application)
Video services (including TV and video-on-demand)	Layer 5 (content)
Online information services	Layer 5 (content)
Search services	Layer 3
Leased line services	Layer 2
Mobile services	Layer 2

Sources: ELM and Mindel and Sicker (2006).

In exhibit 2.3 some examples of telecoms services are given, together with the corresponding layers where the markets for these services are located.

Layer 6: final consumption

A key conceptual feature in ELM lies in the addition of layer 6, a consuming layer. This makes explicit the important role played by final consumption and the co-evolution of this consumption. Firms in layers 1–5 sell products and services to the final consumers in layer 6. At the same time the identification of layer 6 also draws attention to the importance of the intermediate demand and intermediate markets that exist within and between layers 1–5.

Elaborations of the ICT ELM

In what follows, two elaborations of ELM will be developed. The first involves adding various sectors to ELM while the second involves an identification of some of the major firms that have specialised in these sectors.

The ICT ELM B: adding selected sectors and companies

How do the various sectors of the ICT ecosystem, and the companies in these sectors, map onto the ELM? In exhibit 2.4, a selection of some of the more important sectors is provided.

Exhibit 2.4. *The ELM B: layer, function and sectors*

Layer	Function	Selected Sectors
6	Final consumption	
5	Content, applications and services	1 Content 2 Applications 3 Services (e.g. Yahoo!, eBay, YouTube)
4	Middleware, navigation, search and innovation platforms	1 Middleware 2 Navigation (browsers) 3 Search (e.g. Google, Baidu)
3	Connectivity	1 ISPs (e.g. Tiscali, T-Online, Orange)

TCP/IP Layer

Layer	Function	Selected Sectors
2	Network operating	1 *Core network operators* a Telecoms operators (fixed and mobile) b Cable TV operators c Broadcasters (terrestrial, satellite) d Others (e.g. electricity firms) 2 *Access network operators* a Fixed b Cellular mobile c Other wireless (e.g. BT, France Télécom, Vodafone)
1	Networked elements	1 *Devices* a Microprocessors b Memories c Other (e.g. Intel, AMD, NEC, TSMC) 2 *Systems* a Telecoms equipment b Computer hardware and system software c Consumer electronics (e.g. Ericsson, Alcatel–Lucent, Samsung)

Source: M. Fransman.

Exhibit 2.5. *The four-layer ELM model*

Layer	Functionality
4	Final consumption
3	Contents, applications, services, innovation platforms, search, navigation and middleware
2	Network operating
1	Networked elements, including telecoms equipment, computer hardware and software, and consumer electronics

Source: M. Fransman.

The four-layer ELM model

In order to ease exposition, the six-layer ELM model may be aggregated into a four-layer ELM model, as is done in exhibit 2.5. The aggregation to get the four-layer ELM model from the six-layer ELM involves two separate aggregations. The first is the aggregation of layers 2 (Network operating) and 3 (Connectivity) in the six-layer model in order to get layer 2 in the four-layer model. The second is the aggregation of layers 4 (Middleware, navigation, search and innovation platforms) and 5 (Content, applications and services) in the six-layer model in order to get layer 3 in the four-layer model.

The reason for the first aggregation is that connectivity has been vertically integrated – for example, by most telecoms operator incumbents – even though there are also independent ISPs (Internet service providers) who also contest this market (such as AOL and Tiscali). Furthermore, new entrants who have entered on the basis of LLU (local loop unbundling) also contest this market, but their activities are the result of the regulation of the telecoms operator incumbents.

The reason for the second aggregation is that, as we shall see later in this book, activities such as navigation (typified by Google's offerings) – which were in layer 4 of the six-layer ELM model – are intimately connected with the provision of content, applications and services. Furthermore, middleware products are increasingly also being provided by firms involved in navigation, content, applications and services. It therefore makes sense to include them in one layer. Exhibit 1.3 (p. 9) shows this four-layered ELM.

3 | *The new ICT ecosystem as an innovation system*

The widespread adoption of the Internet has transformed the ICT sector, giving birth to what has been referred to as the 'new ICT ecosystem'.[1] But how does this ecosystem work, and what changes it over time? These questions are explored in this chapter, using some of the insights of Schumpeterian evolutionary economics.

To summarise, it can be shown that innovation – the endogenous creation of new knowledge in the ecosystem – has emerged largely from six key symbiotic relationships. These relationships are shaped by both competition and by institutions, which include financial institutions, regulation and competition law, standardisation and universities. It is these processes of innovation that make the new ICT ecosystem the restless, incessantly changing system that it is.

The evolution of the new ICT ecosystem

The essential point to grasp is that in dealing with capitalism we are dealing with an evolutionary process . . . Capitalism . . . is by nature a form or method of economic change and not only never is but never can be stationary . . . the fundamental impulse that sets and keeps the capitalist engine in motion comes from the new consumers' goods, the new methods of production or transportation, the new markets, the new forms of industrial organization that capitalist enterprise creates . . .

[It is this] process of industrial mutation – if I may use that biological term – that incessantly revolutionizes the economic structure from within, incessantly destroying the old one, incessantly creating a new one. This process of Creative Destruction is the essential fact about capitalism. It is what capitalism consists in and what every capitalist concern has got to live in.[2]

---

[1] An earlier version of this chapter appears in Fransman (2007a: 1–22).
[2] Schumpeter (1943: 82–3).

Although Schumpeter did not himself apply Darwin's evolutionary theory to the changing capitalist system he did, as the above quotation makes clear, regard the process of change in this system as an *evolutionary* process. It was left to more recent scholars who have been inspired by the ideas of both Schumpeter and Darwin – some of whom are referred to in appendix 4 – to make the connection. The task that we face in this chapter is to show how the ideas of Darwin and Schumpeter can be brought to bear in developing a deeper understanding of the new ICT ecosystem, an understanding that will help to meet the challenges facing Europe that were identified in chapter 1.

Change in the new ICT ecosystem as an evolutionary process

Darwin's great genius was to discover the causes driving evolution. Essentially, these are two-fold: first, processes that *generate* variety; and, secondly, processes that *select* from that variety. How might such evolutionary thinking be applied in analysing the process of change in the new ICT ecosystem?

The first step is to identify the processes in the new ICT ecosystem that generate variety. But this raises the first problem: variety with regard to what? It is in answering this question that the link may be made to Schumpeter. As the above quotation makes clear, Schumpeter believed that change in the capitalist system (and therefore in the new ICT ecosystem which is part of the capitalist system) comes from four different forms of innovation:

1. New or improved products or services
2. New or improved processes or methods of production (including technologies and transportation[3])
3. New or improved forms of organisation
4. New markets.

In other words, innovation leads to variety in one or more of these four areas. We therefore have the first part of an *evolutionary process*. The second part involves *selection*, a process of winnowing from the variety that has been generated.

---

[3] Although, clearly, Schumpeter had the transport of 'atoms' (or goods) in mind, the same argument applies to the transport of 'bits' (digitised information), particularly important in the new ICT ecosystem.

The topographical structure of the new ICT ecosystem

The architecture of the new ICT ecosystem may be depicted in terms of four modularised, hierarchically structured layers, as is done in exhibit 3.1. This layer model of the ecosystem has already been discussed in detail in chapter 2.

Problems with this depiction of topographical structure

While exhibit 3.1 adequately captures the functionalities of the ICT ecosystem and their hierarchical organisation, it fails to show the *dynamics* of the system, including the innovation processes that are a key part of these dynamics. Essentially this topographical depiction of the structure of the ICT ecosystem is static, in much the same way that the topographical map of a city fails to capture the dynamics going on within it. We therefore have now to introduce an account of these dynamics.

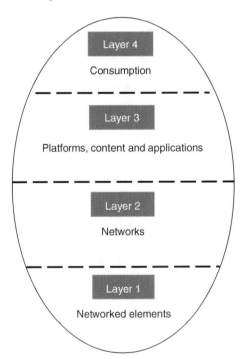

Exhibit 3.1. *A simplified model of the new ICT ecosystem*

Exhibit 3.2. *Six symbiotic relationships*

Relationship

---

1 Relationship between networked element providers and network operators
2 Relationship between network operators and content and applications providers
3 Relationship between content and applications providers and final consumers
4 Relationship between networked element providers and final consumers
5 Relationship between networked element providers and content and applications providers
6 Relationship between network operators and final consumers

Generating variety in the new ICT ecosystem

In the spirit of the Schumpeterian–evolutionary approach we need to explain how new products, new processes, new forms of organisation and new markets come about, since it is these innovations that are, in Schumpeter's words, the 'prime movers' of the system. It is proposed in this book that these innovations largely emerge from six symbiotic relationships that occur within the ICT ecosystem:[4] symbiosis exists when the members of different species live together in close inter-action, with consequences that may or may not be beneficial for all the parties concerned.[5]

The six symbiotic relationships

The six symbiotic relationships that occur between the layer players in the new ICT ecosystem are depicted in exhibit 3.2.

---

[4] R&D expenditures may constitute an important part of a symbiotic relationship. However, there are many forms of innovation that do not involve R&D as conventionally measured. In this chapter reference is made to six symbiotic relationships at the level of aggregation of the new ICT ecosystem used here. A more disaggregated analysis of this ecosystem would allow for a larger number of symbiotic relationships to be examined.

[5] The biologist Lynn Margulis has criticised Darwin's claim that evolution occurs primarily through the competition of different species. She argues that cooperation and mutual dependence play a significant role in the evolutionary process and this includes symbiosis. According to Margulis and Sagan (1988), '*Life* did not take over the *globe* by *combat*, but by *networking*' (emphasis in the original).

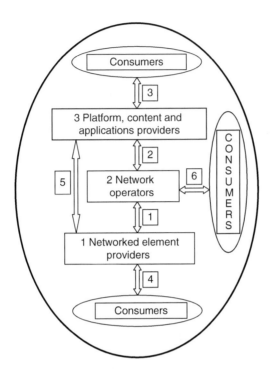

Exhibit 3.3. *Six symbiotic relationships in the simplified model of the new ICT ecosystem*

Essentially, the six symbiotic relationships refer to the interactions between the four groups of players in the new ICT ecosystem: the networked element providers; the network operators; the content and applications providers; and the final consumers. This is shown in exhibit 3.3.

Another way of depicting the six symbiotic relationships is to show the interactions directly, abstracting from the layers within which the players are situated. This is shown in exhibit 3.4.

The multidimensionality of the symbiotic relationships

These six symbiotic innovation relationships are multidimensional. More specifically, there are four dimensions to each of the relationships, depicted as A–D, as shown in exhibit 3.5.

First, each symbiotic relationship involves the purchase–sale of goods or services – that is, Dimension A. For example, in Relationship 1

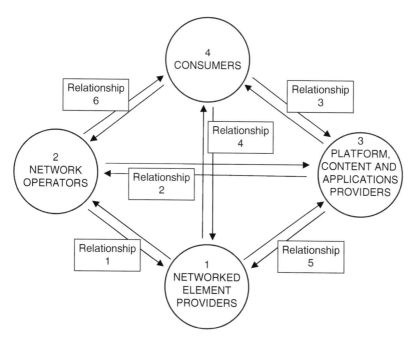

Exhibit 3.4. *Symbiotic relationships between the four groups of players in the new ICT ecosystem*

Exhibit 3.5. *Dimensions of the symbiotic relationships*

	Dimension
A	Purchase–sale (financial flow)
B	Input–output (material flow)
C	Information flow
D	Input flow into the innovation process

(exhibit 3.2) a network operator purchases networked elements from a networked element provider (e.g. switches, routers, systems software). This results in a *financial flow* from the purchaser to the seller. In some cases, however, the purchase–sale is indirect and this can affect the relationship between the parties concerned. For example, in Relationship 3 – the relationship between content and applications providers and final consumers – although a service may be provided by the former to the latter, the latter may not directly pay for the service. Payment may be made by a third party. For instance, Google or YouTube may provide a search service or content to final consumers who may not have to pay. However, the payment comes indirectly since the consumers provide their 'eyeballs' (i.e. their attention) which can be sold on to advertisers vying for this attention, for which they are willing to pay.

In Relationship 2 – the relationship between network operators and content and applications providers – the relationship may also be complicated. While the latter may pay for the network services they directly consume, they do not pay for the network services that their customers use. This lies at the heart of the so-called 'net neutrality conflict' (over whether network operators should be able to charge content and applications providers a premium in providing them and their customers with network services that are superior to those enjoyed by the ordinary Internet user).

Dimension B of the symbiotic relationship is an input–output relationship which involves a *material flow* (consisting of atoms or bits) between the groups of players concerned. It is here that a link is made between the ICT layer model and input–output and filière models that have been analysed by economists (the latter referring to upstream–downstream supply chain relationships). More generally, the first group provides inputs that are used by the second group to produce its output.

Dimension C of the symbiotic relationship involves *flows of information* through a variety of channels. This is a two-way flow that provides each of the parties to the relationship with information about the other. For instance, the seller by selling to the buyer and doing everything this requires gets information about the buyer, whether the buyer is an intermediate buyer in layers 1–3 or a final consumer in layer 4. Simultaneously, the buyer gets information about the seller. The information is partial and rarely provides the party with the full set of relevant information.

Dimension D involves using the fruits of the other three dimensions in order to *innovate*. For example, as we shall now show, a networked element provider (e.g. a provider of telecoms equipment) involved in a symbiotic relationship with one or more network operators – that is, involved in a Relationship 1 – will use the revenue that it receives

(Dimension A), together with relevant inputs it has purchased from other networked element providers (Dimension B), and the information that it has gathered (Dimension C) in order to generate innovations, such as an improvement in one or more of the networked elements it provides (Dimension D).

Example 1: symbiotic Relationship 1 between the telecoms operators and their networked element suppliers

The symbiotic relationship between the operators and their suppliers involves *close cooperation* and *mutual dependence*. One of the most important outcomes of this relationship is innovation. Indeed, so close is the symbiotic relationship between these two 'species' that the one, literally, could not exist without the other.

Let us examine more closely the nature of this relationship. In the first instance the relationship may be characterised as an input–output, buyer–seller relationship. The supplier, the seller, provides the inputs (the networked elements) to the buyer. At this level the relationship is both technical and economic. Technically, inputs are made available from which outputs (services) will be provided. Economically, a market transaction occurs with the purchase/sale of the elements at market prices.

However, this account does not capture crucial aspects of the relationship. Far more happens in the relationship between operator and supplier than input–output provision and purchase–sale. The reason is that the relationship between the operator and its supplier does not end with the purchase of the networked element. Indeed, in many ways it begins before the purchase and continues long after it.

Often it begins with the operator-user beginning to specify precisely what is needed. The process of specification itself is frequently an innovation process involving exploration, search and experimentation. And the innovation process continues after the purchase as the operator uses the networked elements within the context of its telecoms networks and discovers more about their strengths, weaknesses and limitations. This knowledge is, in a later round, passed on to the supplier (or to other suppliers) as the elements are upgraded, modernised and improved.

Central to the process just described is the triad: learning; knowledge accumulation; and innovation. It is this three-pronged process that makes the relationship between operator and supplier far more than an input–output and a purchase–sale relationship, although the latter two certainly are key parts of the nexus. It is important to stress that the learning, knowledge accumulation and innovation processes that we are analysing are themselves a joint output, produced by the symbiotic relationship between operator and supplier. In essence it is a cooperative, mutually dependent relationship from which both parties benefit.

The role of investment . . .

More needs to be considered about the role of *investment* in this symbiotic relationship. There are two key points here. The first is the essentially complementary relationship between investment and innovation. The second key point is that the bulk of the investment expenditure comes from the operator rather than the networked element supplier.

The process that we are talking about here starts with an investment decision. More specifically, a network operator invests in networked elements in order to be able to have a telecoms network that will provide services that can be sold at a profit to customers. (A virtual network operator is not buying the elements themselves, but rather the services of an existing operator.)

. . . and the intimate relationship with innovation

But in reality the process soon becomes more complicated. The complications will to a significant extent depend on the environment within which the investment decision is being made. For example, in a highly competitive environment the operator will want to invest not just in any networked elements but in those which, strung together in the form of a network, will provide services that are in some way superior (cheaper or of better quality) to those offered by competing network operators. It is here that the incentive to innovate enters the symbiotic relationship. The operator wants innovative elements; the supplier has an incentive to provide them. The supplier's incentive comes both from an opportunity (to receive a significant share of the operator's investment expenditure) and a threat (if it does not provide the innovative element it is possible, and over time likely, that a competing supplier will).

As this brief account of the symbiotic relationship between operator and supplier makes clear, the relationship at one and the same time involves investment and innovation. Both are intimately intertwined.[6]

Example 2: symbiotic Relationship 6 between telecoms operators and final customers

Traditional telecoms symbiotic relationship

Traditionally, Relationship 6 has involved the provision of fixed-voice services to final customers. Over time, however, these services have expanded to include mobile services and Internet access. However, in general, the latter two services are not too different from fixed-voice services, involving similar kinds of interactions with customers and similar organisational routines.

One of the characteristics of Relationship 6 is that final consumers are relatively passive. In competitive markets they choose their telecoms operators according to their perceptions of price and quality of service, but they then play little further role. This is very different, however, from the symbiosis in Relationship 3 – that is, the relationship between the platform, content and applications provider in layer 3 and the final customer in layer 4.

Example 3: symbiotic Relationship 3 between content and applications providers and final customers

A new symbiotic relationship

Relationship 3 is fundamentally different from Relationship 6, particularly since the evolution of the Internet has created the so-called Web 2.0. Web 2.0 is characterised by new forms of interaction with users who now play a key role in the content-creation and innovation processes. The telecoms operator that diversifies into layer 3 – becoming a platform, content and applications provider – must form a very different pattern of interaction with final customers in layer 4. This is shown as Relationship 3.

---

[6] For studies on the importance of user–producer interactions in the innovation process, see Ake (1988); von Hippel (1988, 1998); Thomke and von Hippel (2002).

The distinctiveness of symbiotic Relationship 3

It is crucial to understand that there is a fundamental discontinuity between Relationship 6 and Relationship 3. This discontinuity is caused by the significantly different competencies that are required in the two relationships. It is this discontinuity, and the associated different competencies, that explains an important characteristic of the new ICT ecosystem, namely that it is *new entrants rather than the incumbents from layers 1 and 2 who dominate layer 3.*

Web 2.0 and Relationship 3

It is valuable to read the seminal 2005 publication by Tim O'Reilly, which did much to establish the widespread adoption of the Web 2.0 terminology, as essentially an account of symbiotic Relationship 3.[7] As O'Reilly points out, this symbiotic relationship requires a number of important innovation capabilities. At the heart of these capabilities are the software skills needed to create, manage and improve an interactive database that allows the Internet content and applications provider (ICAP) to interact in a variety of ways with its customer-users. In O'Reilly's words: 'Database management is a core competency of Web 2.0 companies' (O'Reilly 2007).

However, the innovation capabilities needed go far beyond the software skills required in the management of databases. How to get customer-users closely involved in the content and applications of the site, and to keep them involved, is a key part of the capabilities required. The reason is that it is their involvement that adds value to the site, generating additional content and contributing directly to innovation in the content and applications. In turn, this generates network effects, a crucial part of the Web 2.0 concept whereby the value of the site increases the greater the number of users.[8] But getting customer-users involved is no easy matter, particularly since there is a large amount of competition on the Web for their attention.

---

[7] O'Reilly's original article, 'What is Web 2.0: Design Patterns and Business Models for the Next Generation of Software,' published on 30 September 2005, is to be found on his web site, www.oreilly.com. This article has how been republished (O'Reilly 2007), as part of a special issue on Web 2.0. Other publications on Web 2.0 include Levine *et al.* (2000); Kelly (2003); and Tapscott and Williams (2006).

[8] As O'Reilly concludes: 'The lesson: Network effects from user contributions are the key to market dominance in the Web 2.0 era.'

There are other important dimensions to the innovation capabilities that are needed. One example is perpetual beta development, whereby applications are constantly improved and tested through interaction and feedback from the customer-users who in effect become co-innovators. This requires trust in the users. As O'Reilly (2007) recommends: 'Engage your users as real-time testers, and instrument the service so that you know how people use the new features.'

The key point to understand is that these innovation capabilities are very different from those involved in the provision of telecom services to customers, such as fixed and mobile voice and Internet access (included in Relationship 6). In short, the company that has mastered Relationship 6 has not yet begun to master Relationship 3. Indeed, to go one step further, having mastered Relationship 6 may well be an obstacle to mastering Relationship 3, since the organisational routines and mindsets required for the former may impede the development of those needed for the latter. As noted, this explains why in all countries the Internet content and applications providers in layer 3 are new entrants and not the incumbents from layers 1 and 2.

Example 4: symbiotic Relationships 2 and 5 between networked element providers/network operators and content and applications providers

A symbiotic relationship also exists between networked element providers and network operators, on the one hand, and content and applications providers, on the other. An example is the relationship between element providers (such as Cisco, Dell and Microsoft) and telecoms operators (such as AT&T, France Télécom and Neuf Cegetel), on the one hand, and Internet content and applications providers (for example, Google, Yahoo!, eBay and MySpace), on the other.

In this symbiotic relationship, the former provide a production and innovation platform for the latter. Without this platform the latter would not be able to offer their content and applications to their customers. Furthermore, they would be unable to innovate, offering new content and applications. It is precisely this symbiotic relationship that is captured in the architectural conceptualisation of the layer model. The content and applications providers in layer 3 'sit on top of' the platform provided by layers 1 and 2.

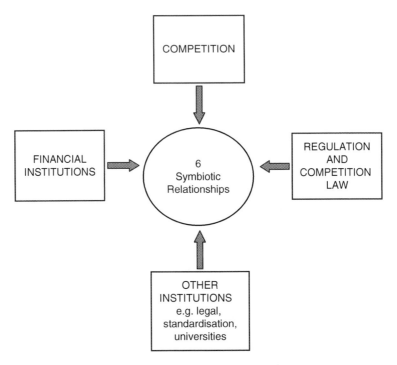

Exhibit 3.6. *The context of the symbiotic relationships*

The context of the symbiotic relationships

Each of the symbiotic relationships occurs within a specific *context* that shapes the nature of the relationship. It is here that both competition and institutions enter the picture, as depicted in exhibit 3.6.

Four sets of influences on the symbiotic relationships are depicted in exhibit 3.6. The first is *competition*. For example, the relationship between a networked element provider and a network operator is affected, as we have seen, by the degree of competition that element provider faces from other competing element providers. The degree of competition will influence the relationship between the element provider and the network operator, as well as the kinds of innovation that the former makes. This underlines how important competition is as a determinant of innovation.

The second influence is *financial institutions*. An example, referred to elsewhere in this book (including appendix 1), is the telecoms 'boom and bust', when the functioning (and malfunctioning) of financial markets – including the cost and terms on which financing was provided as well as more general expectations regarding the returns that were to be made – had a significant effect on the functioning of the entire ICT ecosystem.

The third set of institutions is *regulation and competition law*. These institutions determine the 'rules of the game' under which the symbiotic relationships operate. In turn, this influences the outcomes produced by these relationships, including the processes of innovation.

Finally, *other institutions* are involved, including legal institutions (such as intellectual property laws), standardisation (which crucially affects the way in which the ICT ecosystem's module producers operate, and in turn the interoperability of the system) and universities (which do research, producing some of the new knowledge which through the symbiotic relationships drives change in the system – see appendix 1 for examples – provide trained person-power and incubate entrepreneurs).

Intra-layer and intra-firm innovation processes and relationships with other ecosystems

Intra-layer and *intra-firm* innovation processes and relationships with other ecosystems are also important. An example of a significant intra-layer symbiotic relationship is that between semiconductor providers and those who produce systems using their devices, a relationship that occurs within layer 1. This relationship involves learning and innovation.

Innovation relationships and processes also occur within firms. Some firms, for instance, use their own products and services. Users and providers within the firm interact in order to make improvements (a specific example being the relationship in telecoms operators between the division providing network services and the division using those services in order to sell retail to final customers). Another example, used by Arno Penzias, former head of research in Bell Labs, is the relationship between basic researchers and their 'customers' in applied research in R&D laboratories.

Interactions also occur with other ecosystems. One important example is interactions between the new ICT ecosystem and the financial ecosystem, finance being treated here as part of the environmental context within which the players interact. Important though these

are as part of the overall process of innovation in the new ICT
ecosystem in the interests of simplification they will not be discussed
further here.

Innovators and Schumpeterian entrepreneurs

Until this point in the discussion it has been assumed that innovation
emerges from the symbiotic relationships in the new ICT ecosystem,
contextualised by competition and institutions. But more needs to be
said about how this process of innovation occurs. Let us go back to the
example of the symbiotic relationship between networked element
suppliers and network operators. We have seen that this relationship
provides the supplier not only with information about the needs of the
operator-user and the uses to which the networked elements are put,
but also with the resources that are necessary to produce the elements
and, over time, improve them.

But in order to improve the elements, to innovate, someone (or
some people) needs to produce ideas (new knowledge) regarding the
kinds of changes that would constitute 'improvements' within this
context. In other words, a *cognitive process* is necessary, one that
involves experimental thought and conjecture. The conjectures that
are finally selected are then implemented and tested within the symbiotic relationship, finding either acceptance or rejection. In this way the
symbiotic relationship acts as both a variety-generating and a selection
process.

It is here that Schumpeter's analysis of entrepreneurship enters the
picture. For Schumpeter, it is entrepreneurs who make the innovations
that fuel the system. In general Schumpeter was less concerned
with incremental improvements that essentially left the status quo
unaltered than he was with radical innovations that created the new
while destroying the old. It is these radical innovations that he referred
to as 'new combinations'. The Schumpeterian entrepreneur is a quirky
character. She/he has a different view of the world than others, seeing
opportunities and holding beliefs that they do not. Moreover, the
Schumpeterian entrepreneur has the strength of conviction and motivation to obtain the resources that are needed and to put them into
effect in order to achieve the planned outcome. The result of such
entrepreneurial action is the disruption of the system, disequilibrium
rather than equilibrium.

Not surprisingly, as Metcalfe (2004) has observed, orthodox economics has found it difficult to incorporate such unconventional characters into a conceptual framework characterised by optimisation and equilibrium. The result is that 'Economic theory and the entrepreneur have never made easy travelling companions.'[9] Metcalfe notes: 'Here is a paradox, with which any observer of modern economics must contend. Entrepreneurial behaviour is pervasive yet economic theory, with one or two very significant exceptions, has virtually nothing to say about either its significance or about its origins.'[10]

While entrepreneurship in this sense may be carried out by individuals it may also be undertaken by teams in new or existing firms, small or large. What all these cases of entrepreneurship have in common is the injection of novelty into the ICT ecosystem through new knowledge created in the process of conjecture, experimentation and testing in the market.

Arguably, by focusing on radical innovation Schumpeter underestimated the cumulative significance over time of incremental innovations. Certainly, much of the innovation that takes place in the new ICT ecosystem, over time transforming it, is of the latter kind, emerging as we have seen from symbiotic relationships. Indeed, in his later work, Schumpeter emphasised the extent to which the innovation process in the modern capitalist system has been routinised in the R&D organisations of large companies. However, while this is the case, the Schumpeterian entrepreneur has played, and will continue to play, a key role in generating the variety that transforms the new ICT ecosystem.

Incumbents and new entrants

It is worth pointing out, particularly in a section on the generation of variety in the new ICT ecosystem, that Schumpeter believed that entrepreneurial new entrants played an important role in the dynamics of the capitalist system. In Schumpeter's words:

it is not essential to the matter – though it may happen – that the new combinations should be carried out by the same people who control the productive or commercial process which is to be displaced by the new. On

---

[9] Metcalfe (2004: 157).
[10] *Ibid.*: 158.

the contrary, new combinations are, as a rule, embodied, as it were, in new firms which generally do not arise out of the old ones but start producing beside them; . . . in general it is not the owner of stage-coaches who builds railways.[11]

There are industries where incumbents have survived and prospered for long periods of time, adapting to the novelty injected into the system by the new entrants and, at times, even beating them at their own game. But in these industries the challenges mounted by new entrants have been important in keeping the incumbents on their toes by forcing them to confront the new. The beneficiaries have been the system as a whole and the users of its output.

Consumers as co-evolving innovators

We have already seen how intermediate consumers – that is, consuming companies in layers 1, 2 and 3 – play an important role in the innovation process in the new ICT ecosystem. Final consumers in layer 4 are also crucial. However, there are differences between their role in the system and that of the intermediate consumers.

As Nobel Laureate Amartya Sen stresses, it is only final consumers in socio-economic systems who are both a means (through the labour they provide) and the end (i.e. the purpose) of the activity of the system. Not only do final consumers consume the output of the ICT ecosystem; they also have a say over how the system should work. As the exercisers of political power, consumers influence the organisations that change institutions (at the same time as they are influenced by the institutions they are changing).[12] It is for this reason that some governments and regulators distinguish between consumers and citizens.

But consumers have another dual existence in the new ICT ecosystem. Through their demand they are part of the selection mechanism responsible for the selection of innovations. But consumers are also shaped by the innovations they have selected, and this has consequences for second and subsequent rounds of selection. In this way co-evolutionary processes are generated with consumer demand, consumer behaviour and innovations co-evolving.

[11] Schumpeter (1961: 66).
[12] See n. 13.

Exhibit 3.7. *The changing role of final consumers*

- As *sources of revenue*
- As *user-feedback providers* (e.g. von Hippel 1998)
- As *sources of knowledge* (e.g. open-source software, Wikipedia)
- As *sources of information* (e.g. Web 2.0)
- As *content creators*
- As *conversers* (e.g. social networking, blogging)
- As *activist citizens*

An important example is the co-evolution of one key innovation in the new ICT ecosystem – the Internet – and consumer behaviour. Selected by consumers, the Internet is radically transforming the way in which they behave and the role they are playing in the socio-economy. As highlighted in exhibit 3.7, final consumers play a multi-dimensional role in the ecosystem, a role that has been enhanced and further varied by the Internet's evolution.

The Internet, itself a radical Schumpeterian creative–destructive innovation, has therefore created new ways for final consumers to become part of the innovation processes of the new ICT ecosystem. Through its aggregative and interactive properties, its widespread availability and its low cost and ease of use, the Internet has incorporated final consumers as never before into the innovation process, not only in the ICT ecosystem but in the economy as a whole.

The generation of variety and selection

It is in this way – through the symbiotic relationships occurring within specific contexts of competition and institutionality, through Schumpeterian entrepreneurs and through innovative new entrants – that variety is generated by the production of new products, processes, forms of organisation and markets. However, not all of this variety will survive.

The reason is the *selection mechanisms* that exist within the new ICT ecosystem that winnow from the variety, selecting some forms and rejecting others. Particularly powerful is market selection, where intermediate and final customers, through their decisions and choices, determine which products and services – and therefore which suppliers – will be selected. But there are also many other selection mechanisms in the ecosystem. Examples include intra-firm, pre-market mechanisms and others driven by government that are not fully determined by market criteria.

The restless new ICT ecosystem

Through these processes, the new ICT ecosystem is in a constant process of flux. In appendix 1 a brief history of the ICT sector is provided to show the main innovations that have driven the evolution of this sector since it began around the time of the Second World War (with some earlier antecedents). Over time, these changes have had a profound effect on the ecosystem itself and its internal boundaries. If we were to provide a topographical structural depiction of the ecosystem pre-1995, when the Internet took off as a mass phenomenon, it would not have the Internet content and applications providers in layer 3. Indeed, arguably, the content provided by 'old media' was produced by an entirely different ecosystem.

The boundaries – shown in our depiction of the new ICT ecosystem in exhibit 1.3 (p. 9) as dashed lines – also shift over time, changing the functionalities provided in the different layers. One key example, fundamental to the operation of the entire new ICT ecosystem, is the changing boundary between networked element providers and network operators, as depicted in exhibit 3.8.

Until around the mid-1980s, as discussed in more detail in appendix 1, most of the research and a significant part of the development of the telecommunications part of the ICT ecosystem were carried out by the network operators in layer 2. This R&D was done in their central research laboratories, such as AT&T's Bell Labs, France Télécom's CNET and BT's Martlesham Laboratories. Typically, the research resulted in the creation of prototype new networked elements (such as switches and transmissions systems) that were tested in the laboratories and then transferred to the suppliers in layer 1 for production.

Over time, however, for reasons examined in appendix 1, the networked element providers became more and more sophisticated. (Data on the R&D of these two groups of players is discussed in chapter 4.) As this happened network operators gradually began transferring more network-related activities to their suppliers in layer 1, shifting the boundary between the two layers upwards, as shown in

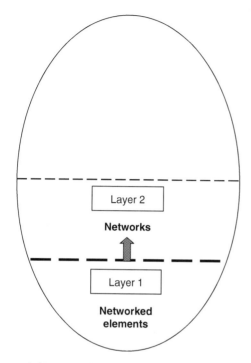

Exhibit 3.8. *The shifting boundary between layers 1 and 2*

exhibit 3.8. This is just one example, though an important one, of dynamic change occurring over time in the structure of the new ICT ecosystem.

This serves to reiterate the point made at the beginning of this chapter, that the topographical structural depiction in the layer model is static, valid for a point in time. However, the hierarchically organised architecture of the functionalities necessary for the operation of the new ICT ecosystem continues. Networked elements, however much they may change over time, are still needed for the construction of networks which, although they too change, are necessary as a platform on the basis of which content and applications are provided.

Conclusion

In this chapter, the new ICT ecosystem has been viewed as an innovation system, as a system which generates endogenously the innovations in

products, processes, forms of organisation and markets that transform the system itself as it evolves over time.[13] These innovations
largely emerge from the symbiotic relationships between the four
groups of players that have been identified at the level of abstraction of the new ICT ecosystem used in this book, interacting within
their environment (although the importance of intra-layer and intra-
firm innovation processes and interactions with other ecosystems,
while not examined in detail here, has also been acknowledged). It is
this innovation that drives the new ICT ecosystem, making it the
restless system that it is and fuelling its contribution to the dyna-
mism of the social and economic systems.

[13] Little has been said here about the transformation process of institutions.
Suffice it to say that in this connection an insight by Nobel Laureate Douglass
North is relevant. North distinguishes between institutions, which he defines as
the 'rules of the game,' and organisations (such as companies, political parties
and trade unions) that exert the power to change institutions. The interaction
between the two is mutual, since organisations themselves operate under the
rules of the game that the institutions they are changing determine. See North
(1990).

4 | *The new ICT ecosystem: a quantitative analysis*

In order to throw further light on the working of the new ICT ecosystem we have constructed a database with information on 157 leading ICT companies divided according to the three layers in the layer model. Analysis of this data reveals, for example, the key contribution made by the networked element providers in layer 1 to the total amount of R&D undertaken in the ecosystem. It also highlights the importance of the network operators who provide the bulk of capital expenditure in the system. A further important finding is that the returns to telecoms operators in layer 2 is relatively lower than the returns to players in the other two layers.

The companies and their assignment to layers

In constructing our database, we selected the top 157 ICT companies (according to market capitalisation) from Thomson Financial.[1] A second source was also used: UBS.[2] We then allocated these companies to the three layers in the ICT ecosystem.[3] The outcome of this procedure and the classifications we have used are shown in exhibit 4.1.

As can be seen from exhibit 4.1, layers 1, 2 and 3 contain 54, 50 and 53 companies, respectively. Layer 1 companies are broken down into two further categories (in sub-sectors A); IT companies (which include system software providers) and telecoms equipment companies. It should be noted that some companies are included in both categories. The IT and telecoms equipment companies are broken down (in sub-sectors B) into European, US and Asian companies.

---

[1] In addition, the following were also used: (i) annual reports and (ii) the DTI R&D scoreboard.

[2] UBS (2007).

[3] A full list of the companies in the database, organised by layer, is to be found in appendix 10.

Exhibit 4.1. *Database classification*

Layer	Functionality	Sub-sectors A (not mutually exclusive)	Sub-sectors B
Layer 1 (54 companies)	Networked elements	IT (incl. system software providers)	European IT, US IT, Asian IT
		Telecoms equipment	European telecoms equipment, US telecoms equipment, Asian telecoms equipment
Layer 2 (50 companies)	Networks	Network services (incl. telecoms, cable, and satellite network operators)	European network services, US network services, Asian network services
		Telecoms services (telecoms network operators)	European telecoms services, US telecoms services, Asian telecoms services
Layer 3 (53 companies)	Platforms, content and applications	Software and services (incl. content and applications software providers)	European software and services, US software and services, Asian software and services
		Internet and e-commerce (Internet-based providers)	European Internet and e-commerce, US Internet and e-commerce, Asian Internet and e-commerce

The companies in layer 2 are divided into two categories (in sub-sectors A), namely network services companies (which include telecoms, cable and satellite network operators) and telecoms services companies (which include only telecoms network operators). Again, each of these two categories is further divided (in sub-sectors B) into European, US and Asian groups.

In layer 3 the companies are divided into two categories (in sub-sectors A); software and services companies (which include content and applications software providers) and Internet and e-commerce companies (that are primarily Internet-based providers). The two categories are further broken down (in sub-sectors B) into European, US and Asian groups.

The individual companies, and the sub-divisions into which they are divided, are shown in appendix 10.

It is important to note that some companies have been included in more than one layer. Microsoft is an example. Most of Microsoft's activities are based on its Windows operating system. Since in our classification system software (which is a networked element) is included in layer 1 these Microsoft activities are included in layer 1. However, Microsoft also is involved in layer 3 (for example, through Microsoft's MSN portal). In order to reflect correctly Microsoft's multilayer involvement we have assumed that 80 per cent of its activities are in layer 1 with the remaining 20 per cent in layer 3. Accordingly, we have assumed that 80 per cent of its market capitalisation is attributable to layer 1 and 20 per cent to layer 3. The companies that have been dealt with in this way are shown in appendix 10.

It should also be noted that the data in our database runs from 2002 to 2006. The reason for choosing 2002 as the starting year is the telecoms 'boom and bust' which distorted figures from the late 1990s until around 2002.

The dynamics of the ICT ecosystem

In this sub-section we use the data provided in our database in order to gain further insights into the dynamics of the ICT ecosystem.

Key investment role played by network operators in layer 2

As exhibits 4.2a and 4.2b show, network operators in layer 2 play a key role in the ICT ecosystem through their capital expenditure, largely in network infrastructure.

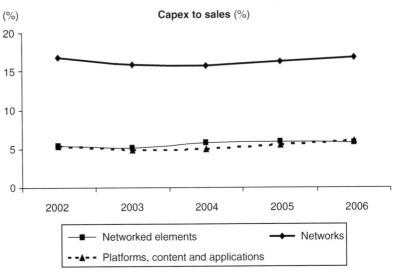

Sources: Thomson Financial and annual reports.

Exhibit 4.2a. *Capital expenditure (capex) intensity, by layer, 2002–6*

Exhibit 4.2b. *Capex, by layer: telecoms sector and Internet companies, 2002–6*

	Average per layer						Distribution	
	2002 (%)	2003 (%)	2004 (%)	2005 (%)	2006 (%)	Av. 2002–6 (%)	2002–6 (%)	2006 (%)
Telecoms equipments	5	4	4	4	3	4	7	6
Telecoms services	17	16	16	17	17	17	92	91
Internet and e-commerce	4	5	5	5	8	5	2	3
Whole ICT eco-system	10	10	10	10	10	10	100	100

Sources: Thomson Financial, annual reports.

As is evident from exhibit 4.2a, the network services providers in layer 2 (including telecoms, cable and satellite network operators) are significantly more capital-intensive than their counterparts in layers 1 and 3. In 2006, for example, the capital expenditure: sales ratio for layer 2 companies was about 17 per cent, while for the other two layers the figure was around 6 per cent.

The key investment role played by network operators in layer 2 is even more apparent in terms of the absolute capital expenditure by each layer. In 2006, for example, according to our sample 70 per cent of the total capital expenditure made by companies in all three layers came from network service providers in layer 2. The IT companies in layer 1 provided 26 per cent of total capital expenditure, leaving the companies in layer 3 to take care of the remaining 4 per cent. As these figures clearly show, it is the *layer 2 companies that play the dominant role in making the investments that are needed to develop the networks (including the Internet) on which the ICT sector and the entire economy depend.*

A similar conclusion emerges from exhibit 4.2b, which confines attention to telecoms operators, telecoms equipment providers and the Internet-based companies in layer 3. Here in 2006 91 per cent of the total capital expenditure undertaken by these players in the three layers was made by the telecoms operators in layer 2. According to our sample, only 6 per cent of total capital expenditure came from the telecoms equipment providers in layer 1, leaving the remaining 3 per cent to be undertaken by the layer 3 Internet-based firms.

It may be concluded, therefore, that the network operators in layer 2 in general, and the telecoms operators in this layer in particular, play the key role in making the investments that are necessary to develop the networks (including the Internet) on which the ICT sector itself, and the economy as a whole, depend. This conclusion, however, raises an important further issue that will be mentioned here and returned to later in the chapter. In order to finance their investments layer 2 companies need to be sufficiently profitable. This will allow them to finance investment from retained profits and to raise additional capital on capital markets at reasonable cost.[4] In a later section we shall examine the relative profitability of layer 2 companies and return to this issue.

Key R&D role played by networked element providers in layer 1

In this sub-section we examine the R&D role played by companies in the three layers. Exhibits 4.3a and 4.3b provide the data.

---

[4] To be more precise, it is the expected future profit margin that matters.

Exhibit 4.3a. *R&D intensity, by layer, 2002–6*

	Average per layer						Distribution	
	2002 (%)	2003 (%)	2004 (%)	2005 (%)	2006 (%)	Av. 2002–6 (%)	2002–6 (%)	2006 (%)
Networked elements	8	8	8	7	7	8	75	73
Networks	1	1	1	1	1	1	11	11
Platforms, content and applications	3	3	4	4	4	4	13	16
ICT eco-system WW	5	5	5	4	4	4	100	100

Sources: Thomson Financial, DTI, annual reports.

Exhibit 4.3b. *R&D, by layer: telecoms sector and Internet companies, 2002–6*

	Average per layer						Distribution	
	2002 (%)	2003 (%)	2004 (%)	2005 (%)	2006 (%)	Av. 2002–6 (%)	2002–6 (%)	2006 (%)
Telecoms equipments	11	11	10	10	10	11	66	63
Telecoms services	1	1	1	1	1	1	26	25
Internet and e-commerce	9	10	9	8	9	9	8	12
ICT eco-system WW	5	5	5	4	4	4	100	100

Sources: Thomson Financial, DTI, annual reports.

As exhibit 4.3a shows, on the basis of our sample it is the companies in layers 1 and 3 that are the most R&D-intensive. Indeed, there is only a small difference in R&D intensity between these two layers, the average intensity between 2002 and 2006 for layer 1 being 8 per cent while that for layer 3 was 4 per cent. However, the R&D intensity for the network operators in layer 2 is significantly lower, averaging 1 per cent for the same period.

A somewhat different picture, however, emerges if we look at absolute expenditure on R&D. In 2006, 73 per cent of the total R&D expenditure undertaken by all the companies in all three layers was done by the networked element providers in layer 1. By contrast, 11 per cent was undertaken by the network operators in layer 2, with 16 per cent being done by the companies in layer 3 (the difference is due to rounding). In terms of absolute expenditures on R&D, therefore, the companies in layers 2 and 3 played a fairly similar role. What is striking, however, is the *dominant role played by layer 1 companies, which contribute three-quarters of the R&D expenditure undertaken by the entire ICT ecosystem.*

In exhibit 4.3b, attention is focused on the telecoms operators, the telecoms equipment providers and the Internet-based companies. Here a similar picture emerges in terms of R&D intensity. Both layer 1 and layer 3 companies have a similar R&D intensity, averaging between 2002 and 2006 11 per cent for the former companies and 9 per cent for the latter. By contrast, the telecoms operators in layer 2 had an R&D intensity of 1 per cent.

However, once again a different picture becomes apparent when we examine absolute R&D expenditures. In 2006 the telecoms equipment providers in layer 1 accounted for 63 per cent of all R&D undertaken in all three layers of the ICT ecosystem. The corresponding figure for the telecoms operators in layer 2 was 25 per cent while the Internet-based companies in layer 3 accounted for the remaining 12 per cent. It may be concluded, therefore, that in terms of R&D it is the companies in layer 1 that play the key role. Insofar as R&D is a driver of change in the ICT ecosystem, it is these companies that are major change agents.

Having said this, however, it is important to distinguish, as we have done in earlier chapters, between R&D and innovation. Following Schumpeter, we distinguished between four different forms of innovation:

1. Changes in products and services
2. Changes in technology and processes
3. Changes in forms of organisation
4. The development of new markets.

While R&D may be a determinant in all four of these areas, non-R&D-based innovation may also be important. Furthermore, as we noted earlier, companies may play a key role in the innovation process as users of the products and processes of supplier companies, and in this way may make important contributions to the latter's innovation, although this contribution may not be reflected in the R&D figures. Specifically, the network operators in layer 2 to some extent play this role *vis-à-vis* their networked element providers in layer 1. An example of non-R&D innovation is the development of electronic billing that has in many areas replaced paper bills. It is important to remember this qualification in discussing R&D and innovation in the ICT ecosystem.

Profitability in the new ICT ecosystem

Where is profitability highest in the new ICT ecosystem? Information to answer this question is provided in exhibits 4.4a and 4.4b.

Exhibit 4.4a shows that profitability (measured by operating income to sales, our preferred measure) is more or less the same in layers 3 and 2, but significantly lower in layer 1.

As is clear from exhibit 4.4b, the ratio of operating income to sales is highest for the Internet and e-commerce companies in layer 3 (over 20 per cent in 2006), second highest for telecoms services companies in layer 2 (around 15 per cent in 2006), and lowest for telecoms equipment companies in layer 1 (just under 10 per cent), although the figure for the latter companies has increased since 2002 at which time they were still feeling the impact of the telecoms bust and the excess capacity that existed.

Obviously, sufficient rates of profit are necessary for companies to continue playing their respective roles in the ICT ecosystem. For example, as was noted earlier, appropriate rates of profit are necessary if telecoms operators are to continue making the investments that are needed to upgrade telecoms networks, including the Internet. Such profit is needed for these firms to finance their investments internally and to raise capital on external capital markets. However, from the point of view of investors in these companies the return on their investments may be more important than the profitability of the companies. What has happened to returns in the new ICT ecosystem?

Returns in the new ICT ecosystem

Two measures of returns are used in this sub-section; return on equity (ROE)[5] and returns on invested capital (ROIC). These are shown in exhibits 4.5 and 4.6.

---

[5] It is important to note that ROE may be affected by debt.

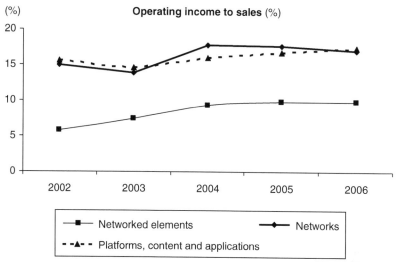

Sources: Thomson Financial, annual reports.

Exhibit 4.4a. *Profitability in the entire new ICT ecosystem, 2002–6*

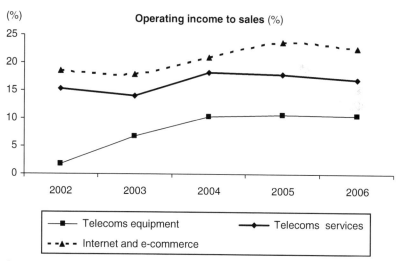

Sources: Thomson Financial, annual reports.

Exhibit 4.4b. *Profitability in the new ICT ecosystem: telecoms sector and Internet companies, 2002–6*

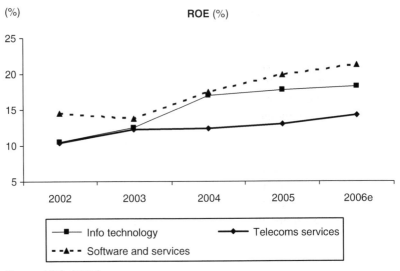

Source: UBS, (2007).
Note: e = Estimated.

Exhibit 4.5a. *ROE in the new ICT ecosystem, 2002–6*

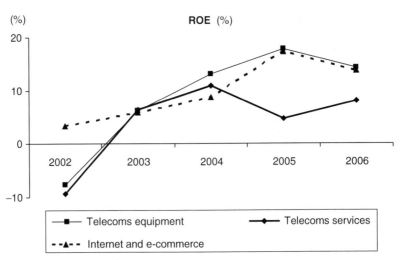

Sources: Thomson Financial, annual reports.

Exhibit 4.5b. *ROE in the new ICT ecosystem: telecoms sector and Internet companies, 2002–6*

As exhibit 4.5a shows, the ROE is highest in software and services (layer 3), second-highest in IT (layer 1) and lowest in telecoms services (layer 2). In 2006, according to the UBS survey,[6] the return in software and services was slightly over 20 per cent, while for telecoms services the figure was about 13 per cent.

A similar picture emerges if we confine attention to telecoms services, telecoms equipment, and Internet and e-commerce companies, as is shown in exhibit 4.5b. Here, too, telecoms services companies in layer 2 earn the lowest rates of return, although for 2006 there appears to be some convergence between returns in the three layers. However, the returns to telecoms equipment companies in layer 1, at around 15 per cent, are higher than those to telecoms services companies, which are about 10 per cent.

The ROIC is shown in exhibits 4.6a and 4.6b. As can be seen from exhibit 4.6a, the ROIC is the lowest for telecoms services companies, somewhat over 10 per cent. This compares with over 40 per cent in software and services and slightly over 30 per cent in IT.

A similar picture emerges if attention is confined to telecoms services and equipment and Internet and e-commerce, as is shown in exhibit 4.6b. Here, too, the return to telecoms services companies in layer 2 is the lowest. However, in this case it is telecoms equipment companies in layer 1 that earn higher returns on capital employed (ROCE) than the Internet and e-commerce firms in layer 3. The spread of returns is smaller than in exhibit 4.6a.

Implications of the differential in profitability and returns

All other things equal, a layer that generates relatively low profitability and returns compared to other layers in the ICT sector and compared to other sectors in the economy may be disadvantaged in terms of the supply and/or the cost of capital.[7] Below a certain level of profitability and returns, this may negatively affect the ability of companies in that layer to play their role in contributing to the healthy development of the ICT ecosystem as a whole. For example, telecoms equipment companies may be unable to undertake sufficient R&D to create innovations that might improve the performance of the ICT ecosystem, or telecoms services firms may not be able to make the

[6] UBS (2007).
[7] This assumes equivalent risk in the different layers.

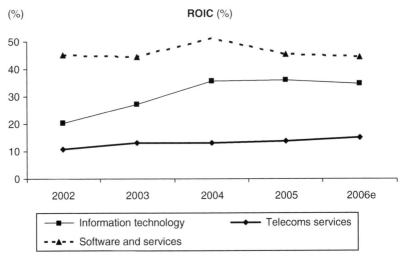

Source: UBS, (2007).

Exhibit 4.6a. *ROIC in the new ICT ecosystem, 2002–6*

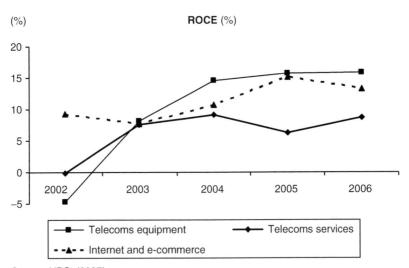

Source: UBS, (2007).

Exhibit 4.6b. *ROCE in the new ICT ecosystem: telecoms sector and Internet companies, 2002–6*

investments that would improve telecoms networks (including the Internet).

It is, however, difficult to be precise about the minimum level of profitability and returns that are needed at a particular time for a healthy evolution of the ICT Ecosystem. One reason is that it is hard to isolate the variables determining the allocation and cost of capital to a specific layer. Furthermore, it is problematical to define what should be understood by a 'healthy evolution' of the system. Having said this, it is clear from the public statements of a number of CEOs of telecoms services companies that they feel that levels of profitability and returns in layer 2 are beginning to threaten their ability to make the investments that are needed to create internationally competitive telecoms infrastructure in their national systems – for instance, investment in next-generation high-speed IP networks.

Global differences in the profitability of telecoms services companies[8]

The argument has been made that the incumbent European telecoms operators face comparatively less competition than their Asian (Japanese and Korean) and US counterparts. It has been argued that the incumbents in Japan and Korea face strong competition from disruptive competitors (such as Softbank in Japan and Hanaro in Korea) who have been far more aggressive and gone much further than competitors in Europe to seize market share from the incumbents. Similarly, it has been suggested that the incumbent telecoms operators in the USA (specifically AT&T and Verizon) face significantly stronger competition from cable companies than their counterparts in the larger European countries (although in some small European countries, such as the Netherlands and Belgium, competition from cable is important). Is there any evidence to throw light on this hypothesis?

---

[8] The telecoms services companies included in each region are:

- **Europe:** Belgacom, BT, Colt, Deutsche Telekom, Eutelia, Fastweb, France Télécom, Freenet, Iliad, KPN, Mobile Telesystems, Neuf Cegetel, Portugal Telecom, Swisscom, Tele2, Telecom Italia, Telefonica, TeliaSonera, Tiscali, Vivendi (SFR), Vodafone
- **USA:** ATT/Bellsouth, Bellsouth, Level3, Qwest, SprintNextel, Verizon
- **Asia:** KDDI, KT, NTT, SKT

One way of approaching the question is to examine the profitability and returns of telecoms operators in Europe, Asia (largely Japan and Korea and excluding China, as is discussed in appendix 9) and the USA. All other things equal (such as taxation requirements and regulatory regime) it would be expected that if European incumbents enjoyed greater market power than their counterparts as a result of less competition they would earn relatively higher profits and generate relatively higher returns than the incumbents in Asia and the USA. Is there evidence to support this hypothesis? Information on the relative profitability and returns of these telecoms operators is provided in exhibits 4.7–4.9.

As exhibit 4.7 shows, in 2002 and 2003 European telecoms operators had the lowest profitability of the operators in the three regions. However, in 2004 and 2005 they had the highest profitability. By 2006 the relative profitability of the European operators had declined so that although they were more profitable than the Asian and US companies there was little difference between the two.

But were European operators able to generate relatively greater returns? Data to examine this hypothesis is given in exhibits 4.8 and 4.9. From exhibit 4.8 it can be seen that the ROE in the US and

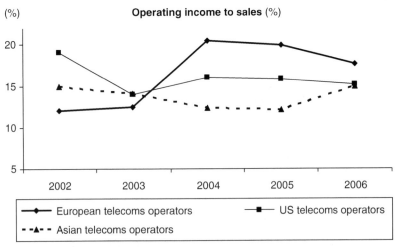

Sources: Thomson Financial, annual reports.

Exhibit 4.7. *Profitability of telecoms operators in Europe, Asia and the USA, 2002–6*

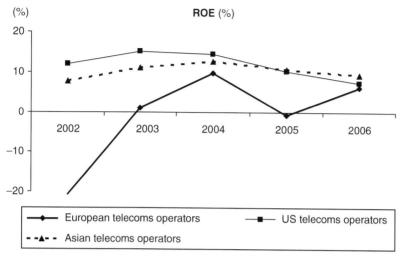

Sources: Thomson Financial, annual reports.

Exhibit 4.8. *ROE of telecoms operators in Europe, Asia and the USA, 2002–6*

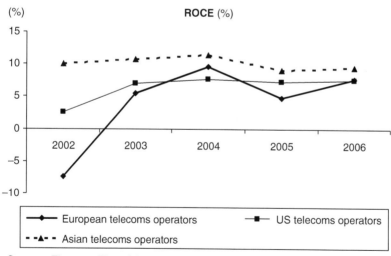

Sources: Thomson Financial, annual reports.

Exhibit 4.9. *ROCE of telecoms operators in Europe, Asia and the USA, 2002–6*

Asian telecoms operators (excluding China) dominates that of the European companies. In four of the five years 2002–6, the ROE of the US companies has exceeded that of the European companies. In 2006 the ROE of the European companies was equal to that of the US firms. The ROE of the US firms also dominated that of the Asian firms, except for 2006 where the latter's return was slightly higher.

The ROCE is shown in exhibit 4.9. Here the Asian companies (again excluding China) dominate those from the other two regions in all of the five years 2002–6. In three of the five years the return in the US companies is greater than that in the European companies. In 2006 the return in the European companies is equal to that of the US firms.

From this data on profitability and returns it may be concluded that there is no strong evidence to suggest that European telecoms operators have significantly more market power than their Asian and US counterparts. Although the profitability of the European companies was higher than that of the firms in the other two regions in 2004, 2005 and 2006, in the latter year there was little difference between the European and Asian companies. Furthermore, the data on the ROE and ROCE show that, comparatively speaking, the European firms have performed worse than their Asian and US counterparts.

Conclusion

Four general conclusions may be derived from the data analysed in this chapter. The first conclusion is that the networked element providers in layer 1 are the most important contributors to R&D in the new ICT ecosystem. However, as has been stressed in this chapter and elsewhere in this book, R&D is only the tip of the innovation iceberg (although an important tip). Not only do many of the companies in layers 2 and 3 undertake a significant amount of R&D, they also make important contributions to innovation in the new ICT ecosystem through their role in the symbiotic relationships examined in chapter 3.

The second conclusion is that it is the network operators in general, and the telecoms operators in particular, in layer 2 that make the major contribution to capital expenditure in the new ICT ecosystem, although once again the companies in the other two layers also make significant capital expenditures. These two conclusions highlight the interdependence and symbiosis between the various layers of the ecosystem stressed in this book.

The third conclusion is that the returns to telecoms operators in layer 2 appear to be lower than the return to players in the other two layers. Further research is needed on the implications of this finding.

Finally, data on returns show that European telecoms operators perform worse than their Asian and US counterparts.

5 | *Telecoms regulation*

Regulation is an important institutional influence in layer 2, the network operation layer. Regulation in layer 2 has effects throughout the new ICT ecosystem. In chapter 4, for example, it was shown that the network operators in layer 2 accounted for the bulk of investment in the ecosystem. The networked element providers in layer 1 are symbiotic beneficiaries of the investments made in layer 2. Content and applications providers in layer 3 utilise the networks that are created through layer 2 investments. Telecoms regulation in layer 2, therefore, has systemic repercussions. In this chapter, and in appendix 2, a closer look is taken at the dominant approach to telecoms regulation in the new ICT ecosystem. In the final part of the chapter the possible impact of evolutionary changes in the ecosystem on the framework of regulation is considered.

Europe in the global new ICT ecosystem

In 2007, *The Economist*, in a special report on European business, concluded that 'Europe has 29 per cent of the world's leading 2,000 or so companies, broadly in line with its 30 per cent share of world GDP. It punches its weight in most global industries *except IT* where America is leaps ahead.'[1] Exhibit 5.1 provides a more detailed picture of Europe's position in the global new ICT ecosystem. This exhibit is based on the *Financial Times Top 500 Companies* (according to market capitalisation). The ICT companies were extracted from the *Top 500* and then distributed into the three layers of the ICT ecosystem. The companies in each layer were then

---

[1] *Economist* (2007: 4, emphasis mine). Only about 16 per cent of the companies in this sector were from Europe.

Exhibit 5.1. *ICT companies in the* Financial Times: Top 500 companies, *by market capitalisation, from the USA, Japan, Europe and East Asia (Korea and Taiwan)*

Layer	Total number of companies	Number of companies, by region
Platform, content and applications	9	USA 6, Japan 2, Europe 1
Network operators	18	USA 5, Japan 3, Europe 8, East Asia 2
Networked elements	29	USA 12, Japan 9, Europe 6, East Asia 2

Source: M. Fransman, calculated from *FT Top 500*, (2006).

divided into regions – USA, Japan, Europe and East Asia (Korea and Taiwan[2]).

The following observations may be made on the basis of exhibit 5.1. First, layer 3 (the platform, content and applications layer) is dominated by US companies. Of the total number of nine companies in layer 3, six are from the USA and two from Japan. Europe has only one company in this layer (Vivendi Universal from France).

Secondly, layer 1 (networked elements) is dominated by companies from the USA and Japan. The USA has twelve of the twenty-nine companies in this layer, while Japan has nine. Europe's position in this layer is somewhat misleading. Although there are six European companies, one of them, namely Philips, is there more for its non-ICT products than for its ICT ones. A second European company, Siemens, has begun making a significant exit from the ICT sector. The two East Asian companies in layer 1 are Samsung Electronics from Korea (the sixth top company, after Microsoft, Cisco, IBM, Vodafone and Intel) and Taiwan Semiconductor Manufacturing Company.

Comparatively speaking, Europe does best in layer 2 (the network operator layer). Of the total number of eighteen companies in this layer, eight are from Europe compared to five from the USA, three from Japan and two from East Asia.

Regulation is an important institution shaping the activities of the network operators in layer 2. In this chapter, we take a closer look at the role of regulation in this layer.

---

[2] There were no companies from other Asian countries.

The dominant regulatory paradigm in telecoms (DRPT) and innovation in the new ICT ecosystem

The co-evolution of regulation

Regulation has co-evolved with the industry it has been governing. The watershed occurred in the mid-1980s, when three countries, for different reasons, decided to abandon the natural monopoly conventional wisdom (according to which it was assumed that monopoly was the only efficient solution for the telecoms services market) and allow competition to their hitherto monopolist telecoms services providers. In the USA, Sprint and MCI were allowed to compete with the incumbent AT&T in long-distance services; in Japan, DDI, Japan Telecom and Teleway Japan were given permission to compete with NTT; and in the UK, Cable & Wireless (through Mercury) competed with BT.

But this decision raised a significant problem in all three countries: how to deal with the dominant incumbent, who had 'significant market power' (SMP), until such time as sufficient competition would remove the need for regulation? It was this question that set the conceptual ball rolling, defining the agenda for telecoms regulatory theory and policy and shaping the co-evolution of telecoms regulation and the telecoms sector which it governed.

In dealing with this problem, telecoms regulators turned to academic economists for help. The latter were quick to oblige, coming up with an increasingly sophisticated theoretical framework with important implications for regulatory policy. By the end of the millennium a dominant regulatory paradigm in telecoms (DRPT) had emerged and had diffused to virtually all developed countries.[3]

The DRPT

To simplify, the conventional approach to telecoms regulation when a dominant player in a market is judged to possess SMP has been to attempt through regulation to achieve the same market outcome as would have been achieved had conditions of substantial competition existed. Take, for example, the case of a new-entrant telecoms network operator wishing to compete with a former monopolist incumbent in a telecoms service market. The incumbent, by definition, is already

---

[3] An outstanding example representing this paradigm is Laffont and Tirole (2000).

connected to most of the customers through its network. The customers, however, have little incentive to switch to the new entrant who, because of the high fixed cost of telecoms networks and the time required to provide wide coverage, can be assumed to have a small network with few subscribers relative to the incumbent. If the incumbent's customers were to switch, and if the networks were unconnected, they would only be able to communicate with a significantly smaller number of people. Left to market forces, therefore, the new entrant is likely to make little progress and sustainable competition is unlikely to occur.

Accordingly, if competition is to be fostered, regulation is necessary. The incumbent must be compelled to allow the new entrant to connect its network to that of the incumbent. This will give the new entrant's customers the opportunity to also reach the subscribers to the incumbent's network. At the same time it will give the incumbent's customers the option to switch to the new entrant. But this raises a further problem. If interconnection is to be enforced, what price should the new entrant pay the incumbent for accessing its (the incumbent's) network? It was in tackling this problem that the academic economists were able to use one of the most potent tools in their conceptual armoury, namely *price theory*.

A large and sophisticated body of theory in this field had been accumulated which analyses the welfare implications (that is, the net benefit to producers and consumers) of the prices that would emerge under different market conditions. These market conditions ranged from perfect competition at the one extreme through a continuum to monopoly at the other. It was this body of knowledge that the economists drew on in order to attempt to calculate the *optimal price* that should be paid by the new entrant for interconnection (that is, the price that would result in maximum welfare).

An example is the forward-looking long-run incremental cost (LRIC) principle. According to this the new entrant should pay a cost-based interconnection price, the cost determined by the long-run additional cost.[4] This principle was based on the theoretical demonstration that under strong competition, where static welfare will be maximised, price will tend to equal incremental (marginal) cost. Although this principle became widely adopted, economists have pointed to some of its shortcomings. For example, Laffont and Tirole (2000) noted that:

---

[4] For more details, see Laffont and Tirole (2000: 148–61).

This broad regulatory consensus in favour of LRIC unfortunately is supported by little economic argument. As a matter of fact, an economic analysis reveals several concerns about the whole endeavour. First, LRIC regulation gives regulators a key role in managing entry. On the one hand, the determination of long-run incremental costs is highly discretionary. On the other hand, long-run incremental costs, even if they can be obtained costlessly and impartially, preclude operators from making money in the access activity and give them strong incentives to favour their competitive affiliates by biasing access against their competitors. These perverse incentives call for heavy-handed supervision of incumbent operators. Both factors imply a high cost in terms of regulatory staff resources and also create scope for interest-group politics in which the different parties try to influence the regulators' exercise of discretion. This outcome is at odds with the official goal of making regulation more light-handed. Second, even if long-run incremental costs could be determined objectively and rivals' exclusion could be prevented costlessly, the associated access prices would still not be the efficient prices and thus would imply economic distortions.[5]

However, despite important shortcomings such as these and despite the debating and modification of the details, the desirability of interconnection prices based on forward-looking costs has remained, as Laffont and Tirole (2000) themselves observe, part of the 'broad regulatory consensus'. It is important to note that this approach to regulation also requires: (a) that relevant markets be defined; and that (b) a practical methodology be established for calculating when a player is able to exercise SMP in that market. The reason, simply, is that regulatory intervention is necessary only if there is such dominance in a market.

Problems with the DRPT

In recent years, growing disenchantment has emerged with the conventional paradigm in telecoms regulation. This disillusionment has been given additional impetus by the changing practice of the Federal Communications Commission (FCC) in the USA in 2004–5 that abandoned some of its previously key policies of networked element unbundling (i.e. making elements of the local access network available to an incumbent's competitors).

Three of the most important problems with the DRPT are summarised in exhibit 5.2. These problems are expressed here in the form of assertions – assertions which, it should be stressed, are controversial, still need to be supported by more evidence and are currently hotly contested.

---

[5] *Ibid.*: 148–9.

Exhibit 5.2. *Problems with the DRPT*

Problem	Details
1	The requirement that incumbents must provide competitors with access to their networks, and the regulated prices at which they must do so, *does not leave the incumbent with sufficient incentive to invest* in upgrading the network so that it becomes internationally competitive. Furthermore, cheap (arguably subsidised) access to the incumbent's network by new entrants *also reduces the incentive of these entrants to invest in their own networks and engage in facilities-based competition.*[1]
2	The focus on optimal access prices is justified by a static theoretical framework that *does not deal adequately with the dynamics of innovation and change.* Accordingly, *endogenous innovation is left out of the equation.* The implications of regulatory measures for the innovation process, and therefore international competitiveness, go unexamined.
3	The *costs of possible regulatory failure* must be weighed against the benefits of regulation (such as increased competition). Examples of regulatory failure include: the creation of regulation-induced uncertainty; the politicisation of the regulatory process as it becomes a contested arena between opposing interests; the mismatch between the inherently slow regulatory process and the speed of market-driven technical change and innovation; and the inherent knowledge and information deficiencies by which regulators are constrained.

Note: [1] More specifically, regulated access has generally involved legacy networks (that is, existing 'old' networks). More controversial, and more debated, is the question of what should be done with new optical fibre networks. Regulated access to these networks, and the terms according to which access is given to competitors, will affect the return to investors in the networks and therefore their incentive to make the investment.

Discussion of the first two problems

The DRPT does not leave the incumbent with sufficient incentive to invest

In the USA there is a strong body of opinion (though it is contested) that a significant proportion of the increased investment undertaken by the two main consolidated telecoms incumbents – AT&T and Verizon – has been caused by the dropping of the unbundling requirements by the FCC in 2004–5. However, this period has also seen increased convergence between telecoms and cable TV networks and services and increased competition between telecoms operators and cable operators, making a causal separation of the two causes of investment – deregulation and increased competition – difficult.

In Germany, Deutsche Telekom, with the support of the German government, has argued against the European regulatory authorities in Brussels that without a regulatory holiday (forbearance) they have little incentive to invest in a new high-speed fixed network (next-generation network, NGN).

In Japan, NTT has argued that although it has gone ahead with its NGN and is now the world leader in optical fibre to the premises (FTTP) this has, due to excessive regulation, been at the expense of profitability which is threatening the company.

In all three countries these arguments are currently being hotly debated. At the heart of these debates is the hypothesis that the methodology used in the DRPT for the calculation of regulated access prices is flawed since it does not leave sufficient incentive for the investment that is needed in the nation's telecoms infrastructure if it is to provide internationally competitive telecoms services.

Furthermore, some have argued that this incentive deficiency applies not only to the incumbent but also to its competitors, who are given access to the incumbent's network at favourable prices (arguably, subsidised prices), therefore reducing the incentive of the competitor to invest in its own network and engage in facilities-based competition, which many regard as the most potent form of competition in telecoms. Clearly, this debate will continue.

The DRPT does not deal adequately with the dynamics of innovation and change

As shown earlier in the discussion on the co-evolution of regulation, the key question to which regulatory theory and policy in telecoms responded since the mid-1980s was: What regulatory measures should be taken when a market is dominated by a player with SMP? However, it is argued under problem 2 in exhibit 5.2 that the body of knowledge that has been produced in answer to this question leaves little conceptual room for endogenous innovation and therefore the dynamics of change driven by it, including the international competitiveness which almost always depends on innovation. By starting with a different key question – How well is a country innovating and what forms of governance (including regulation) would enhance innovation processes? – the conceptual ball would be set rolling in different directions, leading to different theories and policies.

It does seem clear that innovation, when it is dealt with in the DRPT, is treated in a limited way. For example, there are only two references to innovation in the index to Laffont and Tirole (2000). The first is 'innovation,' dealt with on pp. 272–3, and the second is 'innovators, monopoly power of,' referred to on pp. 134–6. In the former, on p. 272, innovation is seen as one of the 'unsettling factors' upsetting the 'traditional paradigm for utility regulation [which] rests on the regulation of a well-defined set of services offered by a well-identified operator (or small group of operators) in a well-circumscribed geographical area.' The authors go on to acknowledge that: 'Recent evolution in telecommunications has shattered each of these foundations' (p. 272). Several pages later the authors include these considerations among the 'shortcomings of the regulatory framework in the new telecommunications environment' (p. 279). There are four items in the index under 'technological progress,' all of which are dealt with on pp. 152–6. This underlines that innovation is not a key concern in the theory underlying the DRPT.

More pragmatically, the DRPT largely ignores key aspects of the innovation process.[6] For example, any attempt to understand innovation in the network operator layer, layer 2, would of necessity have to include an examination of the innovation process involving telecoms operators and their equipment suppliers in layer 1, as shown in chapter 3. Such an examination, however, does not emerge in the DRPT. To the extent that innovation is included as a regulatory objective (and this is frequently the case in many countries) innovation is tacitly assumed to be exogenous, emerging in unexplored and unproblematical ways from layer 1. The regulatory problematic then becomes one of creating the optimal conditions – i.e. competition – that will

---

[6] It is important to note, however, that it is not being suggested in this book that regulation under the DRPT has had no impact on the innovation process. Rather, it is proposed that the framework which the DRPT uses does not deal adequately with endogenous innovation. One example of regulation influencing innovation is the regulation of the prices that dominant incumbent network operators are allowed to charge. This price regulation, arguably, creates an incentive for the regulated to make cost-reducing innovations. However, such regulation may bias the innovation process towards process innovations and away from product/service innovations that may be important for the ICT ecosystem. The point emphasised in this book is that the DRPT's approach tends to lack a focus on endogenous innovation generally and the ways in which such innovation might assist the attainment of objectives for the ICT ecosystem.

incentivise the network operators in layer 2 to adopt the innovations that have appeared from layer 1, helped by their own R&D and innovation. At best, this offers only a partial view of the innovation process in the new ICT ecosystem; at worst, it obscures key determinants of the dynamics driving the entire system.

Moreover, it is crucial to note that competitive markets, which *may* be necessary for innovation (though this is not always true – see, for example, the innovation that occurred during the monopoly era in telecoms until the mid-1980s), are not always *sufficient* for internationally competitive innovation. For example, the academic field of innovation studies, which includes studies of the economic performance of national innovation systems, highlights the key role played by *institutions* in the innovation process. These include legal and financial institutions, standardisation and the role of universities. Even in the presence of competitive markets, as defined by competition law and regulation, institutions may prevent the achievement of the innovation necessary for international competitiveness. This begs the question: How can innovation be brought into the theoretical and policy analysis of the new ICT ecosystem?

Are the DRPT and the Schumpeterian approach complementary?

Are these two paradigms – the DRPT and the Schumpeterian Evolutionary Economics Paradigm (SEEP)[7] – logically and empirically compatible? Probably the best answer is that in some respects they are compatible while in other respects they are not.

First, the compatible areas. The key compatibility is the shared assumption that *competition* is a key determinant of performance. In the DRPT, competition generates an optimal equilibrium outcome in which social welfare is maximised. In the SEEP, competition is a key driver of the innovation process which, in turn, is an important determinant of performance. In assessing whether particular markets are competitive or not, and whether particular firms have SMP or dominance, there is likely to be a good deal of agreement between the two paradigms. In areas such as these, therefore, there is compatibility.

However, there are also incompatibilities. For the DRPT, the existence of sufficiently strong competition *logically implies* (i.e. is the same

---

[7] A brief introduction to Schumpeterian evolutionary economics is provided in appendix 4.

thing as) a social welfare maximizing equilibrium outcome. However, for the SEEP there are two links in the causal chain. The first is strong competition that creates conditions for *innovation* (which is also shaped by institutions). Secondly, it is innovation that is a key determinant of *performance* (however performance is measured). However, this innovation, which requires knowledge, learning and institutional support, cannot be assumed to occur either automatically or costlessly.

In view of compatibilities and incompatibilities such as these, what should be concluded regarding the role of the two paradigms in thinking about the way forward for Europe in the new ICT ecosystem? The position taken in this book is that the two paradigms should be treated as being *complementary*. The main reason is that competition is seen as being a central determinant of performance in both. However, it is necessary to bear the differences between the two paradigms in mind. Particularly important is to identify the principal questions that are being addressed. To the extent that these questions relate to innovation, the SEEP conceptualisation of the joint competition–innovation process will normally be judged more appropriate.

Coming changes in telecoms regulation?

There have recently been some significant signs that the conventional paradigm that has dominated telecoms regulation is beginning to change. One place where these signs are evident is the publications of the UK regulator, Ofcom. During 2005 and 2006 Ofcom commissioned a number of studies focusing on the changes occurring in the communications industry and the implications for regulation. These studies were published by Ofcom as *Communications – The Next Decade: A Collection of Essays Prepared for the UK Office of Communications*, edited by Ed Richards, Robin Foster and Tom Kiedrowski (Ofcom 2006).[8]

In their introduction to the collection Foster and Kiedrowski summarise the main trends that are predicted by the authors who contributed to the study. These trends are shown in our summary provided in exhibit 5.3.

Foster and Kiedrowski then go on to examine the implications for regulation as proposed by the authors of the study. Some of these implications are summarised in exhibit 5.4.

---

[8] www.ofcom.org.uk/research/commsdecade/.

Exhibit 5.3. *Trends predicted in Communications – The Next Decade (Ofcom 2006)*

Problem	Trends
Disruptive competition, blurring boundaries and new competitors	• The telecoms sector is changing *from* relative stability, high entry barriers and monopoly *to* rapid change and disruptive competition as both inter-platform and intra-platform competition increases (15)[1] • *Boundaries are blurring* between fixed and mobile, broadcasting, entertainment and publishing, suppliers and consumers (15) • *New bottlenecks are emerging* in different parts of the value chain, e.g. in search tools, premium content and control of digital rights management (15) • *Powerful media companies and Internet application service providers* may increasingly enter telecoms markets with bundled service offerings (16)
New content relationships	• The *relationship between consumers and the providers of content and services* is being transformed (15)
Increasing power of content and applications providers in layer 3	• There is a change in the *relative positioning of network providers and applications service providers*, partly as a result of the movement of intelligence to the edges of the physical network (15) • This *could shift some control from the underlying network to end-users and applications and content providers*, altering the balance of power between players in the sector (15)
Need for increasingly global perspectives	• The implications of global technology adoption as well as cross-border policy and business decisions *will require policy-makers to take an increasingly international perspective* (15)

Note: [1] Page numbers in Ofcom 2006.
Source: Edited author's summary from Ofcom (2006).

Exhibit 5.4. *Some implications for regulation in Communications – The Next Decade (Ofcom 2006)*

Problem	Implications
Changing market boundaries	• Much of the focus of economic regulation in communications to date has been on promoting competition to monopolies – or, where this has not been feasible, replicating the effects of competition through regulatory pressure on costs and prices. In most countries where *ex ante* regulation is applied to a network operator a finding of *dominance, or market power,* in a defined relevant market, is required first. (19)[1]
	• However, *convergence is leading to the blurring of boundaries between products and services* and this means that new market definitions will be needed. (19)
Dynamic approaches	• Philip Booth argues that it is important for regulators to *concentrate on the competitive process* and less on trying to recreate the hypothetical outcome that would result from perfect competition. (20)
	• This means a different approach to balancing the risks inherent in any regulatory decision – worrying more about the risks that *regulatory intervention might stifle innovation or distort market decisions* than the risk that competition might prove not to be as effective as hoped. (20)
Investment in next-generation facilities	• Reed Hundt (former head of the FCC) raises the issue of *communications sector infrastructure,* and the role that it plays in providing wider competitive advantages for nations and their citizens. Electronic communications networks are not – for the most part – tradeable across national boundaries, but they are an essential input into business and society in each country. (21)
	• Therefore, a premium should be placed on *high-quality, cutting-edge and affordable telecoms networks* in order to improve efficiency and secure economic growth and jobs. (21)
	• *Governments have a responsibility to ensure that their citizens do not come off worst in the competitive battle between countries,* which means that support is required for the creation

Exhibit 5.4. (cont.)

Problem	Implications
	of high-quality, modern and efficient broadband networks – and regulators have a role to play in ensuring that the environment is conducive to this goal. (21)
Potential for new bottlenecks	• *Ex ante* regulation at one level could be risky, as it could *favour one level over another and therefore distort the market*, since companies' investment decisions would be influenced by arbitrary regulatory distinctions rather than commercial realities. (22)
	• Regulators will have to *balance the need to secure access to bottleneck platforms with the need to ensure incentives for efficient investment and innovation*. (22)
Need for new models	• As Steve Burdon notes in his survey of developments in Asia, many regulators are adopting what he terms a 'proactive' approach to managing emerging competition, which involves *setting national interest goals – such as investment in modern infrastructures – as part of the overall regulatory framework*. (25)
Conclusions	• Many of the authors of the report call for a radical rethink of the approach to regulation over the next five–ten years. They argue for a focus on *investment and innovation*, and for the reinvention of approaches to public interest content and other social objectives. (30, emphasis added)
	• The authors of the report are impressed by the overall optimism about the potential for the communications sector to be a *driver of economic growth* and a *generator of great cultural benefits* – and the confidence that policy and regulation can evolve fully to realise those benefits. (31)

Note: [1] Page numbers in Ofcom 2006.
Source: Edited author's summary from Ofcom (2006).

Implications

The message emerging is clear. Radical changes are transforming the entire communications industry. Since, as we saw earlier, telecoms regulation is a co-evolving phenomenon this implies that radical changes will also need to occur in the regulatory frameworks that play an important role in governing this industry. Although it is still too early to be precise about the form that the new frameworks will take, it does seem clear that innovation is likely to play a far more prominent role in thinking about the governance of the new ICT ecosystem than it has until now.

Conclusions

In this chapter, the DRPT has been examined, and two weaknesses noted. The first is the relative absence in the paradigm of endogenous innovation – that is, processes of innovation generated within the new ICT ecosystem. The second weakness, although more controversial, is that the paradigm does not provide sufficient incentives for investment.

In this chapter the DRPT has also been compared briefly with the SEEP. It is shown that although there are some areas of compatibility between these two paradigms, there are also areas of contrast. In particular, competition is dealt with in different ways in the two approaches. Nevertheless, despite these differences, it is concluded that DRPT and SEEP are complementary approaches.

Finally, the results of a forward-looking Ofcom study (Ofcom 2006) are reported which suggest that important changes in the regulation of communications are on the cards. The objective of innovation is likely to feature strongly in the evolving new regulatory frameworks.

6 | Policy-making for the new ICT ecosystem

Governments can, and in the author's view should, monitor and benchmark the performance of their new ICT ecosystem–innovation system (NIE–IS). (As this chapter primarily concerns systems, we shall use the acronym 'NIE' for 'new ICT ecosystem' and 'IS' for 'innovation system' here.) Government should regularly publish and publicise what their performance objectives for the national NIE–IS are, and how actual performance compares with the best in the world and with other comparable NIE–ISs. This will serve to focus attention on what should be done.

Policy-making at the national and regional level

How should policy-makers go about the task of making policy for the NIE? The aim of this chapter is to put forward some suggestions in answer to this question. But first it is necessary to say something about policy-making at national and regional levels.

In this book we have been concerned with the evolving NIE and the way in which it has changed over time. In chapter 3 it was shown that innovation – that is, new products/services, new technologies and processes, new forms of organisation and new markets – drives the evolution of the NIE. It was suggested, further, that each NIE contains an innovation system (IS) which generates the innovations. In this chapter reference will be made to the NIE and its innovation system, NIE–IS.

Each country has a NIE–IS. However, the NIE–IS in each country is different. One reason why NIE–ISs differ is international competitiveness. For example, the USA has excelled in producing Internet content and applications companies that are headquartered there and make an important contribution to its ICT ecosystem. East Asian countries – Japan, Korea, Taiwan and more recently China – dominate global markets in areas such as consumer electronics and some semiconductors. Their companies play a key role in their national ecosystems. At the same time, the leading companies from the USA and East Asia have significant global involvements. In a few countries the providers in the three layers of the NIE–IS are domestic companies; in most countries significant providers are foreign firms or local firms using imports.

Another reason why NIE–ISs differ from country to country is that they are influenced by domestic institutions which themselves are moulded by domestic organisations which have the political power to change them.[1] Political processes and institutions, as we well understand, differ from country to country. This is largely why the NIE–IS in, say, France, the UK, the USA, Japan and China is very different in terms of objectives, configuration, *modus operandi* and performance.

Since institutions and politics are largely a national matter it makes sense to think of NIE–IS at the national level – that is, the British NIE–IS, the US NIE–IS, the Japanese NIE–IS, etc. However, in regions such as Europe there are also European institutions and political processes such as those of the European Union (EU). By a process of implicit aggregation it may make sense to think of a European NIE–IS which may differ, in various identifiable ways, from the NIE–IS in the USA or Japan. In doing so it must be borne in mind that the European NIE–IS is an aggregation of heterogeneous national NIE–ISs. However, at regional level, such as the EU, there may be regional institutions and organisations that transcend the national level and influence the regional NIE–IS.

Crucially, for these and other reasons, performance differs across NIE–ISs. However, performance differentials create both challenges for individual NIE–ISs and opportunities for learning and catch-up.

Prioritising performance objectives

Each country needs to decide for itself what its overall ICT goals and priorities are. It may well be that in Europe different social and economic goals are chosen compared to, say, the USA or Japan. These goals can then be translated into performance objectives for the national NIE–IS. A common question, however, once the performance objectives have been established, is how effective is the national NIE–IS in achieving them.

[1] Nobel laureate, Douglass North, makes this distinction between institutions (which he defines as the 'rules of the game') and the organisations with political power that shape them.

Benchmarking NIE–IS performance

One way to tackle this question is by benchmarking the performance of the NIE–IS in question against, first, the best in the world and, second, a selected group of comparable countries. This should start to give some idea of comparative strengths and weaknesses in the individual NIE–IS. To some extent, of course, this is already done in all countries. However, it seems that in most cases: (a) the benchmarking is seldom done over a sufficiently wide range of performance measures; (b) it is often not done with sufficient rigour; and (c) it is usually not done regularly or early enough.

Important contributions to benchmarking are made by international bodies such as the Organisation for Economic Cooperation and Development (OECD), whose regular publications such as the *IT and Communications Outlook* (published every other year) contain valuable comparative information, and the International Telecommunications Union (ITU). However, as the reader soon discovers, although some valuable data are provided – for instance, the OECD's information on broadband performance, some of which is used later in this chapter – this tends to fall short of what is needed for a comprehensive comparison of the performance of different NIE–ISs.

There is also the key question of the performance measures that are appropriate for the different parts of the NIE–IS. For example, in Japan the ministry-regulator, MIC, has launched a top-level investigation into the international competitiveness of the Japanese ICT sector. This has involved benchmarking the performance of Japanese ICT companies in layer 1 (the networked element layer). Among the measures chosen are sales, market share and exports. Less clear is how performance should be measured in layer 2, the network operator layer, since networks are not generally internationally traded and therefore measures such as market share are not meaningful as judgements of international competitiveness. For instance, how exactly should inter-nation broadband performance be measured?[2] Measuring performance in layer 3 faces further problems specific to this layer (that will, however, not be pursued here).

---

[2] Currently, attempts are being made to address this question through the development of a composite index of broadband performance that includes variables such as penetration, speed and price.

The relative absence of detailed discussions of questions such as these provides an indication of the low priority that has so far been given to this benchmarking task.

Explaining performance differences

Then comes the really hard task: explaining the differences in performance that have been observed. For example:

- Why is the USA – the country that created the Internet and almost completely dominates the global provision of Internet platforms, content and applications – also the country that lags significantly behind Japan and Korea in terms of broadband speed (see pp. 90, 93, 94 for further details)?
- Why did mobile Internet access and regular use by mobile users of Internet sites succeed from 2005 in Japan – which now has more than 40 million regular mobile Internet users – while in Europe and the USA such services have barely begun?
- But why, simultaneously, are Japanese ICT companies in layer 1 falling behind their US, Korean and Taiwanese counterparts, causing concern among Japanese policy-makers?

Answering questions such as these is not easy, as anyone attempting to do so will soon discover. However, it is important that we try, not merely to satisfy intellectual curiosity (though this may be a valid reason), but in order to gain insights into the way in which different ecosystems work so as to try and make progress in improving them.

The example of broadband

An international benchmarking of NIE–ISs in the area of broadband quickly reveals that Japan is significantly ahead of the rest of the world. Exhibits 6.1–6.5 make this clear.

Exhibit 6.1 shows the fastest broadband download speeds offered by the incumbent telecoms operator in various countries. Japan and Korea are significantly in the lead. Although the USA comes third, it substantially lags the two leaders and is not much ahead of the next few countries which are European. The UK is in sixteenth position.

The fastest download speed offered by the largest cable operator is shown by country in exhibit 6.2. Again, Japan is significantly in the lead. This suggests that in Japan there is a process of competition

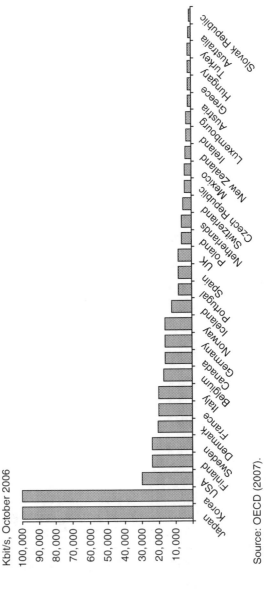

Kbit/s, October 2006

Source: OECD (2007).

Exhibit 6.1. *Fastest broadband download speeds offered by the incumbent telecoms operator, 2006*

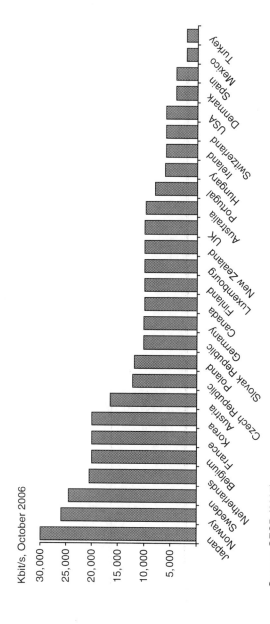

Kbit/s, October 2006

Source: OECD (2007).

Exhibit 6.2. *Fastest broadband download speeds offered by the largest cable operator, 2006*

involving cable network operators who are having to keep up with the incumbent telecoms operator, NTT, and the other telecoms operators. However, surprisingly, the same situation does not seem to exist in the USA where much is made of the competition between these two groups of operators in layer 2. The USA is twenty-third, even though exhibit 6.1 shows the USA in third position with much higher speeds than the country offers in cable. The UK is seventeenth.

Minimum broadband prices are shown in exhibit 6.3. Once again, Japan is by far the leader in, with a price (measured in terms of price per megabit per second) of 0.22 compared to the second country, Sweden with 0.35, and Korea in third place with 0.42. The USA is in thirteenth position with 3.18 and the UK is sixteenth with 3.62.

Why is Japan so far ahead of the pack? The answer is simple: FTTP – that is, optical fibre all the way to the premises of firms and households. (This performance measure is a reflection of the innovation and related investment that has occurred in the Japanese NIE–IS.)

In exhibit 6.4 information is provided on the distribution of different broadband technologies in different country NIE–ISs. Japan is significantly ahead of the other countries in terms of FTTP; in 2006, FTTP provided 23.4 per cent of broadband in Japan compared to 0.1 per cent in the USA and 0.0 per cent in the UK. Significantly, Sweden comes a fairly close second with 17.5 per cent FTTP coverage (suggesting that innovation processes have been occurring in the Swedish NIE–IS that, although they may be very different from those taking place in Japan,[3] have nevertheless produced a performance outcome that is not too dissimilar).

Finally, exhibit 6.5 reveals the extent of optical fibre infrastructure diffusion in Japan, showing the optical fibre innovation investment that has taken place in the Japanese NIE–IS which, in turn, explains the superior Japanese performance measured in the earlier exhibits.

Why is the Japanese NIE–IS so far ahead in broadband?

This question has been dealt with in detail in a book written and edited by the present author (Fransman 2006).[4] The reader is referred to this source and the references it contains for further information.

---

[3] In fact the innovation and investment processes that have taken place in the Japanese and Swedish NIE–ISs are very different. See chapters 2 and 9 on Japan and Sweden, respectively, in Fransman (2006).

[4] See in particular chapter 2 on Japan.

Range of broadband prices per mbit/s, October 2006, all platforms, logarithmic scale, USD PPP

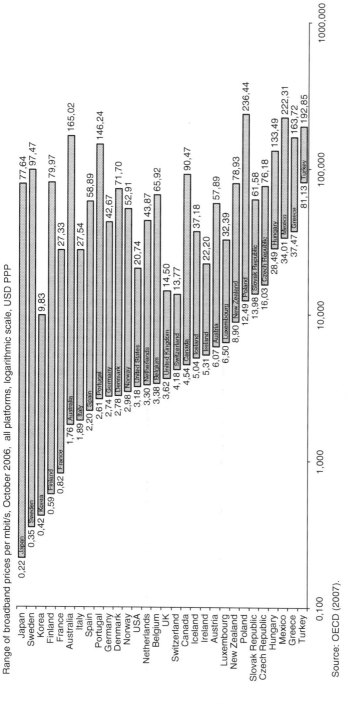

Source: OECD (2007).

Exhibit 6.3. *Minimum broadband prices, by country, 2006*

Exhibit 6.4. *Distribution of broadband technologies, by country, 2006*

Country	DSL (%)[1]	CATV (%)[2]	FTTP (%)	Other (%)
Japan	62.3	14.2	23.4	0.1
USA	36.5	56.4	0.1	7.1
Korea	53.2	32.8	0.0	14.0
EU	80.4	16.9	1.1	1.7
France	93.9	6.1	0.0	0.0
Germany	96.5	2.3	0.0	1.1
Italy	94.0	0.0	3.4	2.6
Sweden	64.6	17.2	17.5	0.6
UK	72.2	27.7	0.0	0.0

Notes: [1] DSL = Digital subscriber line.
         [2] CATV = Cable modems.
Source: Information supplied to the author by MIC, Japan.

Exhibit 6.5. *Optical fibre infrastructure diffusion in Japan, March 2006*

Area	Coverage (%)
Metropolitan areas: *total*	95
Metropolitan areas: *business districts*	98
Cities, population more than 100,000: *total*	90
Cities, population more than 100,000: *business districts*	90
Other cities	70
Nationwide	86

Source: Information supplied to author by MIC, Japan.

Discussion

For many years European regulators and policy-makers, although to some extent aware of what was happening in Japan in the areas of FTTP and broadband, chose largely to ignore it. Little rigorous benchmarking was done and little debate was initiated concerning the implications for Europe of the growing performance differential between the Japanese and European NIE–ISs. When the question was raised it was usually dismissed on the ground that less-expensive high-speed digital subscriber line (DSL) technologies (using the existing copper access networks) would suffice.

It is only since 2006–7, with the increasing desire on the part of both consumers and providers for greater bandwidth to carry exploding demand for video, that European regulators and policy-makers are acknowledging that optical fibre access networks are becoming necessary because of their superior carrying capacity. Only now is debate taking place regarding how to finance the diffusion of optical fibre and whether regulatory forbearance is required to provide the incentives needed for telecoms operators to make the investments. Even the UK – a FTTP laggard – finally accepted, towards the end of 2007, that such investment was necessary since without it the UK's international competitiveness would be threatened.[5]

The problem is that a huge gap has been allowed to open up between Europe and Japan (and to a lesser extent Korea) and there is no agreement regarding how European NIEs will catch up. In the meantime, European telecoms regulators often seem more obsessed with micro-managing the old system (e.g. attempting to reduce short-term prices for consumers) than with figuring out how to facilitate the transition to the new system – that is all-fibre, all-IP NGNs, including optical access networks.

The NIE as an IS: the six symbiotic relationships

Having benchmarked the national NIE–IS and attempted to understand performance differences across systems it is then necessary for policy-makers to decide who should be doing what in order to achieve their performance objectives. In tackling questions such as these a link may be made to the discussion in chapter 3, namely to the consideration of the six symbiotic relationships between the four groups of players in the NIE–IS. It is suggested that these symbiotic relationships – and,

---

[5] The *Financial Times* reported on 17 September 2007 that 'Stephen Timms, [UK] minister for competitiveness, . . . warned in April that ministers and regulators had just two years to find ways to encourage investment in high-speed broadband, or UK competitiveness would suffer. Mr Timms . . . admitted . . . the UK risks falling behind on broadband because countries such as the US, France, Germany and Japan are rolling out fixed-line networks made of fibre-optic cable. These networks will deliver broadband speeds of 50 to 100 megabits a second [Mbps], and should cope with the most bandwidth-hungry businesses and homes. By contrast, BT, the leading fixed-line telecommunications company, is planning to offer UK homes broadband speeds of up to 24 Mbps next year. But', the newspaper continues, 'investors are nervous about BT making any big commitment to fibre.'

more specifically, how well they are working – may provide a useful way of tackling the questions.

An example: i-Mode mobile Internet in Japan[6]

Interestingly, both Europe and Japan embarked simultaneously on the task of developing mobile Internet (partly as a response to slowing growth in mobile voice revenues). Europe created the Wireless Application Protocol (WAP); Japan (more specifically, NTT DoCoMo) created the i-mode. But Europe failed where Japan succeeded. Why?

While the details are available elsewhere,[7] suffice it to say that the explanation is to be found in the working of different symbiotic relationships. In Europe, WAP was essentially driven by telecoms equipment makers hoping to sell WAP equipment to telecoms operators. This was part of symbiotic Relationship 1 (see chapter 3): the relationship between networked element providers and telecoms operators. However, in Japan i-mode emerged essentially from symbiotic Relationship 6: the relationship between a telecoms operator (i.e. NTT DoCoMo) and its final customers.

As explained in Fransman (2002a), the team in NTT DoCoMo that drove the i-mode project (which, significantly, consisted not only of telecoms people but also Internet and media people) designed it from the beginning in such a way as to create content for final customers, eventually selected to be the young and urban. A key part of the project, emerging from symbiotic Relationship 6, involved generating incentives for the creation of content, largely the kind of content that would appeal to this targeted user group. This produced both a demand for mobile Internet services and a win–win situation for the mobile operator, the content and applications creators and the final customers. In Europe, however, no such content emerged. Not surprisingly, neither did the demand for mobile Internet in Europe.[8]

---

[6] This example comes from chapter 9 of Fransman (2002a).
[7] See Fransman (2002a: chapter 9).
[8] Further questions are raised concerning the subsequent mediocre success of i-mode in Europe, introduced through joint ventures between NTT DoCoMo and European mobile operators. However, it is not possible to pursue this question here.

Who should make the policies for the NIE–IS?

Up to this point we have not clarified who should be making the policies for the NIE–IS. The question of agency, however, is tricky. The reason is that by nature government bureaucracy is fragmented and inter-agency coordination is notoriously difficult. The chances are that the bureaucrats in trade/industry, the regulator, the competition authority, finance, science/technology and education have significantly different perspectives on: (a) what their objectives are; (b) what their problems are; and (c) what should be done.

And this does not take account of the networked element providers, the network operators, the platform, content and applications providers and the consumers (including corporate consumers), all of whom will also have their views on these questions and may try to influence decision-making. This problem exists to a greater or lesser extent in all countries.

These difficulties, it should be noted, may be incorporated into an analysis in a particular NIE–IS of the six symbiotic relationships analysed in chapter 3. As mentioned earlier, symbiotic relationships can be mutually beneficial, but they may also be harmful to one of the parties. In large part the problem stems from the complexity of a NIE–IS, with its component parts crossing the jurisdictions of many different government and private agencies. The consequence, however, is that in *no country does a single authority have responsibility for the NIE–IS as a whole*. As a result, policy regarding the NIE–IS is often fragmented, uncoordinated and, at times, even contradictory.

How can this problem be dealt with? I do not think that there is a simple answer (or even a complex one). Perhaps all that can be said is that with an awareness of the difficulties and of the need to understand the NIE–IS as a whole, it may be possible to make some progress in devising solutions. Each country will find its own way, and we can be sure that the ways will differ, causing over time the generation of further variety in the global system. The same holds at the regional level – for example, at the level of the EU. It is of some comfort, however, to be reminded that variety is one of the sources of evolutionary change so that this should be healthy for the longer-term development of the system as a whole.

Some caveats and suggestions

Governments are never omniscient or omnipotent. This is never more so than when they are trying to deal with a highly complex system that, to paraphrase Friedrich Hayek, no one person knows in its entirety.[9] Accordingly, our ability to centrally and rationally plan and deliver outcomes in complex socio-economic systems should always be doubted. But this does not mean that governments are impotent and have no positive role to play in improving the national NIE–IS. In this section some of the positive roles that governments can play will be considered, leaving the question of regulation to the following section.

To begin with, governments can, and in the author's view should, monitor and benchmark the performance of their NIE–IS, as discussed earlier in this chapter. Governments should regularly publish and publicise what the performance objectives for their national NIE–IS are, and how actual performance compares with the best in the world and with other comparable NIE–ISs. This will serve to focus attention on what should be done.

Although this data may well be a cause of embarrassment to some, and provide ammunition for others, significant performance differences will sooner or later in any event come into the public domain. From the point of view of policy and the improvement of the national NIE–IS it is just as well that they come out sooner. Recent examples of public controversy and debate over the lagging performance of the national NIE–IS are the discussion in the USA about relatively poor broadband performance (that was even an issue in the 2008 American presidential election) and in the UK regarding the lag in broadband speed (for the latter, see the *Financial Times* quotation in n. 5, p. 95).

Frequently, performance objectives will be achieved by market forces, such as inter-firm cooperation and competition, without the need for specific government interventions. Government intervention can also be soft-touch – for example, signalling priority areas and opportunities, highlighting weaknesses without moving directly to

---

[9] 'The economic problem of society is . . . a problem of how to secure the best use of resources known to any of the members of society, for ends whose relative importance only these individuals know. Or, to put it briefly, it is a problem of the utilization of knowledge which is not given to anyone in its totality' (Hayek 1945: 519–30).

deal with them or providing incentives (such as forbearance from regulation or tax incentives).

At times, however, government intervention of one kind or another may be judged by the authorities to be desirable (typically, this kind of judgement will differ from country to country). For example, as already mentioned, even the British government (through its minister for competitiveness, Stephen Timms),[10] although usually more reluctant than most of its European counterparts to intervene, seems ready to entertain the possibility of some kind of direct intervention to increase broadband speeds.[11] The failure of the market to deliver on social objectives – such as communications access in remote areas or the narrowing of the digital divide – provides a more conventional rationale for direct government intervention of various kinds.

Overall, however, it is worth government policy-makers remembering that it is variety, together with selection processes, that drives evolution. A healthy NIE–IS will generate variety – in technologies, in forms of organisation and in ideas, even though not all these forms of variety will survive the selection processes. However, in a world of uncertainty generated by rapid change variety can provide some safeguard for the future. The creation of variety in the NIE–IS should, therefore, be a key objective.

To conclude, therefore, government does have a positive role to play in making and implementing policy for the national or regional NIE–IS, even though it is to be expected that the question of what precisely this role should be will be answered in different ways in different countries and regions.

The role of telecoms regulation and competition

Telecoms regulators, it is suggested, have a crucial role to play in improving the performance of the national or regional NIE–IS. *Ex ante*, sector-specific regulation, although controversial, has given them an important resource; a deep understanding, particularly of layer 2 of the NIE–IS, and knowledge of the players, technologies and markets

---

[10] Since August 2009, Timms has been a Treasury Minister charged with putting through the government's Digital Britain Strategy.

[11] *Financial Times*, 17 September 2007.

of this layer. This understanding and knowledge is great relative to that of most other government agencies. Counterbalanced against this, however, are some disadvantages. One of these is that their knowledge and focus is largely (though not exclusively) on layer 2, the network operation layer (where most of the bottlenecks of the NIE which they regulate are located). Their knowledge of layers 1 and 3, though still significant, is inevitably more limited.

In this book it has been suggested that regulators have tended to focus more on competition than they have on innovation and related investment.[12] Frequently, it seems, competition is seen as an objective itself, separated from the performance, innovation and related investment objectives. Regulators often assume implicitly that it is sufficient to ensure that markets are competitive (and, where they are not, to regulate them in such a way as to mimic a competitive outcome). They assume that competition is sufficient to achieve the main objectives of policy, including the achievement of international competitiveness. The evidence provided in this book, however – which includes the evidence on global broadband competitiveness discussed in this chapter – suggests that although competition may be necessary, it is not sufficient.

From the perspective of the NIE and its IS developed in this book it may be suggested that regulators, like policy-makers, *start* with the performance objectives that the country has chosen for its NIE–IS and *then* proceed to identify the conditions that need to be met in order to achieve these objectives.

This way of proceeding immediately leads on to a consideration of *innovation and related investment*, because the achievement of performance objectives will almost always require some form of innovation (defined in this book as new products/services, new technologies/processes, new forms of organisation and new markets). This takes the discussion on to the local innovation system and its

---

[12] It might be more accurate to say that although innovation has been a focus it has tended implicitly to be assumed to be exogenously, rather than endogenously, generated. In part, this may have resulted from the exclusion of symbiotic Relationship 1 (the relationship between networked element providers and network operators) and Relationship 2 (between network operators and content and applications providers) from the view of telecoms regulators based on the assumption that the networked element market is an effectively competitive market.

strengths and weaknesses in delivering the innovation and related investment needed to achieve the performance objectives.

It is at this point that *competition rightly moves to centre stage*. If there is evidence that a lack of competition is impeding the innovation processes needed to achieve the performance objectives then regulators will be able to use their well-honed tools to try and ensure that the necessary competition materialises. In this way, competition will be a means to serve the end of innovation and related investment and be tightly aligned to the attainment of the performance objectives.

Conclusion

As the discussion in this chapter makes clear, policy-making in the NIE–IS is a complex matter. There are no easy solutions. But this does not mean that the policy issues raised here can, or should, be avoided. The reason, simply, is the serious challenges that Europe faces which were identified in chapter 1. The seriousness of these challenges forces Europeans, not simply to sit back and let things happen as they will in their NIE–IS, but to take steps as best they can to improve performance (including international competitiveness), even if they are not guaranteed success.

7 | *The way forward: the message to policy-makers and regulators*

It is widely accepted that the ICT sector is of key importance in all economies. It makes a major contribution to productivity, economic growth and employment and provides the information and communications infrastructure without which, in the modern world, the economy will not function. However, the ICT sector is itself undergoing radical change, largely as a result of the evolution of the Internet which began to be widely diffused only from around 1995. The evolving Internet has created added complexity in the ICT sector. For example, it has incorporated and transformed previously unrelated sectors, such as media, into the ICT sector; it has created new groups of key players in this sector – such as Internet content and applications providers like Google, Yahoo!, eBay, Amazon and MySpace; and it is transforming consumer interaction and behaviour in fundamental ways. In this book the phrase 'new ICT ecosystem' has been used to encapsulate these changes.

It is suggested here that in order to understand the ICT ecosystem it might be useful to conceptualise it in terms of a number of hierarchically structured modularised layers that together constitute a functioning system. The four-layer model proposed here for this purpose includes the networked element, the converged network and the platform, content and applications layers as well as, lastly, the final consumer layer. The major part of this book is devoted to an analysis of how this ecosystem works.

As part of the restless capitalist economy the ICT ecosystem is in an incessant process of change, producing the fuel that constantly transforms it. This fuel is *innovation*. In other words, the ICT ecosystem is also an innovation system. In chapter 3 some of the main processes of innovation in the ICT ecosystem are examined through the identification of six key symbiotic relationships involving the four main groups of players in the ecosystem.

While the ICT ecosystem has a global existence it simultaneously takes different forms in different regions and countries. For example, in various parts of this book (including appendix 7 and 8) it is noted that US Internet content and applications providers (such as Google, Yahoo!, eBay, Amazon and MySpace) have dominated layer 3 of the ecosystem while East Asian companies are particularly strong in parts of layer 1 in areas such as semiconductors, computer hardware and consumer electronics. Europe has been relatively strong in areas such as telecoms equipment and services.

The best way to identify relative strengths and weaknesses in different national ICT ecosystems is by *benchmarking*. Specifically, it is suggested that regions/countries need to benchmark their ICT ecosystems, first against the best systems in the world and, second, against other selected comparable systems. One country where this is done (as discussed briefly in chapter 1) is Japan where the ministry-regulator, MIC, uses a layer model very similar to that used here to analyse the ICT ecosystem and benchmarks the performance of the Japanese system against that in countries such as the USA, Korea, China and India.

It is in examining the regional/country ICT ecosystem that questions of policy emerge. Policy-makers need to analyse the system in their region or country in order to understand its comparative strengths and weaknesses. They then need to decide what, if anything, can be done to improve the performance of the system. It is suggested in this book that in the analysis undertaken by policy-makers a key focus should be on the innovation process in the ICT ecosystem. The reason, simply, is that it is this innovation process that drives the performance of the system (as is shown in many places in this book, including appendix 1). But it is also necessary to remember, as is stressed in this book, the *complementarity* between innovation and investment.

It is in analysing the strengths and weaknesses of the innovation process that competition enters the picture since competition, by creating pressures and incentives, is a major driver of innovation. However, it has been stressed in this book that competition alone is not sufficient for the achievement of internationally competitive performance. One reason is that institutions also play a key role in determining innovation and performance, and the necessary institutions need to be in place and performing effectively if internationally competitive performance is to be achieved. These institutions include financial institutions such as venture capital (discussed, for example, in appendix 7 which explores why US Internet content and applications providers dominate layer 3), universities (that provide knowledgeable person-power and incubate entrepreneurs) and standardisation bodies (that facilitate the functioning and interoperability of the modularised ICT ecosystem). However, ensuring that the required institutions exist and operate as they should may be just as difficult as ensuring that markets are competitive and stable.

This raises the issue of telecoms regulation that is discussed in several parts of this book. Three points may be made in this connection. The first is that the telecoms regulators have been justifiably concerned with establishing where markets are not competitive and seeking remedies to deal with SMP and dominance in these markets. These concerns are justifiable since the telecoms services market in layer 2 was monopolised until the mid-1980s (and even later in many countries) and since factors such as high fixed and low marginal costs, economies of scale and scope and network externalities continually threaten competition.

However, secondly, it is suggested in this book that this justifiable concern with competitive markets should not crowd out a focus on the innovation process in the ICT ecosystem. If competition could be relied upon to automatically produce internationally competitive performance in the regional/country ICT ecosystem then an exclusive focus on competitive markets would be sufficient. Unfortunately, it cannot – for theoretical and empirical reasons that are discussed in many parts of this book. Innovation, including the institutions that shape it, is also necessary for the achievement of an internationally competitive performance. A further issue here, as highlighted in several parts of this book, is that the conceptual theory of competition that underlies the DRPT leaves little room for innovation. This is an important shortcoming, the implications of which need to be dealt with.

The third point follows from the conventional scope of responsibility of the telecoms regulator. This scope is limited to layer 2 of the ICT ecosystem, the network operation layer. The limitation of this scope, however, raises a potential problem, which stems from the interdependencies that exist between the different layers of the ecosystem and between the players in these layers. Some of these interdependencies have been analysed in detail in this book. These include, for example, six important symbiotic relationships in the ICT ecosystem (only two of which will be referred to here).

The first is the symbiotic relationship between network operators and their networked element suppliers, a relationship that involves both innovation and investment. The second is the relationship between the companies in layers 1 and 2 that collectively provide the innovation platforms (notably the Internet) on the basis of which many players in layer 3 provide their content, applications and services. The important implication that follows from these interdependencies is that the regulators, in layer 2 and elsewhere, must take care in making their regulations that they are not negatively impacting either the functioning of some of the other layers – or, indeed, the functioning of the ICT ecosystem as a whole. One of the advantages of the present conceptualisation of the ICT ecosystem is that it helps to identify these interdependencies and therefore may assist regulators to perform their task.

The suggestion that the strengths and weaknesses of the regional/country ICT ecosystem need to be analysed in order to go on and formulate policy raises a further important issue – one of *coordination*. To put the problem bluntly: who has responsibility for overseeing the ICT ecosystem as a whole and assessing its strengths and weaknesses? In all countries (including the more planned East Asian countries) it is not inaccurate to conclude that not only is there no single agency that plays this role, but that different agencies with different agendas and perspectives all have a finger in the ICT ecosystem pie. Examples are agencies such as regulation authorities, competition authorities, ministries of trade and industry, science and technology, education, finance, standardisation bodies, etc. This 'governance fragmentation' raises questions regarding coordination and coherence in policy-making for the ICT ecosystem.

However, the view taken here is that the solution to these problems does not necessarily lie in the creation of a super-agency with policy-making responsibility for the whole ICT ecosystem (although that may be one option). Our experience with the management of highly complex evolving systems such as the ICT ecosystem (as in the case of the financial system) surely teaches us that there are no simple solutions. Indeed, attempts to centrally manipulate and control such systems very often fail. Accordingly, there is much to be said for decentralisation and for evolutionary rules of thumb such as 'generate variety and rely on selection mechanisms, including but not only the market, to shape the outcomes'.

But in the present writer's view it would also be wrong to go too far in the *laissez faire* direction, leaving all questions about the shape and performance of the ICT ecosystem to the decisions of multiple actors in the private sector with a minimalist role for government policy-making. At the very least, it may be suggested, government does have a positive role to play in attempting to benchmark and identify the strengths and weaknesses of its ICT ecosystem, although what happens after that will differ from country to country. The present book, it is hoped, may provide some ideas regarding how this may be done.

Appendix 1: The evolution of the new ICT ecosystem, 1945–2007: how innovation drives the system

The central argument of this book is that it is innovation that drives the ICT ecosystem, innovation in products and services, technologies, forms of organisation and markets. It is for this reason that government policy-makers and regulators involved in the governance of this system should have as one of their main focuses the process of innovation and the factors which facilitate it. In this appendix a brief account of the evolution of the ICT ecosystem in the post-war period is provided, paying particular attention to the key innovations that have driven the system and their ramifications.

The importance of new and improved technologies

What are the forces that drive change in the new ICT ecosystem? When Joseph Schumpeter asked this question, not for this particular sector but for the capitalist economy as a whole, the conclusion that he came to was that 'new combinations' constitute the engine of change. By 'new combinations' Schumpeter meant new products, processes, forms of organisation and markets. These new combinations, introduced by entrepreneurs and the innovations of companies, unleashed – as Schumpeter famously observed – waves of creation–destruction that subvert the old and herald the new.[1]

Schumpeterian new combinations have been a major driving force in the ICT sector since its inception.[2] The origins of the communications part of this sector go back to the telegraph and telephone. As these networks expanded – driven by the network externalities that created increasing benefits for their users – so more resources and greater incentives became available to those who created the elements of these networks. In turn, this led to important innovations.

---

[1] See Schumpeter (1934, 1943).
[2] For an account of the technical changes driving the ICT sector, see Freeman and Louca (2002).

One trajectory of improvement, for example, took place in the switches that connected telephone users. Manual switches were soon replaced by mechanical switches which themselves rapidly improved in sophistication, capacity and speed. Mechanical switches were later substituted first by electrical and then solid state electronic switches. Digital switches soon followed. Complementary changes took place in the transmissions systems that carried the switched signals.[3]

Some of the seeds of the information part of the ICT sector grew within the womb of the communications industry. More precisely, the information industry developed in part from the devices that were incorporated into the switches and transmissions equipment of telephone networks. First relays then vacuum tubes and transistors were incorporated into the early computers that began to appear around the time of the Second World War. Indeed, the transistor that provided a great boost to the computer industry with its added speed and low power consumption was invented in a telephone company. It was in 1948 that the patent was registered for the transistor that Shockley and his colleagues had invented in AT&T's Bell Laboratories, work that won Shockley a Nobel Prize. Research on this key device emerged in Bell Labs out of an attempt to improve telephone transmissions.

The computer gave rise to IT and the information age. However, until the 1950s communications technologies and information technologies and the economic activities that surrounded them remained largely distinct areas. It was only from the 1960s that telecommunications switches incorporated stored programme control and in effect became computers. For the first time a process of convergence took place that resulted in the birth of an increasingly integrated sector, the information and communications (ICT) sector.

In this way information and communications technologies became increasingly interdependent, changes in one area having immediate repercussions in the other. The Internet, which began in the late 1950s as an attempt to share information between computers using telephone lines, increased this interdependence.[4] The advent of the Internet led to a fundamental metamorphosis of the ICT sector.

---

[3] For the authoritative guide to the history of switching, see Chapuis and Joel (1990) and for a study of the corresponding development of switching systems in Japan, see Fransman (1995a).

[4] See Abbate (1999).

The widespread commercial adoption of the Internet from the mid-1990s led to the creation, not only of new forms of interaction and interdependence between information and communications appliances, but also to a powerful new platform of Schumpeterian innovation. The Internet, itself a new combination, gave birth to further new combinations that included different forms of organisation and different markets. The TCP/IP interface facilitated the emergence of new layers of functionality and economic activity, as depicted in the six-layer model of the new ICT ecosystem that was discussed in chapter 2. At the same time as providing completely new services (such as emailing and later blogging) the Internet allowed many old services to be provided in new, often advantageous ways (for example, online newspapers have the added advantage of being searchable). The Internet also facilitated completely new forms of organisation (for instance, the ability of remotely located collaborators who do not know one another to jointly create knowledge, as in Wikipedia or open source software).

The creators of new technologies

As the last section highlights, new technologies and associated innovations have been a major driver of change in the ICT sector. But who have the creators of these technologies been, and how have they created them?

Until the mid-1980s: telecoms operators dominate

Until the mid-1980s telecoms networks in almost all countries were run by monopolies that were state-owned. The conventional wisdom at the time was that monopoly was the only efficient way of organising telecoms services. According to this reasoning, the very high fixed costs of developing, running, maintaining and improving telecoms networks implied significant economies of scale. In turn, these economies of scale implied that only by having one operator could costs be minimised. For this reason telecoms was seen as a 'natural monopoly'.

In the most industrialised countries the monopolist telecoms operator soon developed central research laboratories in order to improve telecoms equipment, networks and services.[5] Although these operators

[5] For a detailed history of the development of telecoms central research laboratories see Fransman (1995a).

were monopolists they were motivated to ensure that improvements took place. Motivating factors included the political pressures that were brought to bear by populations at first simply wanting access to telephone services and then demanding improvements and new services. In addition, demonstration effects between countries occurred as governments and citizens compared both the availability and the quality of telecoms services in their own country with what existed elsewhere. Furthermore, both cooperation and competition took place as telecoms executives and their proud R&D staff (often excellent scientists and engineers) vied with those in other countries to lead the world in introducing advanced services. These motivations constituted a powerful force for improvements in technologies and services and for substantial reductions in cost in the monopolised telecoms industry.

As a result a number of highly creative and technologically powerful central research laboratories emerged. The best known included Bell Laboratories, part of AT&T in the USA, which later boasted the largest number of Nobel Prize winners of any industrial (as opposed to academic) laboratory. Other excellent laboratories included BT's Martlesham Laboratories in the UK, France Télécom's CNET and NTT's Electrical Communications Laboratories in Japan. In addition to doing more applied R&D these laboratories also undertook a significant amount of basic research (aided by the fact that monopoly status together with government ownership meant that there was less pressure than emerged later to prove that investments in basic research yielded attractive commercial rates of return). Typically, R&D in these laboratories took the form of first researching and then developing new prototypes of equipment (mainly switches and transmissions systems). Once this equipment was tested and found to be suitable (reliability being a particularly important requirement) mass manufacture was entrusted to specialist telecoms equipment suppliers (located in layer 1, see exhibit 2.2).

Different forms of industrial organisation emerged in the advanced countries in order to coordinate the activities of the monopoly telecoms operators in layer 2 and their equipment suppliers in layer 1 (exhibit 2.2). At the one extreme were the Japanese. In Japan the Ministry of Communications (*Teishinsho*) and later the spun-out NTT developed a close cooperative relationship with a number of equipment suppliers. These firms were referred to as the 'Den Den Family'.

Its main members were NEC, Fujitsu, Hitachi and Oki. With the exception of Hitachi these firms entered into technology agreements with leading Western telecoms equipment suppliers. Notably, NEC teamed up with Western Electric (which supplied AT&T) while Fujitsu linked with Siemens which supplied the Deutsche Bundespost (later Deutsche Telekom). In this way a form of organisation that the present writer has called 'controlled competition' emerged in Japan.[6] However, the Japanese equipment suppliers were separately owned and remained legally distinct from NTT.

In marked contrast, however, in the USA a pattern of vertical integration was followed. AT&T, the operator, owned and incorporated its single main supplier of telecoms equipment, namely Western Electric. Further differences appeared in Europe, where the typical pattern was for a dominant national telecoms equipment supplier to emerge – GEC in the UK, Siemens in Germany and what later became Alcatel in France – although there were usually also other competitors who played a lesser role.

However, the division of labour that existed between telecoms operators and their suppliers in creating the new technologies that drove the telecoms sector did not remain static but evolved in important ways. The main drivers of the change were the interlinked processes of specialisation and the expansion of the market that Adam Smith had identified more than two centuries earlier as the cause of the wealth of nations. In the ICT sector these drivers would lead to a transformation of the dynamics of layers 1 and 2.

From the mid-1980s: specialist telecoms equipment suppliers dominate

Over time, the competencies of the specialist equipment suppliers increased and they became increasingly sophisticated. This was the consequence of learning. The learning, in turn, resulted from their increasing output (as they were given ever larger orders for equipment from their telecoms operator expanding its networks) and from the greater effort that they made to improve their equipment. The telecoms operators continually demanded lower costs and higher quality. And if the equipment supplier was unable or unwilling to provide

[6] See Fransman (1995a).

them there were always other suppliers (or potential suppliers) who were both able and willing.

Furthermore, although until the mid-1980s operators in the main industrialised countries were reluctant to turn to equipment suppliers from other countries, the latter competed in countries that did not have their own equipment suppliers. These third-country markets became increasingly important for equipment suppliers, who soon came to the conclusion that stronger R&D competencies were a necessary condition for survival. The result was that the specialist equipment suppliers gradually became more sophisticated in researching and developing telecoms equipment than their former mentors, the telecoms operators. This increasing relative sophistication became evident in the resources that each group devoted to R&D. In short, the equipment suppliers soon became far more R&D-intensive than the telecoms operators (as was shown statistically in exhibits 4.3a and b, p. 60). The causation became cumulative. The stronger the suppliers became, the more the operators came to rely on them for both the research and the development of the equipment. This process of specialisation and division of labour resulted in the R&D engine of the telecoms part of the ICT sector moving away from layer 2 and being located more firmly in layer 1.

These tendencies were strengthened from the mid-1980s when telecoms services markets were liberalised in the USA, UK and Japan as new telecoms operators were allowed into the market to compete with the incumbent. These new operators were also supplied by the existing telecoms equipment suppliers, although in many cases the operators chose suppliers from other countries. The availability of equipment suppliers willing and able to supply competitive equipment at competitive prices significantly reduced the barriers to entry confronting the new operators, allowing them to compete more effectively with the incumbent operators. (The liberalisation process and its aftermath is analysed in more detail from p. 117.)

Nevertheless, the boundary remained in the division of labour between network operators and equipment suppliers in layers 2 and 1, respectively. Equipment suppliers did not become operators and increasingly operators ceased to be equipment makers (the most notable case in point being AT&T's decision to spin off its in-house equipment supplier, Western Electric, which was later re-named Lucent).

Computer hardware and software

Although in a general sense computing can be traced back to the abacus and the work of the English mathematician Charles Babbage, it was around the time of the Second World War that the first effective computers began to emerge. These computers were largely developed in universities (notably in the USA and UK) and in a small number of emerging firms associated with them. In the later 1950s a number of large companies in the USA, Europe and Japan began entering the newly emerging computer industry.[7] In the 1960s, however, a watershed change occurred which fundamentally re-shaped the computer industry. This was the rise of IBM, which quickly came to dominate not only the US computer industry but also the global industry, standing head and shoulders above all the other players.

IBM's success was attributable to its relative technological sophistication, itself the result of a substantial commitment to R&D and close collaboration with government financial backers and users (notably the US Defense Department). But IBM's success was also due to its sophisticated understanding of the needs of its business customers (IBM had begun as a company making business machines before the computer era). This understanding led IBM to introduce a compatible range of larger and smaller mainframe computers in the System 360 series. By the end of the 1960s and into the 1970s IBM's global dominance went virtually unchallenged (despite the noble efforts made by would-be competitors in the USA, Europe and Japan).

However, just when IBM seemed unassailable, its substantial lead began slowly to be eroded. The main agent for change was not a bigger and better competitor but rather a Schumpeterian new combination. The new products in question were increasingly powerful (and increasingly cheap) electronic devices that provided the processing and memory functions of the computer. These new products were incorporated into a new combination, a so-called 'minicomputer' that, although less powerful than most of IBM's mainframes, was adequately suited to many tasks (in places such as universities and medium-sized companies). Significantly, the minicomputer was also far cheaper. This new technology facilitated the entry of new competitors into the

---

[7] For a good account of the emerging computer industry in the USA and Europe, see Mowery and Nelson (1999).

computer industry, some of which – notably Digital Equipment (DEC) – grew rapidly. The writing was on the wall, and the words spelled a radical transformation of the computer industry.

The next wave of technical change was more like a tsunami compared to the ripple that had brought the minicomputer. It began with the invention of the microprocessor, the 'computer on a chip'. But this tsunami had an inauspicious start. Its beginning was in the semiconductor company Intel, that at the time was struggling to find a way of competing with large Japanese companies that were rapidly making inroads into its market for dynamic random access memories (DRAMS). Intel had been asked by a small Japanese calculator company called Busicom to develop the wired logic circuits that would power its calculators. Ted Hoff, the engineer in Intel assigned to the job, came to the creative conclusion in 1971 that he could meet Busicom's requirements by using Intel's knowledge of memory devices to store the necessary software instructions, while integrating sufficient logic circuits on a single silicon chip to perform the operations required by the instructions. In effect, this meant that a simple computer was created on a single chip.

The problem was that what in retrospect became a mountain at the time looked only like a molehill. Indeed, Andy Grove, one of the founders of Intel and its most famous pioneer, later recalled stopping at traffic lights and having heard about Hoff's invention had the thought that the new microprocessor could possibly be used to operate such lights. The microprocessor at this stage had limited capabilities and it was impossible to even think of it doing the job of the existing logic circuits that powered computers and sophisticated military applications.

But great things sometimes have modest beginnings. By the late 1970s hobbyists, geeks and even a few start-up firms (such as Apple started by Steve Jobs and Steve Wozniak) were beginning to use microprocessors to create simple computers. But these activities were generally confined to the cognoscenti. It took a practical application that would propel the emerging microcomputer into a wider market: the spreadsheet. With this useful application non-geeks – including small businesses and householders – could rapidly appreciate the value of this new machine.

The rest is well-documented history. Sensing the emergence of a relatively minor new market opportunity in the microcomputer, IBM made the decision to enter. In order to do so, however, it established a new business separately located and managed so as not to interfere with its more important mainframe activities. In order to go rapidly to market IBM made the famous (some say fateful) decision to out-source both the operating system and the microprocessor for the new IBM PC. The operating system went to Bill Gates and Microsoft while the microprocessor was given to Intel, both companies retaining proprietary rights over their contributions.

With this move a rapidly growing global industry was born. Having retained the property rights, Microsoft and Intel were able to supply not just IBM – that gave respectability to this new appliance – but also its competitors, the so-called 'IBM clones'. And competition brought both increasing quality (further enhanced by the improvements simul-taneously being made by the makers of microprocessors – largely Intel and Motorola) and, equally importantly, falling cost. But perhaps even more significantly, the microcomputer based on the so-called 'Wintel standard' created a new widely available platform for innovation. Software application developers were encouraged to develop all sorts of applications for this new ubiquitous device. And just as was the case in the early diffusion of the telephone, network externalities kicked in with the microcomputer and Wintel, too, with the benefit to users increasing as more users joined. A standard system meant that *interoperability* became possible and users could share files.

Convergence between telecoms and computing: the Internet

Around 1995 a new tsunami burst over the ICT sector, this one even bigger and more powerful than its predecessor. However, it had begun almost forty years earlier as a small swell. In 1958, the Advanced Research Projects Agency (ARPA) was established in the USA in response to the Russian launch of the Sputnik artificial satellite in 1957. It was this agency that was to launch the first version of what would later morph into what we now know as the Internet. In 1972 ARPANET was first demonstrated as a viable system.

Independent of this project, however, another of the triad of key technologies underlying the Internet had begun to emerge. This was packet switching that allowed data (including voice) to be broken up into small 'packets', allowing each packet to be independently routed through the data and telecommunications networks to be re-assembled at the receiving end. The flexibility in this way designed into the communications system had the added advantage of allowing the system to be more resilient, limiting the potential damage that could be caused by a Russian attack, and therefore allowing ARPA to achieve one of its primary objectives. In the early 1960s packet switching was invented independently by Paul Baran of the Rand Corporation in the USA and Donald Davies of the British National Physical Laboratory, based on the notion of 'message switching' that went back to the postal and telegraph systems.

The second of the triad of key Internet technologies was TCP/IP (discussed on p. 26 in connection with the layer model). It was in 1973 that Vinton Cerf, often referred to as the 'Father of the Internet', was invited by Robert Kahn to develop a system for inter-working between dissimilar networks (i.e. for the Internet). In 1974 this led to the specification of a Transmission Control Protocol (TCP), part of the basic architecture of the Internet. In 1978 they split the TCP protocol into two separate parts; a host-to-host protocol (TCP) and an inter-network protocol (IP). IP would simply pass individual packets between machines (from host to packet switch or between packet switches); TCP would be responsible for ordering these packets into reliable connections between hosts. In this way the transfer of packets across different networks, using different technologies, was facilitated.

In 1990 the third of the triad of technologies emerged. It was the first incarnation of the World Wide Web, created by Tim Berners-Lee, Robert Cailliau and others at CERN, the particle-physics research establishment in Switzerland. In January 1993, Mosaic was introduced, the first World Wide Web browser, based on research done at the University of Illinois. In April 1994, Mosaic Communications was established, a firm that soon became Netscape Communications Corp. that was floated on the stock exchange on 8 August 1995.

There is evidence that Bill Gates began to understand the implications of the Internet only in 1995. Although Gates and Microsoft were immersed in the development and shipping date of Windows 95 (eventually released on 24 August 1995) and until mid-1995 did not pay too much attention to the Internet, Gates' vision of the future of computing and Microsoft had come to encompass the importance of networked computing. On 6 October 1994, Gates wrote a memorandum titled 'Sea Change' that spelled out plans for networked computing for Microsoft. Earlier, in May 1993, Gates had approved work on Marvel, an online service that would be offered by Microsoft (and later become MSN, currently a competitor to Google and Yahoo!). Marvel, however, was not intended to be Internet-compatible.

Until early-to-mid-1995, it is clear that Gates saw Microsoft as the dog of networked computing and the Internet, at best, as a rather insignificant tail. In Gates' own words: 'I wouldn't say it was clear [at this time] that [the Internet] was going to explode over the next couple of years. If you'd asked me then if most TV ads will have URLs [web addresses] in them, I would have laughed.' By 1995, however, some 20 million people were accessing the Internet without using Microsoft's software. On 26 May 1995, Gates issued a memorandum, 'The Internet Tidal Wave', that finally confirmed his conversion to the view that the Internet had become the dog, with Microsoft, after all, only its tail.

Competition and market structure

As the last section makes clear, Schumpeterian new combinations – new technologies (i.e. new products and processes), new forms of organisation and new markets – are a 'prime mover' (in Schumpeter's words) of change in the ICT sector. However, new combinations do not directly cause the final outcomes. Rather their effect is mediated through markets and other institutions that shape what eventually happens. In this section we shall examine in more detail the impact that competition, market structure and one particular institution – regulation – have had on the dynamics of layer 2 in the ICT sector.

Telecoms operators in layer 2: liberalisation and new competitors

In the mid-1980s a significant change in mindset occurred when the decision was taken in three of the world's leading countries to abandon the natural monopoly presupposition and introduce competition in layer 2 to the hitherto monopolist telecoms operators. The three countries were the USA, Japan and the UK. Significantly, however, this path-breaking change in these three countries was unconnected; each country was led to this conclusion for different internal political reasons. In the USA the debate was dominated by anti-monopoly moves against AT&T while the change in Japan was motivated more by a wider process of administrative reform against the backdrop of national budget deficits. In the UK, by contrast, the move reflected the views of the new Prime Minister, Margaret Thatcher, whose ideology emphasised the unleashing of market forces and the privatisation of state-owned enterprises (SOEs) such as BT.

However, the initial moves away from monopoly in the telecoms services markets of these countries and towards a greater degree of competition were cautious. Most cautious of all was the UK, that began by ushering in a period of duopoly; Cable & Wireless was allowed to establish a new subsidiary, Mercury, which would compete with the privatised BT (formerly the British Post Office). In the USA, AT&T was divested, with the long-distance part of the company (the new AT&T) being separated from a number of newly established companies that offered regional and local services, the so-called 'Baby Bells' (the most successful of which later turned out to be Verizon and SBC). Two new long-distance companies were allowed to compete with AT&T: MCI and Sprint. Japan went one step further. While like Britain, Japan finally decided not to break-up NTT (though a vigorous debate took place over this issue), the authorities allowed three long-distance competitors into the market; Daini Den Den, Japan Telecom and Teleway Japan.

De facto *monopolised local telecoms services*

Significantly, however, the local telecoms services markets in all three countries were left under the control of the *de facto* monopolistic incumbents. The reason was, simply, that it was far easier to introduce competition in long-distance services. With the significant amount of traffic going over the long-distance core network, and with long-distance telephone prices initially high as a result of the monopoly era, it was relatively easy to persuade new entrants to contest this market. Facilitating regulations added to the incentive.

By contrast, the local telecoms services market was relatively unattractive (the so-called local access market, or simply the 'last mile', the outermost bit of the network connecting homes and businesses to the local telecoms switch). The reason was that each individual customer generated little traffic while the investment cost of taking new lines to these customers was substantial. The result was that the winds of competition blew far more strongly in the long-distance than in the local market (a fact that was to significantly shape the future evolution of the US telecoms sector in particular, as we shall see).

The second wave of long-distance new entrants

The newly deregulated long-distance market also created market entry opportunities for other smaller players. Their opportunity was enhanced by the rather conservative pricing strategies adopted by the first wave of competitors. Knowing that competition was still very limited the latter tended to price not much below the incumbent but sufficiently lower to make switching a reasonably attractive option for customers (business and private). This gave a break to the second wave of entrants.

One early example was a tiny start-up that began life in September 1983 in a coffee shop in Hattiesburg, Mississippi. One of the founders (who had been a football coach and ran a number of motels) who soon assumed leadership of the company was a rather brash man by the name of Bernie Ebbers. The company later changed its name to World-Com. Other second-wave entrants who entered later included Qwest, Global Crossing and Level 3. In the UK, once the duopoly period was ended by the government, similar second-wave entrants emerged. They included COLT (established by the US financial company, Fidelity), Energis and Scottish Telecom (which later became Thus).

The Internet and the telecoms boom

As we saw earlier, from 1995 the Internet took off as a new rapidly diffusing commercial service creating a huge demand for Internet access. This access was initially provided by a narrowband dial-up service over the copper local access telephone network. But as investors quickly came to realise, the global take-off of the Internet would also generate a substantial derived demand for telecoms capacity and the telecoms companies best placed to satisfy that demand, it was believed, would make substantial profits doing so.

A seminal meeting cemented the link between the Internet and the prospects for telecoms companies in the eyes of investors. In 1995 – the same year that Bill Gates finally acknowledged the significance of the Internet – Gates was invited by Warren Buffett, the billionaire investor 'sage of Omaha' who was to become the second-richest man in the world after Gates, to a private meeting for Buffett's investors in Dublin. It was at this meeting that the link between the burgeoning Internet and opportunities for profit in telecoms was formed in the minds of a number of important US investors. The same connection would soon be made by many others.

At this meeting, Gates spoke about his new-found belief in the potential of the Internet. Attending the meeting was Walter Scott, who was on the board of Buffett's main company, Berkshire Hathaway. Hearing Gates, Scott came to the conclusion that the Internet would become a hugely important phenomenon.[8] Furthermore, he came to understand that the Internet was nothing more than a network of IP networks. This insight led him to create Level 3, one of a new US generation of aggressive new-entrant telecoms operators that was in the same league as other entrants such as Qwest and Global Crossing. (Interestingly, Buffett himself, though a close friend of Scott's, refused to become involved in what became known as the 'Telecoms Boom'. The reason was that he claimed he could not understand the alleged profit proposition in the telecoms sector. Although in the short run this would lose Buffett the confidence of a significant number of his investors, in the longer term his judgement would become prophetic.)

And so began the 'telecoms boom'. Between 1996 and 2001 a total of $1,805 billion was invested globally in the telecoms sector, $890 billion of this took the form of syndicated bank loans, $500 billion was invested by private equity and stock markets and $415 billion was invested by bond markets.[9] Between 1996 and 1999 in the USA alone 144 new telecoms companies went public, raising more than $25 billion.[10]

---

[8] How did Scott react to Gates' comments? 'From my perspective, if Bill really thought the Internet was important and he needed to understand it, I thought it was important and we needed to understand it. And I thought that because I have a lot of faith and confidence in Bill knowing and understanding a lot more about these things than I do. And with the interest that Bill had in it, I just came back and told [my colleagues] that I thought it was something we now needed to do something about.' The result was a substantial series of investments made by Scott in Internet-related telecoms companies. Author's interview with Scott, Omaha, Nebraska, 2002.

[9] Fransman (2002a: 1).

[10] Fransman (2002a: 25).

A consensual vision[11] reigned supreme, proclaiming that super-normal profits were to be made from the Internet and its impact on the telecoms sector, and this vision ruled the hearts, the minds and the pockets of both telecoms companies and investors (institutional and private). Everyone seemed to be happy (except for those that failed to acquire either real or financial telecoms assets and sat on the sidelines watching with envy as their prices inexorably rose). Even the telecoms regulators took comfort from the fact that newly deregulated telecoms services markets seemed to be working well with growing competition as the new entrants grew rapidly and mounted their challenges to the incumbents and billions were poured into the modernising telecoms infrastructure, although as more heat was generated in the markets some of them began privately to wonder whether a bubble was forming.

The telecoms bust

And, indeed, that is precisely what was happening. For a while exuberant financial markets plugged the gap between fantasy and reality, masking the failure of the new-entrant telecoms companies (both operators and equipment suppliers) to turn their huge investments into attractive rates of return. The failure of revenue and profit margins to perform was more than compensated for by the rising financial values of the companies concerned (as typically happens in bubble periods). Eventually, however, the real world asserted itself. Having ignored the nakedness of the emperor for so long, preferring to marvel at the alleged beauty of his clothes, investors and analysts were in time forced by the stubborn failure of the financial variables to perform to come to terms with the fact that the figures simply did not add up.

A large part of the problem was on the supply side which, incredibly, had been largely ignored. Although it is true that the rapid global diffusion of the Internet was generating huge increases in demand, substantial increases were also occurring in supply. We have already referred to the significant increases in investment in the telecoms industry, a large part of which went into increasing the capacity of telecoms networks. Furthermore, rapid technical change meant that

---

[11] See Fransman (2002a, 2004) for a detailed analysis of this consensual vision, its making and its fate.

each dollar of investment was adding much more capacity than hitherto. (One example was the great improvements made in dense wave division multiplexing (DWDM), a technology that made use of the differing wavelengths of different colours of light in order to create multiple channels within the same optical fibre, multiplying its carrying capacity significantly.)

Astoundingly, by September 2001 it was estimated that 'only 1 or 2 per cent of the fibre optic cable buried under Europe and North America has even been turned on or "lit". . . A similar overcapacity exists in undersea links [connecting the continents], where each new Atlantic cable [as a result of improved technology] adds as much bandwidth as all the previous infrastructure put together.'[12] But the problem was also caused by the way financial markets worked. John Maynard Keynes commented that stock markets often work like beauty contests; in both, the punter has to calculate not how beautiful the stock/girl is, but how the judges will see the matter; Keynes (1936). In the case of stock markets, the judges are other large investors.

Beauty contest behaviour was reinforced in financial markets by the widespread practice of benchmarking the performance of financial portfolios against indices such as the FTSE or the Dow Jones. During the time of the telecoms (and so-called dot.com) booms these indices were influenced by the major telecoms and Internet shares that were quickly growing in value. Fund managers who suspected the beauty of telecoms shares in the belief that they were overvalued and who refused to hold them (or were underweight in them) were punished since their portfolios, not containing the rapidly rising telecoms shares, underperformed the index.

This is precisely the fate that awaited the late Tony Dye in the City of London; known in the media as 'Dr Doom', he lost his job at UBS for refusing to purchase telecoms and dot.com shares. It was little comfort for him to learn, only a short while after his dismissal, that from March 2000 the telecoms boom had turned into the telecoms bust. In March 2000 the total global value of telecoms shares was $6,300 billion. By the beginning of September 2001 (just before the 9/11 collapse of the Twin Towers) this value had fallen to $3,800 billion, a total loss of $2,500 billion.[13]

---

[12] Fransman (2002a: 16).
[13] See Fransman (2002a).

Shake-out and consolidation

Virtually all the telecoms operators were left high and dry by the telecoms bust. During the exuberance of the telecoms boom almost all of them had borrowed extensively in order to expand their networks. Those in the strongest positions engaged heavily in mergers and acquisitions (M&As) (further fuelling the frenzy in the financial markets), often using their inflated shares as the acquisition currency and in turn adding additional inflation in financial values. But as the dust began to settle following the telecoms bust the parlous state of their finances became visible.

The largest telecoms operator incumbents were tens of billions of dollars in debt. Many of the new entrants, who were seen as the main challengers to the incumbents (and indeed, in cases like WorldCom, their successors), were on the point of collapse. Indeed, some did collapse. The most dramatic and notorious case was WorldCom itself. Not only did WorldCom become the biggest bankruptcy in US corporate history, its leader, Bernie Ebbers, was convicted for fraudulently distorting his company's financial performance figures.

Similar stories emerged for other high-flying new entrants such as Qwest and Global Crossing. The scandal enveloped not only the telecoms companies but also the financial analysts who had provided much of the alleged rationale justifying the high financial values. The most notable example was Wall Street's Jack Grubman, a former AT&T employee who with his understanding of telecoms technologies was accorded guru status and whose statements could move telecoms share prices. Grubman was accused in court of falsely inflating expectations and was fined and banned from working in financial institutions.

With substantial excess capacity in many telecoms markets adding considerably to the gloom, and financial markets decisively withdrawing their support for the telecoms sector, it was inevitable that a substantial shake-out would occur. And it did: even now the effects have not yet fully worked themselves through.

In the USA the main winners in the shake-out were the regional Baby Bells, SBC and Verizon. The main reason they emerged victorious was that in their regional and local telecoms services markets they were not subjected to the same severe competition that was the fate of their long-distance counterparts such as AT&T, MCI, Sprint, WorldCom, Qwest and Global Crossing. Although the US

authorities had introduced the Telecommunications Act in 1996 with
the specific purpose of facilitating more competition in local markets
(largely with the intention of allowing the long-distance companies to
contest these markets) by the turn of the century it had become clear
that the Act had failed. One of the main reasons for failure was the
successful defence mounted by the Baby Bells in courts and elsewhere
to thwart the aims of the Act and forestall new entrants.

With their market power largely intact, and with rivals weakened
by the telecoms bust, it was no surprise that it was the leading Baby
Bells that emerged victorious from the consolidation process. Thus
SBC acquired both AT&T and Bell South, calling the combined company AT&T (thus keeping the brand name of the most famous
telecoms operator in history). Verizon acquired MCI (that had been
earlier acquired by and merged into WorldCom) and another Baby
Bell, US West.

With this process of consolidation the US telecoms services market
(depicted in layer 2) had come almost full circle. When AT&T was
divested in 1984 the intention was to break-up the monopoly and
create several competitors. By the middle of the first decade of the
twenty-first century, however, only two across-the-board telecoms
operators survived.[14] Many wondered whether the tortuous road that
the Americans had followed in their search for competitive telecoms
services markets had been worth the cost.

The consolidation process in Japan resulted in the survival of three
across-the-board telecoms operators. The first was the incumbent,
NTT, a group of five major companies that included Japan's main
mobile operator, NTT DoCoMo, the second was KDDI. KDD was in
the monopoly era the state-owned provider of international telecoms
services (NTT being restricted to national services). KDD acquired
DDI, the most successful of the three companies originally allowed to
compete with NTT, renaming the company KDDI.

The third is Softbank, a company started by Masayoshi Son, an
Internet entrepreneur. Having been a partner in the layer 3 company,
Yahoo! Japan (that offered broadband through a successful subsidiary,
Yahoo! BB), Softbank went on to acquire first the fixed network of
Japan Telecom and then the mobile subsidiary of this company,
J Phone. (Japan Telecom was originally acquired by the mobile

---

[14] The somewhat different case of mobile operators is examined later.

company Vodafone which at first was interested solely in J Phone. Japan Telecom's fixed network was accordingly sold to Softbank. But later, after failing dismally to make an impact on the Japanese mobile market, Vodafone, under considerable shareholder pressure due to its worsening financial performance, sold J Phone to Softbank.) After its consolidation, therefore, Japan has been left with three across-the-board telecoms operators in contrast to the USA's two.

In Europe, consolidation has meant that the incumbent telecoms operators have remained the largest across-the-board operators. However, a combination of intra-European diversification, regulation and convergence has meant that these incumbents have come under increasing competitive pressure. For example, in the mobile area European incumbents compete with their counterparts in the latter's markets (e.g. France Télécom's Orange is a major competitor in the UK) and the same thing happens in fixed markets although to a lesser extent (for instance, Telecom Italia offers broadband services in France in competition with France Télécom). The regulation of LLU (allowing competitors to the incumbent to install their equipment in the incumbent's local network and directly access its customers, all at a low, regulated access price) has encouraged a group of new, often aggressive, entrants. This has also motivated companies from previously distinct industries for whom convergence has created new market opportunities. One example is Sky, the media company owned by Rupert Murdoch's News Corporation, which now uses BT's unbundled lines to compete with it, offering triple-play services (voice, TV and broadband Internet).

Mobile communications

So far, most of the story told here about telecoms operators has been about those offering fixed services. Where does mobile fit in?

The concept of cellular communications, used by all conventional mobile operators, was invented in Bell Laboratories in 1947. The first publication on cellular mobile communications was by Shulte and Cornell of Bell Labs in 1960. A decade later, in 1970, the first civilian standard for modern cellular telephony began to be specified in Scandinavia, leading to the Nordic Mobile Telephony (NMT) standard introduced in 1981.[15]

---

[15] See Fransman (2002a: 72–3).

However, as with the microprocessor discussed earlier, and many other technological revolutions, the mobile revolution had an inauspicious beginning. The commercial attractiveness of mobile communications was at the start clouded in uncertainty. For example, in the early 1980s when AT&T asked the consulting company McKinsey to predict how many cellular mobile phones would be in existence globally by the year 2000, their answer was around 900,000. In the event, the figure was about 400 million.

According to Kurt Hellström, President of Ericsson, the world's largest producer of mobile systems: 'When I joined Ericsson in 1984 Radio Communications was something odd happening on the outskirts of Stockholm.'[16] At that stage, Ericsson's main focus was on the development of its new digital switches for fixed telecommunications. Furthermore, the focus of state-of-the-art research at the time was on optical-fibre transmissions systems capable of providing huge capacity. Radio communications, whose signals were susceptible to electromagnetic interference, was seen as a distinctly inferior transmissions technology. As these events make clear, in the early 1980s mobile communications was not perceived to be the bonanza that it became in the late 1990s. From around 1997, however, the demand for mobile communications exploded, at first in the rich countries. One of the main companies to benefit was Vodafone, which quickly became the dominant global mobile player.

The mobile sunrise and sunset

As Vodafone's history dramatically illustrates, mobile was a boom industry from the late 1990s. As the whole telecoms sector went from boom to bust after 2000, mobile provided the single source of hope. Almost all of the incumbent telecoms operators had mobile subsidiaries and it was these that came to provide the major source of growth in revenue and profitability.

For a while Vodafone continued to successfully ride the mobile wave. The mergers and acquisitions engineered by Chris Gent and his financial advisers in the City in London made Vodafone one of the darlings of the stock market. Shortly after-wards, boom turned to bust and the heavily indebted telecoms incumbents began to suffer

---

[16] *Financial Times*, 26 July 1999.

seriously, but Vodafone continued to prosper. Praised by analysts as a 'single-play' mobile company, and with the demand for mobile phones still rising significantly, it was felt that Vodafone was largely immune from the problems plaguing the across-the-board incumbents. But the optimism was not to last, neither for Vodafone nor for the mobile industry in the rich countries (although continuing rapid diffusion in poorer countries continues to provide a source of growth and profitability, particularly in countries such as China, where China Mobile and China Unison continue to prosper, and in India where Vodafone has recently become more involved).

Vodafone suffered from four significant problems. First, saturation in its main European mobile markets became a growing problem. Second, increasing competition from other mobile companies began to eat into its profits. Third, its minority holding in Verizon Wireless in the USA proved to be problematic. The fourth problem was Vodafone's misadventure in Japan. Having long warily eyed its main rival – Japan's NTT DoCoMo – Vodafone under Gent's successor, Arun Sarin, decided to enter the Japanese market. In order to do so it purchased the mobile subsidiary of Japan Telecom, J Phone. However, this proved to be a serious miscalculation.

Japan has the most sophisticated and competitive mobile market in the world. The leading company by market share is DoCoMo, the mobile subsidiary of the incumbent NTT. DoCoMo's lead is underpinned by its substantial R&D expenditure and capabilities and by its inventive cooperative relationship with its equipment suppliers and mobile phone makers. Although not as successful as DoCoMo, KDDI was also a strong competitor in mobile. With phones that were inferior, Vodafone just could not compete. Under pressure for relatively quick results in Japan (since Vodafone's overall revenue and profitability was disappointing financial analysts) Vodafone soon made the embarrassing decision to exit. J Phone was sold to the third Japanese telecoms player, Softbank.

In addition, Vodafone, like other mobile companies, has to cope with two further problems. The first of these is uncertain consumer demand. It is unclear what consumers want over their mobile phones and how much they are willing to pay. The second problem stems from disruptive technical change. Two technologies are particularly important. Voice-over-the-Internet (with flat-rate Internet access charges) in effect means that consumers can talk for free over the

Internet. Wireless Fidelity (WiFi) in some circumstances provides an alternative radio technology to cellular mobile, allowing users to make some mobile calls while by-passing the cellular mobile network.[17]

Vodafone is developing several strategies to cope with these problems. In order to deal with falling voice revenues, for example, it is attempting to increase its data traffic through its content site, Vodafone Live, and providing music and TV over mobile phones. Vodafone has also entered into an agreement with BT to use the latter's network in order to offer fixed broadband services. This is a significant change for a company that once prided itself in being a 'single-play' mobile company.

However, if Vodafone's lacklustre share price performance and its boardroom battles are anything to go by, the jury is still very much out regarding its ability to bounce back and prove that it will remain a growth company. Realising this, Vodafone is now pinning a substantial part of its strategy on increasing involvement in high-growth emerging countries.

Broadband Internet[18]

Fortunately for the telecoms companies (both network operators and equipment suppliers) a new wave of technologies would once again inject new opportunities for profit and growth into the evolving ICT ecosystem. These technologies would help to counteract the twin hammer blows of the telecoms bust coupled with saturating mobile voice markets in some of the most important rich countries.

The technologies provided broadband Internet access. Until the early 2000s Internet access was provided mainly on a narrowband dial-up basis. But the connection took a relatively long time to make, the speed was slow and a further disadvantage was that the telephone line was fully occupied, preventing incoming calls. Having rapidly adopted the Internet in the latter half of the 1990s, consumers soon became frustrated with their new toy. The tribulations of consumers were matched by the desire of the telecoms operators to find new high-growth markets to help deal with their post-bust woes. One technical

---

[17] BT Fusion, for example, offers a bimodal mobile phone which uses cheaper WiFi in the home or office and automatically switches to cellular (using Deutsche Telekom's T-Mobile cellular network) when the user is on the move and WiFi connections are unavailable.

[18] This account draws on Fransman (2006).

fix that seemed to provide a solution was the Integrated Services Digital Network (ISDN),[19] and from the late 1990s many telecoms operators began to offer high-speed ISDN connections. However, an even better solution was also available. This was the digital subscriber line (DSL) that soon became, with cable modems, the most important way of providing broadband Internet.

DSL

Asynchronous digital subscriber line (ADSL) is a technology that allows broadband data to be sent over the traditional copper telephone lines that connect most homes and small businesses. It has also been referred to as the incumbent telecom operators' broadband technology because it is these companies that own the copper telephone lines (also known as the local loop, the loop consisting of two copper wires that connect the customer's premises with the local telephone network). It is called 'asynchronous' because the download speed is faster than the upload speed.

ADSL was first developed in the late 1980s by Joseph W. Lechleider, formerly of Bellcore Laboratories (spun off from Bell Laboratories when AT&T was divested, Bellcore's mission being to do research for the separated Baby Bells). For the Baby Bells and their researchers a key question was whether they would be able to use their copper local loop for TV and video. If so, they would be able to diversify into new markets in competition with the satellite and cable TV companies. It was Lechleider who first demonstrated, in a mathematical paper, that this was possible. This made technically feasible a new service called video streaming, which in turn facilitated video-on-demand (VoD). Further important research relating to the implementation of ADSL was done by John Cioffi of Stanford University.

Essentially, ADSL involves splitting the telephone line, allowing one channel to provide voice communications and a second, operating at higher frequencies, to deliver high-speed data (thus allowing broadband Internet access). This, in turn, facilitated two of the most important characteristics of broadband communications; always-on functionality and the ability of the user to use the Internet while receiving phone calls (capabilities that did not exist with narrowband,

---

[19] Integrated Services Digital Network, an international standard for the end-to-end digital transmission of voice, data and signalling.

or dial-up, Internet access). In addition, ADSL facilitated flat-rate tariffs while allowing the network to survive the massive increase in traffic that resulted from these changes. It was these characteristics, together with a fourth – faster speed – that initially drove demand for broadband, rather than broadband-specific content, applications or services.

In the event, ADSL at first failed to achieve its initial objective, namely providing a new market for the Baby Bells in TV and video. Given the state of the supporting technologies, the cost of the services and the existence of cheap alternatives (such as video shops), consumer demand failed to materialise. However, something like a decade later, the demand for Internet access (on the part of both consumers and telecoms providers) created a new lease of life for ADSL.

Wireless

In 1896, twenty years after Alexander Graham Bell invented his telephone, Guglielmo Marconi developed the radio transmitter that in 1901 allowed him to transmit long-wave radio signals across the Atlantic. Although an old technology in widespread use, by the 1970s many researchers felt that as a way of transmitting communications signals radio had serious drawbacks. Bell Laboratories went so far as to cut back its research on radio. While radio signals are subject to interference, optical fibre, with its higher carrying capacity and speed and less vulnerability to disturbance, was seen as the transmissions technology of the future.

The development of cellular mobile communications in the 1970s, however, and its widespread adoption in the late 1990s changed these perceptions.[20] The technologists, it became apparent, had focused too narrowly on the techniques of transmission and had ignored the users. Users, it turned out, were willing to put up with interference and, on occasion, lack of signals in return for mobility. Cellular mobile soon provided not only mobility for the user but also a way for the user to be located. These advantages fuelled the rapid global diffusion of mobile communications from the late 1990s. By the early years of the new millennium advanced second-generation and new third-generation

---

[20] The first proposal to use cellular systems in the field of mobile communications, in order to make most efficient use of limited spectrum, was put forward in 1947 and discussed in Bell Laboratories. The first publication on cellular radio was by Shulte and Cornell of Bell Labs in 1960.

cellular mobile systems were capable of offering broadband speeds.[21] Particularly in Japan (through NTT DoCoMo's i-mode service) mobile Internet access became very popular.

Another set of wireless broadband technologies is wireless local area networks (LANs), popularly known as WiFi. This technology allows an over-the-air connection to be made between a radio-enabled client (e.g. laptop or phone) and a base station connected to the LAN (or another client). First discussed in 1990, this technology was developed by the Institute of Electrical and Electronic Engineering's (IEEE's) 802 Committee, winning final approval in June 1997.[22] Since the user can be mobile (within the footprint of a WiFi base station), some analysts believe that WiFi will become a serious competitor to cellular mobile communications. Most incumbent telecoms operators have developed WiFi 'hotspots' (e.g. in airports, stations and coffee houses) and have integrated them into their service offerings.

A further wireless technology is WiMAX (Worldwide Interoperability for Microwave Access), a fixed wireless access technology that covers a far wider area than WiFi. Some believe that WiMax will be able to provide wireless mobile coverage over entire city centres, also becoming a serious competitor to cellular mobile networks. WiMax is covered by the 802.16 standard.

Optical fibre[23]
But the *crème de la crème* of transmission technologies remains optical fibre. The reason, simply, is the speed of light (photons) which significantly exceeds that of electro-magnetic waves. Moreover, light is influenced less by electro-magnetic interference and is able to carry a far higher bandwidth, and it is for these reasons that it provides a more efficient transmission mechanism. Stimulated by the complementary

---

[21] These were offered by two competing standards, both based on code division multiple access (CDMA), a method of spreading spectrum transmission for digital wireless personal communications networks that allows a large number of users simultaneously to access a single radio frequency band without interference. The two standards are wideband code division multiple access (WCDMA), used largely in Europe and Japan, and code division multiple access (CDMA) 2000 (and later versions), used largely in the USA.
[22] This has resulted in a number of WiFi standards, including 802.11b, 802.11a and 802.11g.
[23] For a detailed account of the development of optical fibre and its use in the ICT ecosystem see Fransman (1995a: chapter 5 and appendix 2).

innovations in light-transmitting devices – such as the laser[24] and light-emitting diode (LED) – researchers in the 1960s at first experimented with various kinds of light wave-guides. But it was in 1970 that the key breakthrough was achieved when researchers at the Corning glass company produced an optical fibre with a loss rate below 20 decibels per kilometre (dB/km) that made optical fibre for the first time a viable transmissions technology. Thereafter rapid progress was made with many different kinds of innovations speeding the passage of light through the glass fibre and multiplying its carrying capacity by many orders of magnitude.

However, despite these advantages, there remain several important drawbacks to the use of optical fibre. Among these is the necessity to lay new optical fibre cables, often in new conduits, while one of the competing technologies, ADSL, could use already installed and depreciated copper local loops. This tended to make optical fibre a relatively expensive technology which negatively affected its adoption. Another disadvantage was its fixed nature, which limited its ability to provide mobility, unlike its wireless-based competitors.

Global diffusion of broadband technologies and national innovation systems

In assessing economic impact it is necessary to distinguish between the *emergence* of a new technology (and the processes that led to that emergence) and the *diffusion* of that technology. It is only with the latter that technologies have their economic impact. However, the diffusion process at national levels is always highly complex. Many factors impinge on the rate of diffusion, the choice of alternative technologies that are diffused, the effectiveness with which they are used and the subsequent generations of innovation that accompany diffusion. Some of these factors are economic, such as the impact of

---

[24] A laser is a device that produces amplified light as a result of the stimulated emission of radiation ('laser' being an acronym for Light Amplification by the Stimulated Emission of Radiation). In 1958 Charles H. Townes (then at Columbia University) and Arthur L. Schawlow (of Bell Laboratories) published a paper and patent application that provided the theoretical rationale for laser action. On 7 July 1960, Theodore H. Maiman of the Hughes Research Laboratories in Malibu, California, announced that he had developed the first working optical-frequency laser. In 1964 Townes won a Nobel Prize for his work on coherent radiation, and in 1981 he shared a Nobel Prize with Schawlow for their research on laser spectroscopy.

relative prices and the intensity of competition which influence incentives and therefore outcomes. But non-economic factors can also be important, such as the influence of the institutional environment, the 'rules of the game' and the non-economic contexts within which diffusion occurs. Certainly, it is a mistake to assume, as many regulatory models implicitly do, that competition alone (rarely adequately defined) is sufficient to generate optimal diffusion.

An indication of national diversity in the diffusion of broadband technology was provided in chapter 6. Several distinguishing national features emerged from that discussion. One of the most important was the substantial lead of Japan in FTTP. This superior technology provided for almost a quarter of broadband connections in Japan in 2006, a figure that is rapidly increasing. The adoption of FTTP also explains why Japan leads the world by far in broadband speed (the evidence is provided in Fransman 2006). Sweden, too, for reasons explored in the latter book, is a rapid adopter of FTTP, but the other countries lag significantly behind.

Also outstanding has been the role played by cable modems (CATV) in providing broadband in the USA. Underlying the figures is the competition between telecoms operators and cable TV companies, a competition that has significantly influenced the changing regulatory stance of the FCC, the US regulator, since 2003 as discussed briefly in the following section.

But for present purposes the significance of this data is that it illustrates the extent of national diversity in the diffusion of technology and the performance that is accordingly achieved. This highlights the importance of thinking of innovation processes and performance in terms of national and sectoral innovation systems, as is done here in connection with the ICT ecosystem.

Next-generation networks

A further major change in the new ICT ecosystem took place in the early 2000s with the emergence of so-called 'next-generation networks' (NGNs). These are all-IP networks that enjoy the considerable cost and quality advantages provided by Internet technologies. NGNs are currently in the process of adoption by the world's leading telecoms operators, for two reasons. The first is that they offer considerable cost savings and enhanced flexibility while the second is that they facilitate important improvements in telecoms services. However, NGNs have raised tricky regulatory issues, problems that have led to global regulatory divergence (paradoxically, at the same time as increasing technological convergence has taken place at the technological level within the ICT ecosystem).

Here is the regulatory paradox. In most cases the only telecoms operators in a position to provide nationwide NGNs are the incumbents (that is, the former monopolists). The reasons are that the costs of so doing are enormous and there are substantial economies of scale. However, telecoms regulators are committed to facilitating competitive telecoms markets and, where this cannot be achieved, to regulating the industry by calculating the access prices that would exist if competition ruled.

But if there is to be competition then competitors to the incumbents must either create their own nationwide networks or they must be given access to the incumbents' NGNs. From a competition point of view the first of these options is ideal. With their own NGNs, competitors to the incumbents have strong incentives to improve their networks (innovate to reduce costs and enhance quality) in order to increase their competitiveness. Over time, this facilities-based competition could be expected to yield important innovations and improvements. However, in many countries – as noted for example by the British regulator, Ofcom (Ofcom 2006) – there is currently 'little appetite' on the part of competitors to make the necessary investments.

This means resorting to the second option, namely interconnection to the incumbent's NGN by its competitors. But this raises a key regulatory dilemma. What price should the competitors pay in order to be given access to the incumbent's NGN? The lower the price, all other things equal, the greater the incentive for the competitors (including, perhaps, new entrants) to enter the market, thereby gaining access to the incumbent's customers through accessing its NGN. At the same time, however, competitors have reduced incentives to invest in their own NGNs. This reduces facilities-based competition between incumbent and competitors.

Furthermore, and this is where the paradox comes in, the lower the price, the lower the incentive for the incumbent to invest in the NGNs in the first place. The reason is that regulated interconnection at low access prices reduces the returns that the incumbent is able to appropriate from its investments. (To give an analogy from another industry, it is as if the US government wanted to encourage General Motors to build a new, state-of-the-art car plant which would significantly reduce the cost and increase the quality of cars while at the same time insisting that Ford, Daimler–Chrysler, Toyota and its other competitors be given access to this plant at a low price (i.e. based on long-run incremental cost). The incentive problems that would result are obvious.)

In tackling this dilemma, the responses of regulators in the world's major countries have diverged significantly. At the one extreme is Japan. In Japan, the ministry-regulator, MIC, has insisted that NTT give access to its NGN at low regulated prices[25] to its competitors. NTT, however, has complained that these measures are reducing its profitability and hence its ability to provide adequately for the long-run infrastructural needs of Japan. But MIC has held fast, apparently believing that its measures have not quite killed the goose that lays the golden egg.

At the other extreme is Germany. Here, the incumbent, Deutsche Telekom, has won the support of both the German government and the regulator in arguing that it should not give competitors access to its NGN for a period of five years. The rationale is that this will create a sufficient incentive for Deutsche Telekom to invest in the NGN. Opposition, however, has come not so much from within Germany as from the European Commission, which has argued that the Germans are in violation of Brussels' regulatory framework which insists on competition.

The USA is a little closer to the German side. Initially, the FCC took a strong line, with the incumbents insisting on low interconnection prices for competitors (based on long-run incremental costs). However, after intense in-fighting, largely between the Republican- and Democrat-appointed commissioners (but not solely on partisan lines), the FCC made a major U-turn in 2003. This involved 'forbearance' – that is, deciding not to regulate access to the incumbents' NGN, leaving the matter to the companies themselves to resolve. Banking on competition to the incumbents (AT&T and Verizon) coming from the cable companies, the FCC hoped that this would be sufficient to ensure that the US got its internationally competitive NGNs. (As a result of the technological convergence of their networks both the telecoms operators and their cable rivals are offering so-called 'triple-play' services, namely telephony, Internet access and TV/video.)

---

[25] Technically, these prices are determined by MIC's calculation of forward-looking costs.

Exhibit A1.1. *Global telecoms equipment companies, market share, 2005*

Company	Market share (%)
Alcatel/Lucent	19
Ericsson/Marconi	18
Nokia/Siemens	17
Nortel	7
Cisco	6
NEC	5
Other	28

Source: Nokia, Siemens (based on sales to carriers).

As the present discussion makes clear, there has been a significant divergence between regulators in the USA, Japan and Europe attempting to resolve the regulatory dilemmas and contradictions involved in the creation of NGNs. Time will tell which approach will be the most effective.

Consolidation among telecoms equipment suppliers in layer 1

The telecoms bust and the subsequent substantial fall in capital expenditure by telecoms operators had a significant knock-on effect on the suppliers of telecoms equipment in layer 1. The result was a similar process of consolidation as that which occurred in layer 2, as shown in exhibit A1.1

In 2005–6 three major mergers occurred, resulting in the formation of the top three players shown in exhibit A1.1. The French company, Alcatel, acquired Lucent (formerly AT&T's Western Electric that was spun-out of AT&T), the Swedish company Ericsson acquired the British firm Marconi and the Finnish and German companies, Nokia and Siemens, merged their telecoms equipment operations.

Conclusion

In this appendix, we have provided a brief account of the evolution of the ICT ecosystem in the post-war period. It has been shown that innovation – in products and services, technologies, forms of organisation and markets – has driven the dynamics of the system, providing the new services, such as mobile and the Internet, that have transformed not only the ICT ecosystem itself but also the infrastructure and functioning of the entire national and global economies. From the point of view of the governance of the ICT ecosystem – including government policy-making and regulation – the task is to try and ensure that the measures designed enhance the vitality of the innovation process in a system that now plays so central a role in the economy.

Appendix 2: European regulation of electronic communications, 1987–2003

The aim of this appendix is to examine the making of the European New Regulatory Framework up to its implementation in 2003, showing the main concerns that have shaped this framework. The final section highlights these concerns and discusses some of the problems that have arisen.

The vision for telecoms

Until 1987, generally speaking, very little attention was paid at EU level to telecoms services which tended to be left to member states. From 1987, however – with the liberalisation of telecoms having been put firmly on the agenda by the substantial liberalisations occurring in the mid-1980s in Japan, the USA and the UK – the EU itself began to take a far closer interest in telecoms services.[1] Exhibit A2.1 provides a detailed periodisation of the main EU policies that were adopted in the telecoms field services.

The old regulatory framework

As noted in exhibit A2.1, with the full liberalisation of services and infrastructure provision achieved formally from January 1998, discussion began on a New Regulatory Framework that would establish an appropriate context for the development of telecoms into the twenty-first

---

[1] It is important to note that this section is primarily concerned with telecoms services. In a parallel but largely unrelated set of activities undertaken by different parts of the European Commission, steps were taken by the EU aimed at strengthening European electronics companies, some of which were also the producers of telecoms equipment. The R&D programmes that were established in this area included the European Strategic Programme for R&D in Information Technologies (Esprit) and R&D for Advanced Communications in Europe (Race) programmes.

Exhibit A2.1. *Periodisation of the main EU policies for telecoms services*

Until 1987	Generally, until 1987 little attention was paid at the EU level to telecoms regulation and liberalisation. In 1987 the **Green Paper** was published on telecoms regulatory issues.
1990–9	In 1990, with the adoption of rules on open access (contained in the open network provision (**ONP**) **Framework Directive**), a comprehensive regulatory framework was introduced for the liberalisation of the telecoms market and the achievement of a single market for telecoms services and equipment. Liberalisation was achieved in three steps. **Step 1** involved the partial liberalisation of telecoms services through the harmonisation of network interfaces and rules on open access. In **Step 2**, partial liberalisation of infrastructures was implemented, involving mobile communications networks and cable television networks. **Full liberalisation** came with **Step 3**, introduced from **1 January 1998**. This included the liberalisation of all services, including voice telephony, and all infrastructure provision.
1999–2003	With the full liberalisation of services and infrastructure provision achieved formally from January 1998, discussion began on a **New Regulatory Framework** that would establish an appropriate context for the development of telecoms in the EU and for achieving EU objectives in this area. On 10 November 1999 the Commission presented the 1999 Communications Review to the European Parliament. On 26 April 2000 the Commission presented a communication to the European Parliament on the results of the public consultation on the 1999 Communications Review. On 7 March 2002 the five directives were issued comprising the main part of the New Regulatory Framework. Member states were required to comply with these measures from 25 July 2003.

century in the EU. But what was wrong with the old regulatory framework? The answer to this question is summarised in exhibit A2.2.

The 1999 Communications Review[2]

The first comprehensive document aiming to rectify the problems with the old framework and create a New Regulatory Framework was the

---

[2] European Commission (1999: 539).

Exhibit A2.2. *General and specific problems with the old regulatory framework*

General problem	The old regulatory framework was designed to take the EU from a monopoly regime to one characterised by new entry and competition. However, it was not tuned to deal with many of the detailed problems that would continue after full liberalisation from January 1998.
Specific problems	• Inconsistency in applying rules in the different member states • Insufficient flexibility in coping with rapidly changing or converging markets • Tensions between the old regulatory framework and EU competition policy framework • Individual licensing procedures too complex

1999 Communications Review. In this section, some of the main issues tackled in this Review will be highlighted. In introducing the 1999 Review the Commission made it clear that its objectives in the field of telecommunications were closely tied to its objectives for enhancing the information society in Europe more generally.[3] Enhancing the information society in Europe, furthermore, necessitated increasing the competitiveness of European companies:

Without efficient, high quality communications, European industry, and in particular small and medium-sized enterprises (SMEs), face a major disadvantage in relation to their global competitors.[4]

The Commission was also frank about the shortcomings that remained despite the full liberalisation of all telecoms services and networks in the EU from 1 January 1998:

[Although the old regulatory framework] has transformed a sector traditionally characterised by State monopolies into a dynamic industry ready to take full advantage of the global market ... the process is not complete. The EU telecommunications market remains fragmented and is dominated by incumbent operators in all Member States, notwithstanding the rapid development of competition, as illustrated by falling tariffs and a growing number of operators.[5]

---

[3] In the document mention was also made of the e-Europe initiative examined in more detail on p. 00.
[4] European Commission (1999: ii).
[5] *Ibid.*: iii.

Exhibit A2.3. *The 1999 Communications Review: principles for regulatory action*

1. 'Be based on clearly defined policy objectives'
2. 'Be the minimum necessary to meet those objectives'
3. 'Further enhance legal certainty in a dynamic market'
4. 'Aim to be technologically neutral'
5. 'Be enforced as closely as practicable to the activities being regulated'

The time was ripe, the Commission argued, for a review of existing telecoms regulations in the light of its overall policy objectives. Three such objectives were identified:

1. To promote and sustain an open and competitive European market for communications services.
2. To benefit the European citizen.
3. To consolidate the internal market in a converging environment.[6]

In order to achieve these objectives, the Commission enunciated five 'principles for regulatory action', as shown in exhibit A2.3.

In pursuance of these principles, the Commission proposed a 'design' for a New Regulatory Framework. The design consisted of three elements. The first was sector-specific legislation. This would take the form of a Framework Directive which would identify general and specific policy objectives, and four specific directives dealing with licensing, access and interconnection, universal service, and privacy and data protection. According to the Commission, this legislation would amount to 'a substantial simplification of the current framework, reducing the number of legal measures from twenty to six'.[7]

The second element was 'accompanying non-binding measures'. These would consist of 'recommendations, guidelines, codes of conduct and other non-binding measures' that would allow for a flexible response to changing market conditions. However, these non-binding measures would be created within the framework of general principles set out in EU legislation. (As will be seen later in this section, these 'soft' measures, while arguably enhancing the flexibility of the

[6] *Ibid.*: iv–v.
[7] *Ibid.*: v.

New Regulatory Framework, would also open new possibilities for fragmentation and inconsistencies between the EU member countries.)

The third element related to the measures affecting competition. An important dimension of the design of the New Regulatory Framework would be 'greater reliance on the general competition rules of the Treaty, allowing much of the sectoral regulation to be replaced as competition becomes effective'.[8]

Dominant position and significant market power

'In the early stages of competition', the Commission argued, 'access by new entrants to the incumbent's network is an essential pre-requisite for sustainable competition'.[9] In the old regulatory framework, the concept of *significant market power (SMP)* was used in order to trigger the application of specific obligations on the incumbent to provide effective access to its network by new entrants. SMP was defined as existing when the incumbent had more than a 25 per cent market share in specific markets (e.g. fixed telephony, mobile telephony, leased lines). However, National Regulatory Authorities (NRAs) were given the discretion to take other factors into account and therefore to deviate from a strict '25 per cent rule'. (These factors included: the organisation's ability to influence market conditions; its turnover relative to the size of the market; its control of the means of access to end-users; its access to financial resources; and its experience in providing products and services in the market.[10])

However, as a result of studies done for the Commission examining practice under the old regulatory regime, the Commission concluded that in some cases the concept of *dominant position* or *dominance* – derived from competition law – was a 'more appropriate trigger'.[11] Specifically, the Commission felt that *ex ante* obligations should be imposed on a firm (usually an incumbent) where it held a dominant position, defined and measured as in competition law. (Examples of these *ex ante* obligations given by the Commission included obligations to supply unbundled, cost-oriented, interconnection services and obligations concerning non-discrimination.) Nevertheless, the

[8] *Ibid.*: vi.
[9] *Ibid.*: 49.
[10] *Ibid.*: 50.
[11] *Ibid.*: 50.

Commission felt that the threshold of SMP should be retained for other obligations – the examples it gave were obligations to negotiate access and obligations for transparency, which it saw as 'lighter' obligations. (The definition and measurement of 'dominance' that later emerged in Commission guidelines are examined later in this section.)

NRAs would be required to draw up a list of firms with a dominant position or SMP, using guidelines prepared by the Commission to ensure consistency among member states. In general, the Commission was of the view that the advantage of using *two triggers* for the imposition of obligations – namely, dominance for *ex ante* obligations and SMP for other obligations – was that the 'least burdensome regulation' would be imposed on market players, 'proportionate to the level of competition in particular markets'.[12] More generally, over time as EU communications markets moved towards 'full competition', there would be less reliance on pro-competitive sectoral telecoms laws and more reliance on competition law. Overall, this would imply a lower degree of regulation as market forces replaced sector-specific regulation.

The role of NRAs

In the 1999 Communications Review the Commission was frank about its concern with the inconsistent application of telecoms legislation in different member states: 'Inconsistent application of certain provisions of telecommunications legislation is hindering the development of effective competition and the deployment of pan-European services.'[13] However, despite this concern, the Commission was 'not persuaded that a regulatory body at Community level would currently add sufficient value to justify the likely costs'.[14]

But the Commission also recognised 'the need for a clear regulatory function to be exercised at the level of the Union',[15] while insisting that regulation should be 'implemented close to the market in Member States'.[16] Accordingly, it proposed that 'primary responsibility for achieving objectives set out in sector-specific Community legislation

[12] *Ibid.*: 50.
[13] *Ibid.*: ix.
[14] *Ibid.*: ix.
[15] *Ibid.*: 54.
[16] *Ibid.*: 54.

should rest with the independent national regulators who are best placed to take account of the different levels of competition and market development in Member States'.[17] While this was consistent with the EU's 'subsidiarity principle', whereby decisions would be made and implemented at the lowest effective level, it begged the question regarding the possible trade-off between making the best use of local knowledge on the one hand and achieving harmonisation among member states on the other.

How, in the Commission's view, would harmonisation be achieved? In the 1999 Communications Review, three mechanisms were proposed to achieve harmonisation. First, the Commission, in its directives underpinning the New Regulatory Framework, would provide a 'framework of principles' for NRAs to follow 'rather than to set out detailed provisions relating to the problems themselves'.[18] It was hoped that this framework would produce a significant degree of consistency among member states. Secondly, the Commission proposed the creation of what was called a High Level Communications Group, consisting of NRAs and the Commission, that would discuss consistency problems and propose solutions on the basis of rules agreed at Community level. Thirdly, the Commission proposed that it itself would have to undertake 'monitoring and quality assessment activities to ensure consistent and effective implementation of regulation at national level'.[19]

In the case of the determination of SMP and dominance the Commission proposed that the NRAs would play the leading role. NRAs would prepare lists of firms holding SMP and in a position of dominance, 'in close co-ordination with the national competition authority',[20] on the basis of guidelines drawn up by the Commission. In doing this they would provide determinations of 'relevant markets' and of the positions of market players in these markets.

Public consultation on the 1999 Communications Review[21]

Comments on the 1999 Communications Review were invited by 15 February 2000, and over 200 responses were received.

---

[17] *Ibid.*: 14.
[18] *Ibid.*: ix.
[19] *Ibid.*: 14.
[20] *Ibid.*: 50.
[21] European Commission (2000).

The New Regulatory Framework

On the basis of the public consultation on the 1999 Communications Review (and the inevitable political horse-trading among the stakeholders involved) the Commission cobbled together the package that would come to constitute the New Regulatory Framework. An outline of this new regulatory package is shown in exhibit A2.4.

As can be seen from exhibit A2.4, it is the Framework Directive that provides the overall structure for the other four directives – the Authorisation Directive, the Access and Interconnection Directive, the Users' Rights Directive and the Data Protection Directive. The Liberalisation Directive and the Spectrum decision provide further context for the five directives.

In the following sub-sections particular attention will be paid to three of these directives as well as to several other key components of the New Regulatory Framework not shown in exhibit A2.4.

The Framework Directive[22]

Scope and aim
The scope and aim of the Framework Directive was to establish:

a harmonised framework for the regulation of electronic communications services, electronic communications networks, associated facilities and associated services. It lays down tasks of national regulatory authorities and establishes a set of procedures to ensure the harmonised application of the regulatory framework throughout the Community.[23]

Definition of networks and services covered by the directive
One of the motivations of the whole New Regulatory Framework exercise was to take account of the *convergence* of different communications infrastructures, and this concern is reflected in the Framework Directive's definition of 'electronic communications network':

'electronic communications network' means transmission systems and, where applicable, switching or routing equipment and other resources which permit the conveyance of signals by wire, by radio, by optical or by other electromagnetic means, including satellite networks, fixed (circuit- and packet-switched, including Internet) and mobile terrestrial networks,

---

[22] Directive 2002/21/EC (2002). In the text, this document is referred to as the Framework Document.
[23] Framework Directive, chapter I, Art. 1.1.

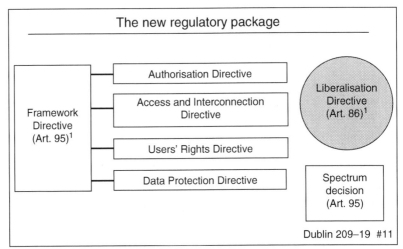

Source: European Commission, (2000).
Note: [1] Framework Directive, chapter I.

Exhibit A2.4. *Outline of the new regulatory package*

electricity cable systems, to the extent that they are used for the purpose of transmitting signals, networks used for radio and television broadcasting, and cable television networks, irrespective of type of information conveyed'.[24]

'Electronic communications services' are defined as services involving the 'conveyance of signals on electronic communications networks', including both telecommunications and broadcasting networks, *but excluding services involving content*.[25]

National regulatory authorities
The Framework Directive makes it clear that 'Member States shall ensure that national regulatory authorities exercise their powers impartially and transparently'.[26]

SMP, market definition and market analysis
The definition of '*SMP*' in the Framework Directive is shown in exhibit A2.5.

[24] *Ibid.*: chapter I, Art. 2.a.
[25] *Ibid.*: chapter I, Art. 2.c.
[26] *Ibid.*: chapter II, Art. 3.3.

Exhibit A2.5. '*SMP*' *according to the Framework Directive*

'An undertaking shall be deemed to have significant market power if, either individually or jointly with others, it enjoys a position equivalent to dominance, that is to say a position of economic strength affording it the *power to behave* to an appreciable extent *independently of competitors, customers and ultimately consumers*'. (Emphasis added)[1]

Note: [1]Framework Directive, chapter IV, Art. 14.2. This concept of dominance has been defined in the case-law of the European Court of Justice.

The Framework Directive also distinguishes where two or more firms are in a 'joint dominant position' (the criteria used in making such an assessment being spelled out in annex II of the directive) and where a firm that has SMP on a specific market may also be deemed to have the same power in a closely related market.

Article 15 of the Framework Directive refers to 'relevant product and service markets' in terms of characteristics that may justify the imposition of regulatory obligations set out in the other specific directives in the New Regulatory Framework. Article 16 requires NRAs to carry out an analysis of such relevant markets. The Framework Directive promised *Guidelines* (2002) that would help NRAs to undertake this task and to encourage consistency between different NRAs. Where a NRA concludes that a relevant market is 'effectively competitive', it shall not impose, or shall withdraw, specific regulatory obligations. However, where a NRA concludes that a relevant market is not effectively competitive, it shall identify the firm/s that is/are in a position of SMP and impose, maintain or amend specific regulatory obligations on it/them. All these actions of the NRA must be consistent with the member state's competition law and, where appropriate, carried out in collaboration with the state's competition authorities.

Commission Guidelines on market analysis and SMP[27]

The steps that a NRA needs to take in identifying 'relevant markets', and deciding whether 'effective competition' exists in these markets, are outlined in exhibit A2.6.

[27] Commission Guidelines (2002). In the text, this document is referred to as Guidelines.

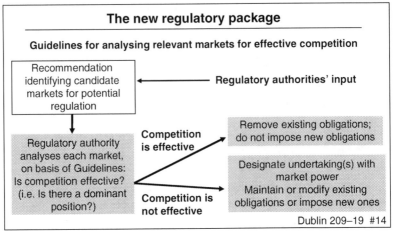

Source: European Commission (2000).

Exhibit A2.6. *Analysing 'relevant markets' for 'effective competition'*

These steps, at first sight, are relatively straightforward:

- **Step 1**: Identify those 'candidate markets' where regulation may be needed.
- **Step 2**: Analyse each of these markets with a view to establishing whether 'effective competition' exists within them.
- **Step 3**: If there is effective competition, remove existing regulatory obligations and do not impose new ones; if there is not effective competition, keep or change existing obligations and/or impose new ones.

However, the devil is in the detail. This is immediately apparent when it is asked what the candidate markets are, and when effective competition can be said to exist in these markets. As will shortly be shown, the answers to these questions turn out to be extremely complex. Nevertheless, competition authorities at both Brussels and member state levels have had a good amount of experience in dealing with these kinds of questions and have developed practice in answering them.

Defining the relevant market
In its Guidelines the Commission frankly recognises 'the difficulties inherent in defining the relevant market in an area of rapid technological change'. However, its confidence in tackling this difficult task

Exhibit A2.7. *The 'relevant market' according to the 2002 Guidelines*

The relevant market 'comprises all those products or services that are sufficiently interchangeable or substitutable, not only in terms of their objective characteristics, by virtue of which they are particularly suitable for satisfying the constant needs of consumers, their prices or their intended use, but also in terms of the conditions of competition and/or the structure of supply and demand on the market in question'. (para. 44)

is based on its 'considerable experience in applying the competition rules in a dynamic sector shaped by constant technological changes and innovation, as a result of its role in managing the transition from monopoly to competition in this sector'.[28]

When is a market 'relevant' from the point of view of the EU's regulatory process? Once this question has been answered, it is then possible to select 'candidate markets' from among the set of relevant markets. Candidate markets are those where one or more firms may be in a position of dominance (as defined in exhibit A2.7). It is then for further analysis to establish whether these firms are in fact dominant. If so, the market will not be effectively competitive and must be regulated.

The key issue, the Guidelines make clear, is the extent of 'competitive constraints on the price-setting behaviour of the producer(s) or service provider(s)' in the particular market.[29] Three competitive constraints are identified:

1. Demand-side substitution
2. Supply-side substitution
3. Potential competition.

'Demand-side substitutability' measures the extent to which consumers are willing to substitute other services if there is a relative price increase in the service in question. Supply-side substitutability measures the extent to which competing suppliers are willing in the short run to increase their supply of a substitutable service (after the firm in question increases the relative price of its service). Potential competition

---

[28] Guidelines: para. 3.
[29] *Ibid.*: para. 38.

measures the extent to which new entrants are prepared to enter the market and supply a substitutable service.[30]

The Guidelines note that 'one possible way' of assessing demand- and supply-side substitution is to use the 'hypothetical monopolist test'. Using this test, the NRA 'should ask what would happen if there were a small but significant, lasting increase in the price of a ... service, assuming that the prices of all other products or services remain constant' (which refers to a relative price increase).[31] An assessment of how demanders and suppliers will respond will reveal the extent of competitive constraints on the price-setting behaviour of the firm in question. To the extent that demanders will switch to alternative services and suppliers will increase their supply of the service in question (or a very closely substitutable service), the competitive constraints on the firm will be great, lessening the need for regulation.

The definition of the 'relevant market' contained in the Guidelines is given in exhibit A2.7.

In the light of this definition of relevant markets, the Guidelines advise NRAs to 'commence the exercise of defining the relevant ... market by grouping together products or services that are used by consumers for the same purposes'.[32] Once this is done it will become apparent that different kinds of services may be used for the same purposes. For example:

consumers may use dissimilar services such as cable and satellite connections for the same purpose, namely to access the Internet. In such as case, both services (cable and satellite access services) may be included in the same ... market.[33]

However, two services that appear to serve the same purpose may in fact be perceived by consumers as having different functions and performing different uses:

paging services and mobile telephony services, which may appear to be capable of offering the same service, that is, dispatching of two-way short messages,

---

[30] 'Supply substitution involves no additional significant costs whereas potential entry occurs at significant sunk costs' and will take more time to occur. Guidelines: para. 38.

[31] *Ibid.*: para. 40.

[32] *Ibid.*: para. 44.

[33] *Ibid.*: para. 45.

may be found to belong to distinct ... markets in view of their different perceptions by consumers as regards their functionality and end use.[34]

It is important to note that in providing an operational definition of relevant markets the Commission was anxious to avoid a static approach in favour of a *dynamic analysis*:

Market definition is not a mechanical or abstract process but requires an analysis of any available evidence of past market behaviour and an overall understanding of the mechanics of a given sector. In particular, a dynamic rather than a static approach is required when carrying out a prospective, or forward-looking, market analysis.[35]

Once the relevant market has been identified, the next step is to define the *geographical dimension* of the market. The Guidelines explain what is meant by this term:

the relevant geographic market comprises an area in which the undertakings concerned are involved in the supply and demand of the relevant products and services, in which area the conditions of competition are similar or sufficiently homogeneous and which can be distinguished from neighbouring areas in which the prevailing conditions of competition are appreciably different.[36]

Assessing SMP (dominance)
Having identified the relevant markets and the geographical dimension of these markets, the next task for the NRA is to assess whether SMP exists.

Dealing with firms with SMP

Once a NRA has decided that a firm enjoys a position of SMP in a relevant market it must ensure that appropriate obligations are imposed on that firm. In the words of the Guidelines, 'NRAs must impose at least one regulatory obligation on an undertaking that has been designated as having SMP'.[37] Some of the possible obligations are listed in exhibit A2.8.

---

[34] *Ibid.*: para. 45.
[35] *Ibid.*: para. 35.
[36] *Ibid.*: para. 56.
[37] *Ibid.*: para. 114.

Exhibit A2.8. *Obligations that may be imposed on firms with SMP*

NRAs apply appropriate remedies for the specific problem, from the following list:
- Price control, including cost orientation
- Transparency
- Accounting separation
- Non-discrimination
- Mandatory provision of specific facilities
- Mandatory access to specific facilities

Dublin 209–19 #11

Source: European Commission (2000).

The Authorisation Directive[38]

The aim of the Authorisation Directive is:

to implement an internal market in electronic communications networks and services through the *harmonisation* and *simplification* of authorisation rules and conditions in order to facilitate their provision throughout the Community.[39]

One of the main features of this directive is to restrict the authorisation required by a member state of a provider of networks and/or services to what is referred to as a 'general authorisation'. In the words of the directive:

The provision of ... networks or ... services may ... only be subject to a general authorisation. The undertaking concerned may be required to submit a notification but may not be required to obtain an explicit decision or any other administrative act by the national regulatory authority before exercising the rights stemming from the authorisation ... The notification ... shall not entail more than a declaration by a legal or natural person to the national regulatory authority of the intention to commence the provision of ... networks or services and the submission of the minimal information ... This information must be limited to what is necessary for the identification of the provider, such as company registration numbers, and the provider's contact persons, the provider's address, a short description of the network or service, and an estimated date for starting the activity.[40]

---

[38] Directive 2002/20/EC (2002).
[39] Authorisation Directive: Art. 1.1, emphasis added.
[40] *Ibid.*: Art. 3.2 and 3.3.

The annex to this directive contains the 'maximum list of conditions which may be attached to general authorisations'.

The Access Directive[41]

The Access Directive 'harmonises the way in which Member States regulate access to, and interconnection of ... networks and associated facilities'. The aim of the Directive is:

> to establish a regulatory framework, in accordance with internal market principles, for the relationships between suppliers of networks and services that will result in sustainable competition, interoperability of ... services and consumer benefits.[42]

The Directive sets out objectives for NRAs regarding access and interconnection and makes provision for the review of regulatory obligations imposed by the authority and the withdrawal of obligations once the objectives have been achieved. It also establishes the rights and obligations of operators and of firms seeking interconnection and/or access to their networks.

Significantly, the directive provides a 'general framework for access and interconnection'. This general framework ensures that firms will be able to negotiate access and interconnection between themselves without requiring authorisation to operate in a member state:

> Member States shall ensure that there are no restrictions which prevent undertakings in the same Member State or in different Member States from negotiating between themselves agreements ... for access and/or interconnection ... The undertaking requesting access or interconnection does not need to be authorised to operate in the Member State where access or interconnection is requested, if it is not providing services and does not operate a network in that Member State.[43]

However:

> Member States shall ensure that the national regulatory authority is empowered to intervene at its own initiative where justified or, in the absence of agreement between undertakings, at the request of either of the parties involved, in order to secure the policy objectives ...[44]

[41] Directive 2002/19/EC (2002).
[42] Access Directive: Art. 1.1.
[43] *Ibid.*: Art. 3.1.
[44] *Ibid.*: Art. 5.4.

The European Regulators' Group

An important part of the New Regulatory Framework is the European Regulators' Group that had its first inaugural meeting in Brussels in October 2002. As noted earlier, the Commission, in preparing for the New Regulatory Framework, soon came to the conclusion that the benefits of a centralised European regulatory authority would be outweighed by the associated costs.[45] It accordingly opted for a guiding framework to be created by the Commission with implementation within this framework being delegated to the NRAs. However, as a further mechanism to create harmonisation and consistency among NRAs, the Commission proposed the establishment of a European Regulators' Group. This group would also provide a coordinating link between the Commission itself and the NRAs. In his opening address at the first meeting of the European Regulators' Group, Erkki Liikanen, then European Commissioner for Enterprise and Information Society, said:

The European Commission and national regulatory authorities need to look together at what specific actions can be undertaken, ensuring that the European markets develop in an efficient and sustainable way. Any actions must take into account two factors: first the need to ensure that the new regulatory framework is fully implemented on time and that it remains stable; second, that the integrity of the European Internal Market and the principles of competition policy are respected.[46]

Reflections on the European New Regulatory Framework

In this section some comments are made on the priority concerns that have shaped the Framework and the bearing that they have on what the 1999 Communications Review suggested was the ultimate objective of

[45] This 'conclusion' was actually the result of different lobbying forces. Initially, an alliance between the large incumbents and the Commission pushed for a single European regulator. The incumbents felt that this was the only way that they would avoid being confronted by inconsistent regulatory rules in different member states while the Commission wanted central control in order to avoid such inconsistencies. In the event, however, the collective views of the member states prevailed. They feared that the Commission might overrule measures that were desirable from an individual state's viewpoint. The final outcome was the regulatory system described and analysed in this appendix.

[46] *Financial Times*, 30 October 2002.

the whole exercise, namely the achievement in Europe of globally competitive communications.

The priority concerns shaping the Framework

As this appendix makes clear, the priority concerns that shaped the European New Regulatory Framework were two-fold and closely related. The first was the concern to create a single market for electronic communications services in Europe within which undertakings would have unrestricted access to customers. The second was to ensure that, where SMP or dominance existed, remedies would be implemented that would limit the negative effects arising from the absence of competition.

Comparative global performance in European electronics communications services markets

It is worth noting that in the formal documentation relating to the New Regulatory Framework little is said explicitly regarding the global comparative performance of European electronic communications services markets. As noted above, in the 1999 Communications Review it was stated that:

Without efficient, high quality communications, European industry, and in particular small and medium-sized enterprises (SMEs), face a major disadvantage in relation to their global competitors.[47]

The clear implication is that the ultimate goal of the New Regulatory Framework is the achievement of efficient, high-quality communications in Europe. However, nothing is said – either here or in the other documentation regarding the New Regulatory Framework – about what is to be understood by 'efficient, high quality communications' nor about the conditions that need to be satisfied for Europe to achieve such communications.

There are two possible interpretations of this absence. The first is that it was tacitly assumed that by creating a single market, by ensuring that as far as possible competitive conditions are established within this market and, where this is not possible, that the remedies laid down in the New Regulatory Framework are implemented,

---

[47] European Commission (1999: ii).

'efficient, high quality communications' would automatically be realised. The second interpretation is that it was tacitly assumed that the Framework, together with other measures taken at the European and/ or national levels, would achieve the desired level of communications.

However, both of these interpretations raise further difficulties. The first interpretation raises the problem, referred to in several places in this book, that while a single market and competition may be necessary – although even this could be questioned, particularly what is meant by 'competition' – they may not be sufficient conditions for the achievement of globally competitive communications. In this book it has been stressed that it is likely that several other factors would also have to play a determining role. These include the contribution of institutions – such as financial and legal institutions, standardisation and the contribution of universities and entrepreneurs – and the intensity of competition, the determinants of which go beyond those discussed in the New Regulatory Framework. The problem raised by the second interpretation is that nowhere is it made clear what these other measures, taken at the European and/or national levels, are and no evidence is provided regarding why they might be expected to generate globally competitive communications.

This leaves a significant problem. If the ultimate aim, as the 1999 Communications Review implies, is the achievement of globally competitive communications, we are left without a robust account of how this outcome might be achieved. In the present book it is proposed to deal with this problem by conceptualising the new ICT ecosystem as an innovation system, by defining explicitly the desired outputs from this system, and by specifying the innovation processes and their determinants that are needed to generate these outputs. Clearly, this is no simple task. But at least it would begin to deal with the important issues of European performance and its determinants, issues that are largely avoided in the European New Regulatory Framework.

Conclusions

To conclude, it is clear that in the European New Regulatory Framework the authorities have been primarily concerned with the extension of the single market in Europe and with the establishment, as far as possible, of competitive conditions within this market. Where such conditions cannot be established due to the existence of SMP, the aim has been to design remedies that will deal with the negative effects of the competitive shortcomings.

However, this appendix has examined a set of problems that relate to the ultimate objective of the New Regulatory Framework exercise. The 1999 Communications Review implied that the ultimate objective is the achievement in Europe of globally competitive communications. The question, though, is: What conditions must be established in Europe for this objective to be achieved?

The New Regulatory Framework implicitly assumes that three conditions are both necessary and sufficient: the establishment of a single market in this area; the establishment as far as possible of competitive conditions in this market; and, where such conditions cannot be established due to the existence of SMP, the implementation of remedies defined in the directives.

However, it is suggested in this book that these three conditions are not sufficient (even if we accept, for argument's sake, that they are necessary). Evidence of both a theoretical and empirical kind is provided elsewhere in this book to suggest that the achievement of global competitiveness requires far more than these conditions. More specifically, a variety of institutions needs to be in place and operating effectively. Furthermore, it is the *intensity* of competition that is crucial – where firms fight and cooperate in order to improve their positions, often using innovation as their key weapon – rather than 'market power' as defined in the Framework. The conclusion that follows is that Europe needs to devote far more attention – based on the measuring and monitoring of comparative global performance – to these key issues.

Appendix 3: Some problems with the dominant regulatory paradigm in telecoms (DRPT)

This appendix is devoted to a discussion of several papers by academic economists that comment on various aspects of the DRPT.

The optimal access price

The attempt to introduce competition into the previously monopolised telecoms services market from the mid-1980s raised an immediate problem. Potential new competitors would find it difficult to enter the market because factors such as high fixed/sunk costs, economies of scale and scope and network externalities work to the incumbent's advantage, acting as barriers to entry.[1] In order to create sufficient incentives for new competitors to enter regulators would have to allow them to interconnect with the networks of the incumbents.

But this raised a further problem: What price should the incumbent be allowed to charge the new entrants? This was a key question. If the price were too high it would disincentivise entry and therefore limit competition. However, if it were too low it would disincentivise

---

[1] *Economies of scale* stem from the high fixed costs that exist in parts of the new ICT ecosystem (e.g. in layer 2, where full-facilities-based network operators face high fixed investment costs). High fixed costs imply that as scale increases, so unit costs fall. This gives an advantage, all other things equal, to larger firms and those that are first able to achieve greater scale. It is economies of scale that lay behind the natural monopoly argument suggesting that telecoms operation should be left to national monopolies. *Economies of scope* occur when it is cheaper to produce and distribute two or more products by the same firm than it is to produce them separately by separate firms. Economies of scope may reinforce the effect of economies of scale, giving advantages to larger early-entrant firms. *Network externalities* occur when the benefit to users of a network increases the more members there are of that network. Network externalities drove the adoption of the original telephone; the more subscribers there were the greater the benefit to existing and new subscribers who could contact more people. They explain the 'snowballing effect' as more subscribers join the network, their benefit-cost ratio (BCR) of so doing continually increasing.

investment by the incumbent, thus threatening the nation's communications infrastructure. (Furthermore, if the price were too low it would also disincentivise the new entrants from investing in their own infrastructure – thus engaging in infrastructure-based competition with the incumbent – perpetuating dependence by the new entrants on the incumbent's infrastructure. This is an important limitation because many believe that infrastructure-based competition is the most effective kind of competition in the telecoms services market.)

In order to solve the problem regulators turned to economic theory in an attempt to calculate the optimal price. Alleman and Rappoport (2005) tell the story of what happened in the USA:

Since the [US] 1996 Telecommunication Act, the FCC has formalized its pricing policy by relying on notions derived from competition theory [i.e. the theory of perfect competition] . . . perfect competition implies that when there are many firms – virtually an infinite number – in the industry, no single firm can affect prices in the market. From the firm's point of view, according to the theory, demand is perfectly elastic and the firm produces where price equals marginal cost. It is then shown that this is the most efficient allocation of resources. Ergo, first-best pricing is price equals marginal cost. (2005: 111)

Alleman and Rappoport observe that 'regulatory communities have accepted the traditional first-best pricing results, and the models on which they are based, to apply to charges for intermediate services such as interconnection or access to the network' (2005: 112). They note that the:

prime example is the rule 'price equals marginal cost' derived from the efficient price rule of conventional economics in a static context. It has been used to justify 'long-run incremental cost' methodology to determine prices. In the United States this has been contextualised as Total Service Long-Run Incremental Cost (TSLRIC). The fundamental idea is that under the neoclassical economics assumption of perfect competition this is the best, most efficient pricing method. (2005: 111)

Problems with the conventional concept of the optimal access price

However, there are three fundamental problems with this conventional thinking about the optimal access price. The first is that the assumptions made in the theory of perfect competition violate the conditions that exist in the real world. In Alleman and Rappoport's words, 'this perfect world does not exist'. The reasons they give are that:

externalities – call and network – distort the simple model; economies of scale and scope eliminate the possibility of an infinite number of providers; indeed in capital intensive network industries such as telecommunications, only a few providers can survive. (2005: 112)

Precisely the same point is made by Booth (2006) in a volume published by the British regulator, Ofcom, which examines changing trends in regulation. Booth points out that the textbook model of perfect competition used in telecoms regulation assumes:

a situation where there is perfect knowledge, and where identical products are sold at a price equal to marginal cost. This leads, when combined with other assumptions, to all opportunities for welfare maximisation being exploited. (2006: 276)

However, he notes:

it should be obvious that a perfectly competitive market cannot exist. If we had perfect competition prevailing, there would be no innovations or product differentiation. If consumers or producers were to discover new knowledge, either it would have to be shared immediately with all others in the market or the state of perfect competition would come to an end. New knowledge and innovations occur continually in real life markets. (2006: 270)

Booth proposes that a very different conception of competition is needed compared to that used in perfect competition. He suggests that:

competition should be understood as being the *process* by which consumers and producers seek new knowledge to enable the production of new goods or existing goods at lower cost, thus enhancing welfare. (2006: 276, emphasis in the original)

More generally, an increasing number of academics are drawing attention to the limitations imposed by the implicit *static* assumptions made in the conventional approach. Technology, costs and demand are given in this approach. This automatically rules out a dynamic world of innovation, co-evolving consumer tastes and demand and uncertainty. That is, it rules out the real world in which all the players in the ICT ecosystem, including policy-makers and regulators, make their decisions. Yet as Alleman and Rappoport complain:

Nevertheless policy-makers have assumed that this perfect world exists; and have attempted to require incumbents to interconnect with entrants at prices that approximate static marginal costs. They have attempted this by producing a variety of engineering cost models to mimic the 'marginal cost' methodology. These models have serious flaws because they lack a fundamental understanding of economics and finance. (2005: 112)[2]

The second problem with the use of the conventional concept of the optimal access price is more practical. Even ignoring the issues raised by the first problem – fundamental though they are – it turns out that there are significant difficulties that arise in attempting to implement the conventional approach. This is pointed out by Shelanski (2005) who notes that the 'FCC ultimately found TELRIC [Total Element Long-Run Incremental Costs] troublesome in three crucial respects'.

The first is that 'the TELRIC rules have proven to take a great deal of time and effort to implement'. Secondly, 'the Commission found the costly proceedings to produce inconsistent results'. In the FCC's own words, 'For any given carrier there may be significant differences in rates from state to state, and even from [legal] proceeding to proceeding within a state'. Thirdly, again to quote the FCC, 'the lack of predictability in . . . rates is difficult to reconcile with our desire that . . . rates send correct economic signals'. The latter leads Shelanski to comment that:

As the FCC's observation about incorrect economic signals indicates, the rate-setting function of monopoly regulation is costly not only in its administrative burdens, but in its effects on the economic incentives of market players. (2005: 29)

---

[2] Alleman and Rappoport (2005) also refer in this context to the theory of *contestable markets*. (A contestable market is a market in which competitive pricing can be observed even though there may be only one firm serving the market. Contestable markets exist as a result of low barriers to entry and exit.) 'Recognizing that this perfect world does not exist, some commentators have developed the theory of contestable markets, claiming that this emulates the competitive solutions . . . We, and others, take issue with this . . . This theory is flawed in that it assumes that the entry into and exit from markets is costless . . . The theory totally collapses if even the smallest cost of entry or exit exists' (2005: 111).

Shelanski's comment points to the third problem with the DRPT. While it focuses on the costs of incumbents in the attempt to calculate optimal prices it largely ignores the costs imposed by regulation. The latter costs go much further than the specific problem of incorrect economic signals. In addition to the regulator's own costs there are other costs imposed on players – incumbents and their competitors alike – that follow from the often cumbersome and time-consuming process of regulation. A particularly important cost arises from *regulation-induced uncertainty.* This uncertainty impacts negatively not only on the investment and other decisions made by incumbents and their competitors but also on the linked decisions made by financial institutions and markets. In short, any benefits that flow from the regulation process must be weighed against all the costs of regulation. It is true to say that until now these costs have not been adequately taken into account.

Competition from new technologies and forms of organisation

Perhaps influenced to some extent by the problems referred to in the last sub-section, some academics and regulators are becoming increasingly aware that the monopoly or quasi-monopoly conditions which the DRPT is designed to remedy are in fact being eroded by new technologies and forms of organisation.

Shelanski is one such academic. He concludes his article with the observation that:

As telecommunications markets in the United States transform, regulation has remained essentially static in its fundamental approach and monopoly assumptions. (2005: 37)

But this is increasingly inappropriate because 'rules remain whose motivating, monopoly conditions no longer hold' (2005: 34). The reason, he argues, is that 'increasing competitive substitution from wireless and Internet-based communications has undermined the rationale for conventional monopoly regulation' (2005: 15). The implications, according to Shelanski, are significant:

As these rules become increasingly obsolete, they risk causing increasing harm to the incentives of incumbents and new entrants alike to invest and compete for the benefit of consumers. (2005: 34)

A Schumpeterian alternative?

Alleman and Rappoport (2005) note that although the Schumpeterian approach is inherently dynamic, focusing as it does on innovation, it has tended to be ignored:

> Dynamic models have been in the economist['s] tool kit for some time, for example Schumpeter's work; unfortunately, they seem to be rarely utilized. The Schumpeterian model is one of those models most often cited, but the policy-makers do not seem to rely on this or other dynamic models in their deliberations. (2005: 113)

In other areas of economics, however, the Schumpeterian approach is gaining an increasing number of influential adherents. One example, relevant to the present book on Europe, is Aghion and Howitt (2006), that seeks to explain the growth gap between Europe and the USA. In this article the authors elaborate a theory of growth policy. One of the mechanisms which they analyse is innovation which 'is a means by which the firm can break away from the constraints of intense competition with a close technological rival' (2006: 280). This article points to the kinds of links that from a Schumpeterian perspective could be made between the process of competition and innovation at the micro level, the level at which regulation has largely been concerned, and growth at the macro level. This is just one indication of the kind of fruit that the Schumpeterian approach in this field may bear.

Appendix 4: A short introduction to Schumpeterian evolutionary economics

In this appendix a brief introduction is given to the Schumpeterian evolutionary economics which provides a conceptual underpinning for much of the thinking in this book.

Joseph Schumpeter's main concern was with what he called 'economic development', a phenomenon that in his view was closely associated with innovation. However, in his book, *The Theory of Economic Development* (Schumpeter 1934), he began by imagining an economic world devoid of innovation. It is in this world, he showed, that the static theory of neoclassical economics found its natural home as equilibrium prices and quantities were established.[1]

The choice of this starting point, however, is to emphasise that the real world of restless capitalism is fundamentally different from the stationary world imagined in our chapter 1. The essence of this real world is that it involves endogenously generated development. Schumpeter defined this development as 'the carrying out of new combinations' – in short, the implementation of internally created innovations. These new combinations included new products, new technologies and processes, the opening of new markets, the creation of new sources of supply of raw materials or manufactured goods and the implementation of new forms of organisation.[2]

It is the carrying out of new combinations that, Schumpeter argued, is the function of entrepreneurs, both the individual entrepreneur (as Schumpeter argued in *The Theory of Economic Development*) and the large corporate 'entrepreneur' that organised the entrepreneurial function in routinised company R&D laboratories (as he suggested

---

[1] 'The theory of the first chapter [of *The Theory of Economic Development*] describes economic life from the standpoint of a "circular flow" running on in channels essentially the same year after year – similar to the circulation of the blood in an animal organism' (Schumpeter 1934: 61).

[2] 1943: 66.

in *Capitalism, Socialism and Democracy*, 1943).[3] It is these new combinations that are primarily responsible for change in the capitalist system, a process that Schumpeter famously called creative–destruction, a process that creates the new while destroying the old. It is this creative–destructive world with which firms, institutions and policy-makers have to deal. It is also a world that requires dynamic, rather than static, theorising.[4]

Schumpeter himself made the link between his concept of creative–destruction and that of evolution. For example, in *Capitalism, Socialism and Democracy* he argued that 'The essential point to grasp is that in dealing with capitalism we are dealing with an evolutionary process ... Capitalism ... is by nature a form or method of economic change and not only never is but never can be stationary'.[5] However, even though he did refer to Darwin, he refrained from directly applying Darwin's theory of evolution to his own task.[6]

Darwin's seminal contribution involved the explanation of evolution in terms of two interrelated determining processes; processes that generate variety and processes that select from this variety, winnowing the options. A watershed occurred in Schumpeterian evolutionary economics when Richard Nelson and Sidney Winter, drawing on various antecedents, married Schumpeterian and Darwinian thinking with modern economics in their path-making book, *An Evolutionary Theory of Economic Change* (Nelson and Winter 1982).

To simplify, Nelson and Winter conceive of the economy as consisting of a population of firms.[7] Crucially, these firms differ from one another as a result of the different routines that each firm develops as it goes about its business in its particular context. These routines are

[3] Metcalfe (2004: 157–76) explains why the Schumpeterian entrepreneur and orthodox economic theory make such bad travelling companions. In this article Metcalfe also explores the differences between the entrepreneurial and the management functions and the difference between Schumpeter's theory and Kirzner's theory of entrepreneurship.

[4] Schumpeter's discussion of the process of creative–destruction is to be found in chapter 7 of *Capitalism, Socialism and Democracy* (1943).

[5] 1943: 82–3.

[6] The comments on Darwin and evolution are to be found in Schumpeter (1934: 57–8).

[7] For a more detailed discussion of Nelson and Winter's ideas, and a comparison of other related theories, see Fransman (1994b: 1–45. For a more recent summary of the Schumpeterian evolutionary approach see Dosi and Nelson (1998: 205–34).

analogous to the genes of biological organisms. It is in their routines that firms store their knowledge. The routines, in turn, influence the specific characteristics of the output produced by the different firms (i.e. their phenotypes).

It is here that selection processes enter the picture – for example, selection by the market processes that are particularly important in economic evolutionary systems. These market processes winnow by selecting the products and services of some firms over those of others. The profits of the selected firms grow relative to those of the deselected firms. This profit allows the selected firms to invest more than the others and therefore to grow faster than them. This process influences market, sectoral and aggregate demand and supply in the economy, which in turn determines the new costs, revenues, profits and growth.

Where does innovation enter this story? In each firm, a particular set of routines exists to carry out the purpose of changing routines – that is, bringing about innovation. These routines involve searching for new combinations in the Schumpeterian sense. Those routines, including search routines, that contribute to the characteristics that are selected by the selection process prosper and are reproduced. In this way routines and the innovation process itself are part of the wider co-evolutionary process. Unlike in the biological world, however, the selection and rejection of routines are incorporated into the *learning processes* that take place in firms.

However, the innovation process in the economic system is shaped not only by the search and R&D processes that occur within and between firms, but also by institutions. For example, intellectual property regimes, financing mechanisms and university and government research institutes all have an influence on the innovation process. Not only do these and other institutions influence the innovation process, they also define the 'rules of the game' according to which the firms operate.[8]

Institutions come to the fore in a stream of literature that emerged from the late 1980s in Schumpeterian evolutionary economics dealing with so-called national innovation systems. The early pioneers in this area include Bengt-Åke Lundval, Christopher Freeman and

---

[8] In Nelson (2002: 17–28), an attempt is made to reconcile the somewhat different approaches to institutions taken in Schumpeterian evolutionary economics, on the one hand, and institutional economics (of the kind proposed by Nobel Prize winner, Douglass North), on the other. North (1990) defines institutions as determiners of the 'rules of the game'.

Richard Nelson.[9] The essential insight in this literature is that innovation processes tend to be different in different countries because institutions and their functioning often vary markedly according to country. Furthermore, since innovation is a key determinant of economic performance, countries frequently differ in terms of their performance in various industries. In *Sources of Industrial Leadership: Studies of Seven Industries* David Mowery and Richard Nelson and their collaborators explain global leadership by US, Japanese and European companies largely in terms of their differing national innovation systems in industries that include computers, software, semiconductors, chemicals, pharmaceuticals and machine tools (Mowery and Nelson 1999).

Studies of national innovation systems, in turn, led on to a new subcategory, namely sectoral systems of innovation, which emphasised that the innovation process and corresponding industrial and institutional organisation were very different in different sectors of the economy. One of the pioneers in this area is Franco Malerba who defines a sectoral system of innovation as:

a set of new and established products for specific uses and the set of agents carrying out market and non-market interaction for the creation, production and sale of those products. Sectoral systems have a knowledge base, technologies, inputs and demand. The agents are individuals and organizations at various levels of aggregation, with specific learning processes, competencies, organizational structure, beliefs, objectives and behaviours. They interact through processes of communication, exchange, cooperation, competition and command, and their interactions are shaped by institutions. A sectoral system undergoes processes of change and transformation through the co-evolution of its various elements.[10]

In a summary as short as the present one it has been possible only to provide a brief taste of some of the issues that have been tackled in Schumpeterian evolutionary economics. The bibliography, however, contains further references to works by pioneers mentioned above for the interested reader. In the present book this economics has shaped the attempt to understand the dynamics of the new ICT ecosystem and in particular to analyse it as a sectoral innovation system. The debt to the writers referred to here, as well as to other writers in this tradition, is clear.

[9] Freeman (1987); Lundval (1988: 349–69, 1992a, 1992b); Nelson (1993).
[10] Malerba (2002: 248).

Appendix 5: Other layer models: OSI and TCP/IP

In this book a layer model was developed in order to help analyse the ICT ecosystem. In chapter 1 it was shown that the Japanese ministry-regulator (MIC) had used a similar model. In this appendix a very brief summary is provided of two of the best-known layer models that have been used primarily by engineers in the areas of computing and telecommunications.

The Open System Interconnection (OSI) model is a seven-layered description of open (non-proprietary) communications and computer network protocols. It was established in the 1980s by the International Standards Organisation (ISO). The definitive account of this model is provided in ISO (1994).[1] The original intention of the OSI model was to understand the hardware and software that comprised a network. The basic OSI model is shown in exhibit A5.1.

The TCP/IP model deals with the communications protocols that are used to connect hosts in the Internet. These protocols are expressed in a modular set of layers. A description of the part played by TCP/IP in the development of the Internet is provided by Cerf (1989).[2] A recent discussion of the OSI and TCP/IP models is to be found in Mindel and Sicker (2006).[3] The TCP/IP model is shown in exhibit A5.2.

It is worth repeating that the two layer models discussed briefly here deal primarily with technical functionalities and relationships. By contrast, the layer model used in this book to analyse the ICT ecosystem, while also having a technical dimension, is simultaneously about economic and institutional relationships.

---

[1] See www.iso.org/iso/en/CatalogueListPage.CatalogueList?ICS1=35&ICS2=100 &ICS3-01.
[2] Cerf (1989).
[3] Mindel and Sicker (2006: 136–48).

Exhibit A5.1. *The OSI model*

Layer	OSI stack
7	Application
6	Presentation
5	Session
4	Transport
3	Network
2	Data link
1	Physical

Exhibit A5.2. *The TCP/IP model*

Layer	TCP/IP stack
4	Application
3	Transport
2	Internet
1	Network interface

Appendix 6: Content, applications and services: definitions

In this appendix definitions are provided for the content, applications and services used frequently in this book.

Content is a commonly used term with regard to the Internet and other electronic media (e.g. television and DVDs). In its broadest sense it refers to material which is of interest to users, such as textual information, images, music and movies.[1]

Applications and services may be defined in the following ways. An application is a program or group of programs designed for end-users. Software can be divided into two general classes; systems software and applications software. Systems software consists of low-level programs that interact with the computer at a very basic level. This includes operating systems, compilers and utilities for managing computer resources.

In contrast, applications software (also called end-user programs) includes database programs, word processors and spreadsheets. Figuratively speaking, applications software sits on top of systems software because it is unable to run without the operating system and system utilities. This is illustrated in exhibit A6.1.

A service is a provider/client interaction that creates and captures value. The following discussion on services comes from an IBM publication available on the Internet.[2]

For instance, almost everyone is familiar with a typical doctor/patient interaction, in which both sides benefit from the transaction – referred to as 'capturing value' in services parlance. The doctor receives a fee; the patient gets a health assessment and (it is hoped) recovers from the illness. This basic principle also underlies the work between a services provider and a corporation.

The provider and client coordinate their work (co-production), and in the process both create and capture value (transformation). Services

---

[1] www.bellevuelinux.org/linmo/content.html.
[2] www.research.ibm.com/ssme/services.shtml.

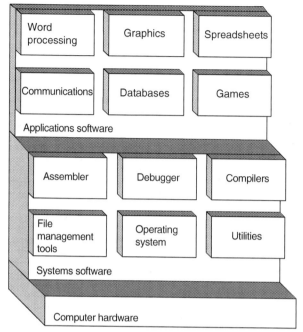

Source: www.webopedia.com/TERM/A/application.html.

Exhibit A6.1. *Computer hardware, systems software and applications software: a diagrammatic depiction*

typically require assessment, during which provider and client come to understand one another's capabilities and goals. In the case of the doctor/patient interaction, the patient checks to see if the doctor is licensed and/or accredited and if he or she has the right speciality for the given illness. The doctor also conducts an assessment to determine the patient's medical history, gather information on the current ailment and verify insurance or payment details. All of these steps factor into both sides capturing value from the services engagement. Obviously, for IT and business services, these assessments can be far more complex, but the processes and measurements are similar.

In business services, if the client does not install the new IT systems and train the necessary people in the re-engineered process, the client firm will not receive the benefit of the service. Thus, the provider in many cases must monitor and assess the way the client is performing its responsibilities. And, of course, the client needs to determine that the provider is likewise applying satisfactory effort and quality controls in the performance of its tasks. These issues become of paramount importance in outsourcing deals, where a client may out-source a component of its business to a provider that is in a different country with different government regulations and national cultures.

Because services depend critically on the co-production relationship, it is very important that the service contract spell out mutual respon-sibilities and expectations. A significant percentage of service engage-ments (estimates range from 10–50 per cent) do not meet the client's or provider's expectations, resulting in poor performance and low satisfaction and, therefore, in less value created and captured than anticipated. This gap is an opportunity for services innovation that will improve returns, performance and satisfaction.

Appendix 7: Why do US Internet companies dominate in layer 3?

A key feature of the ICT ecosystem, as noted in several places in this book, is the dominance of Internet content and applications provision in layer 3 by US companies such as Google, Yahoo!, eBay, Amazon and MySpace. But why do US companies dominate in this space, and why are European and Asian companies so scarce? In this appendix some reasons are suggested.

Introduction

One of the most important distinguishing features of the global new ICT ecosystem is the dominance of layer 3 by US companies. These companies are particularly strong among the Internet-based content and applications providers (ICAPs). Examples are companies such as Google, Yahoo!, eBay, Amazon and YouTube which have very rapidly become globalised household names. This phenomenon begs three questions:

- Why is it US companies that have achieved this prominence?
- Why are there so few European and Asian companies in this space?
- Can anything be done to remedy this uneven development?

In order to examine these three questions, the author has taken a sample of ICAPs and studied their origin. In addition to the five US companies referred to above two other non-US companies were added to the sample – a Chinese and a European ICAP, Baidu and Skype, respectively. Baidu is the main Chinese Internet search company that has the largest market share in the Chinese market, exceeding that of Google. Skype is perhaps the most famous voice-over-IP (VoIP) company which was established by a Swede and a Dane in Europe. By adding these two non-US ICAPs to the sample it was hoped to gain further insights into the dominance of US companies in this area. In the following sub-sections the main lessons that can be learned from this study are presented.

The early bird catches the worm

The first lesson from these companies is that there are significant *first-mover advantages* that exist in the area of Internet-based content and applications. All the seven companies in the sample entered their field as soon as the emerging technology created new market opportunities. This is shown in exhibit A7.1.

The watershed year for the mass adoption of the Internet was 1995. It was in this year that Bill Gates, founder of Microsoft, came to the realisation (prompted by younger researchers in his company who were in touch with unfolding events on US campuses) that it was the Internet that would drive Microsoft, rather than the other way round. The four main Internet pioneers – Amazon, eBay, Google and Yahoo! – all began within one year of 1995 as shown in exhibit A7.1. (That is, the activities began that would later lead to the establishment of these companies.)

The origins of the remaining three companies further support the first-mover hypothesis. Baidu, which started in 2000, had to await the mass adoption of the Internet in China (which itself required acceptance by the Chinese authorities). Skype and then a bit later YouTube had to await the mass adoption of broadband Internet.

Zennström and Friis, the founders of Skype, developed their plans for VoIP several years after the first wave of ICAPs. These plans drew on the peer-to-peer software that had made their controversial music-sharing site, Kazaa, so successful. However, they realised that to achieve the virtual real-time communication that was necessary for acceptable voice conversations it was essential that the users have broadband connections. Broadband began mass diffusion only around 2000.

YouTube also needed the broadband Internet provided by telecoms operators if their bandwidth-intensive videos were to be uploaded and downloaded with a speed that would be acceptable to a mass consumer audience. The market opportunities created by broadband in the areas of voice and video, therefore, were quickly exploited by Skype and YouTube almost as soon as the broadband user-base emerged.

The origins of all seven companies, therefore, supports the first-mover hypothesis. However, for this hypothesis to have explanatory power we need to answer a further question: Why have late-comers been disadvantaged so that generally they have been unable to catch

Exhibit A7.1. *Internet content and applications providers, start-date*

Company	Entrepreneur's name/names and date of birth (DoB)	Start-date[1]
Amazon	**Jeff Bezos:** 12 January 1964[2]	**July 1994**[3]
Baidu	**Robin Li:** Not clear (age can be calculated at 38 as of 2006),[4] so DoB around 1968 **Eric Xu Yong:** Not clear (age can be calculated at 42 as of 2006),[5] so DoB around 1964	**Beginning 2000**[6]
e-Bay	**Pierre Omidyar:** 21 June 1967[7]	**September 1995**[8]
Google	**Larry Page:** 26 March, 1973[9] **Sergey Brin:** 21 August 1973[10]	Search engine research involving the pair which initially went under the name BackRub (**January 1996**).[11] **September 1998** (Google company registered)[12]
Skype	**Niklas Zennström:** 16 February 1966[13] **Janus Friis:** Ten years younger than Zennström[14], so around 1976	**2001** (the two men launched Kazaa)[15] **August 2003** (Skype launched[16] with the partners working on their new idea from 2002)
Yahoo!	**David Filo:** Born in 1966[17] **Jerry Yang:** Born on 6 November 1968[18]	**April 1994** (as indicated by David Filo)[19]
YouTube	**Chad Hurley:** Was said to be 29 years old as of 2006[20], so DoB around 1977 **Steve Chen:** Said to have been born in 1978 or 1979[21]	The domain name 'YouTube.com' was activated on **15 February 2005**.[22] The origins of the company go back to the purchase of PayPal by eBay in 2002, leaving a number of key individuals with large windfalls and a desire to create a new Internet business.

Notes:

[1] Date the activity leading to the company began, **not** set-up date of the company.

[2] www.wordiq.com/definition/Jeff_Bezos: accessed 26 July 2006.

Notes for Exhibit A7.1. (*cont.*)

3 www.wordiq.com/definition/Jeff_Bezos: accessed 26 July 2006.

4 www.forbes.com/lists/2005/74/TW1E.html: accessed 3 July 2006.

5 www.forbes.com/lists/2005/74/TW1E.html: accessed 3 July 2006.

6 http://64.233.183.104/search?q=cache:aX9c8ooBjzcJ:www.baidu.com/about/en/mt_eric.html+eric+Xu&hl=en&gl=uk&ct=clnk&cd=1: accessed 3 July 2006.

7 www.achievement.org/autodoc/page/omi0pro-1: accessed 10 July 2006.

8 www.omidyar.net/corp/t_pierre.html: accessed 13 June 2006.

9 www.nndb.com/people/830/000044698/; http://en.wikipedia.org/wiki/Lawrence_E._Page.

10 www.nndb.com/people/826/000044694/: accessed 11 April 2006; http://en.wikipedia.org/wiki/Sergey_Brin; http://www.imdb.com/name/nm1962236/: accessed 11 April 2006.

11 www.google.com/intl/en/corporate/history.html.

12 FT.com site, 29 April 2004: Article B.

13 *Sunday Times* (London), 27 November 2005.

14 *Sunday Times* (London), 27 November 2005.

15 *Fortune* (Europe), 9 February 2004, 149 (2): 38–46.

16 *Financial Times*, 19 November 2003.

17 http://www.bookrags.com/sciences/computerscience/yahoos-david-filo-csci-04.html.

18 http://en.wikipedia.org/wiki/Jerry_Yang: accessed 2 May 2006.

19 http://xent.com/oct00/1174.html: accessed 3 May 2006.

20 *Financial Times*, 8 October 2006.

21 http://en.wikipedia.org/wiki/Steve_Chen_%28Youtube%29: accessed 11 October 2006.

22 http://en.wikipedia.org/wiki/Youtube: accessed 11 October 2006; *Financial Times*, 8 October 2006.

Source: From individual company profiles by Ian Duff, JETS.

up with, and even surpass, the early birds? The answer to this latter question may be summed up in one phrase: *dynamic increasing returns*. In other words, the first-movers have been able to benefit from several dynamic effects that have over time given them increasing advantages relative to later entrants into their particular markets.

What are these dynamic effects? The first set of effects follows from extremely low marginal costs, one of the great benefits provided by the Internet. Low marginal costs exist for both the supplier and the users. For certain kinds of products distribution over the Internet entails very low marginal costs for the supplier. A good example is provided by Skype. The additional cost to Skype of providing for an additional user (i.e. its marginal cost) is very low because all the user has to do is go to Skype's website and download the free software that will enable the user to speak (with the necessary equipment, such as microphone and speakers) with other Skype users. There is very little extra cost to Skype (if any cost) of providing this facility once the peer-to-peer software and website are already up and running.

Moreover, there is very little extra cost to the user of adopting this innovation and using it. Since most broadband users pay flat-rate tariffs and since the equipment is relatively cheap, the adoption cost is low. Moreover, Zennström and Friis decided to spend little on advertising and marketing. Instead they relied on the extremely low adoption costs and free voice over the Internet between Skype users to generate 'viral advertising', whereby users inform other users via the Internet at no cost to Skype.

With low marginal costs to start the dynamic increasing returns ball rolling, network externalities then kick in to make the ball roll ever faster. Network externalities exist when the value of a network increases the more users there are. In Skype's case, the more users who have downloaded the software, the more people a particular user can contact. In other words, the BCR of adopting the Skype innovation increases the more people become Skype subscribers. This BCR increases, and increases rapidly, over time, making it less likely that a user will switch to other alternative suppliers of VoIP (unless the new entrants are able to find additional benefits, such as additional services). The same network externalities apply to eBay (the more users, the greater the set of products available to buy and the greater the number of potential customers for a seller) and to YouTube (the greater the number of videos that are available for the downloader and the greater the potential audience for the uploader). Many of Yahoo!'s services work similarly.

Further effects that also generate dynamic increasing returns follow from user-generated content (a central component of so-called Web 2.0 thinking). Amazon provides a good example. Two features of the Amazon website increase its value to users. The first is reviews of books provided by other users as well as information regarding the desirability of the book (e.g. star ratings). The second is 'other users who bought this also bought that' information. In aggregate this kind of user-generated information increases the more users there are, increasing the overall benefit of the service. Similar benefits are obviously also present in the offerings of YouTube, MySpace, Second Life, etc.

Beneficial second-round effects follow. These include a rapid increase in consumer demand (as a result of low marginal costs and network effects), rapid globalisation of activities and user base (because of the global ubiquity of the Internet) and a low cost of Internet-based diversification into neighbouring markets. All seven companies provide good examples.

An important third-round effect then follows for companies that have successfully gone through the first two rounds. In this third round financial markets kick in and in successful cases multiply by many orders of magnitude the financial value of the company. This works through events such as a rapid rise in the share price of the successful Internet company (as subscribers, and later profits, increase), IPOs, capital raising and M&As, the latter facilitated by the company's shares serving as an acquisition currency. In turn, these financial processes facilitate further growth and diversification.

For these reasons it is the early bird, rather than the late-comer, that catches the worm. With the passage of time the barriers to entry into the market segment increase, protecting the early-comer and disadvantaging the potential new entrants, who have to think of innovative new ways of entering the market by providing additional new services if they are to stand a chance of succeeding.

To a significant extent this explains the global dominance of the US ICAPs and, conversely, the relative absence of European and Asian competitors. The Internet was invented in the USA and its mass adoption first took place there. Being on the spot, the US companies we have studied were, as a result of the entrepreneurial activities of their founders, first to address the new market opportunities that the new technology (the Internet) was generating. Dynamic increasing returns cemented their lead. However, there is more to the US story. Three other factors that also played a crucial role are discussed in the following sections.

It's in the atmosphere

In analysing the benefits accruing in the industrial districts of Britain during the latter nineteenth century the Cambridge economist, Alfred Marshall, talked of the importance of the 'atmosphere' in these areas. By 'atmosphere' he meant the thinking generated by large numbers of people concentrated in the industrial districts and involved in the technologies and markets of the time, the supplies of knowledgeable people and the many forms of cooperation occurring between firms in the area, including between competing firms. Within this context, ideas concerning the technologies and related markets were 'in the air' and associated knowledge was easily and rapidly transmitted, as what Marshall called externalities were generated.[1]

A similar atmosphere was created in parts of the USA as the Internet took off in the mid-1990s. Silicon Valley is the most celebrated example. However, the creation of the Internet 'atmosphere' began much earlier with the diffusion of stand-alone computers. Exhibit A7.2 provides information on the prior experience of the ICAP entrepreneurs with computers.

Indeed, in looking at the background of the ICAP entrepreneurs one of the striking commonalities is how many of them became 'hooked' on computers when they were children. This interest was reflected in their choice to study computer science (or perhaps engineering) at university. With this background for starters the entrepreneurs were well prepared to go on to the main meal that was available in the atmosphere in their area.

The role of universities

Universities played a particularly important role in contributing to the atmosphere and providing the facilitating incubating environment encouraging entrepreneurial activity. Not surprisingly, in view of Marshall's

---

[1] Marshall (1885, 1889, 1920a, 1920b).

Exhibit A7.2. *ICAP entrepreneurs: country of birth, parents' occupations, prior experience with computers/Internet*

Company	Entrepreneur's country of birth	Parents' occupations	Prior experience with computers/Internet
Amazon	Albuquerque, New Mexico, USA.[1]	His Cuban step-father worked as an engineer for Exxon.[2] His mother worked in a bank.[3] His grandfather had worked as a regional director for the Atomic Energy Commission.[4]	Access to a mainframe at school at 10 years old (1974).[5] In the 11th grade he got an Apple II Plus – and 'continued fooling around with computers'.[6] First used the Internet in 1985 during an astro-physics class at Princeton.[7] While at Princeton he switched from Physics to Computing Science and Electrical Engineering[8] (see 'Universities involved' section in exhibit A7.3). In 1989 the he collaborated with Merrill Lynch in developing intranets and personalised news services for stockbrokers.[9] While working on Wall Street from 1986 to 1994 (for FITEL[10] Bankers Trust Co.[11] and DE Shaw[12]), Bezos was heavily involved in applying computer science to the stock market.
Baidu	**Robin Li:** Chinese (a native of the Shanxi province).[13]	**Robin Li:** Not covered.	**Robin Li:** Studied Computing while at university (see 'Universities involved' section in exhibit A7.3). Following his studies Li worked as a senior consultant for IDD Information Services (May 1994–1997). He then worked as a staff engineer for Infoseek, a pioneer in the Internet search engine industry, from July 1997 to December 1999.[14] At some point during his stay in the USA he was also said to have worked for Dow Jones and to have been involved with the *Wall Street Journal*'s website.[15] He was reported to have patents on Internet search technology going back to the mid-1990s.[16]

	Eric Xu Yong: Chinese.	Eric Xu Yong: Not covered.	Eric Xu Yong: In 1999 he co-founded a company in Silicon Valley that specialized in e-commerce online services and which reportedly became profitable in six months. Additionally he was also said to be active in offering consultancy services to other start-up companies in Silicon Valley.[17]
e-Bay	Born in Paris, France.[18]	His father was a doctor;[19] his mother had studied linguistics.[20]	While he was in the third grade (around eight years old) he was bought a TRS-80 computer from Radio Shack. He learned how to programme Basic on it.[21]
			He studied computer science at university (see 'Universities involved' section in exhibit A7.3). In his junior year at Tufts, Omidyar took a summer internship with Innovative Data Design.[22]
			After leaving university (1988) Omidyar had worked for Claris, an Apple Computer subsidiary, where he helped to write the programme for MacDraw.[23]
			In 1991 he formed Ink Development Corp. with three friends to develop software for pen-based computers.[24] This company later changed its focus from pen-based computing to e-commerce, a change reflected in its new name, eShop Inc. It was eventually sold to Microsoft in 1996.[25]
			By 1994 he seemed to have little more to do with eShop Inc. and took up a separate position as a developer services engineer for General Magic, a mobile communication platform company.[26] Prior to starting eBay he had also started his own Web consulting firm called the Echo Bay Technology Group. Crucially for this story this had its own Web address of www.ebay.com.

Exhibit A7.2. (*cont.*)

Company	Entrepreneur's country of birth	Parents' occupations	Prior experience with computers/Internet
Google	**Larry Page:** born in East Lansing, Michigan, USA.[27]	**Larry Page:** His parents are Carl Vincent Page (deceased[29]), who was a professor of computer science at Michigan State University and Gloria Page, a computer programming teacher at the same institution.[30]	**Larry Page:** The family bought a home computer, the Exidy Sorcerer, when he was only six. Reportedly Page's elder brother was involved in designing the machine's operating system.[34] By adapting this machine the young Page was reportedly able to present his school project in a word-processed form, the first time any pupil at the school had managed such a feat.[35] Page went on to study computing at university (see 'Universities involved' section in exhibit A7.3)
	Sergey Brin: Russian by birth. Born in Moscow, USSR.[28]	**Sergey Brin:** His father, Michael Brin, was an economist with leanings towards mathematics.[31] In 1979, when Sergey was six years old, the family emigrated to the USA. The reason	**Sergey Brin:** Brin states that he had an interest in computers from early on in his childhood. On his ninth birthday he received his first computer, a Commodore 64, as a present from his father.[36] Even back in his first year at primary school he showed an aptitude for mathematics and computing, surprising his teacher by submitting a project in printed form.[37] Brin went on to study computing at university (see 'Universities involved' section in exhibit A7.3)

			for the move was a position for Brin senior in the Maths Department at the University of Maryland.[32] His mother, Genia, obtained a position as a climate scientist at NASA.[33]
Skype	Niklas Zennström: born in Sweden and brought up in the university town of Uppsala.[38]	Niklas Zennström: Both his parents are teachers.[40]	Niklas Zennström: Had studied computer science at university (see 'Universities involved' section in exhibit A7.3) and been involved in Internet development at Tele 2. Here he was responsible for the launch of the European Internet Service Provider (ISP) business known as get2net. He was also the CEO of the everyday.com portal[41] After Tele2 he developed Kazaa (2001).
	Janus Friis: born in Denmark.[39]	Janus Friis: Not covered.	Janus Friis: Also involved with Internet development at Tele2. Prior to joining Tele2 he had spent some time at the help desk of CyberCity, one of Denmark's first ISPs.[42] Apart from developing Kazaa he was also involved in setting up Bullguard.com.[43]
Yahoo!	David Filo: Wisconsin, USA[44]	David Filo: Father an architect; mother an accountant.[46]	David Filo: Had studied Computing while at university (see 'Universities involved' section in exhibit A7.3).

Exhibit A7.2. (*cont.*)

Company	Entrepreneur's country of birth	Parents' occupations	Prior experience with computers/Internet
	Jerry Yang: Taipei, Taiwan.[45]	**Jerry Yang:** Father died when Jerry was two years old.[47] Mother an English teacher (in Taiwan).[48]	**Jerry Yang:** Was studying electrical engineering while at university (see 'Universities involved' section in exhibit A7.3). By 1994 both men had become more interested in mapping the emerging Internet than in pursuing their studies.
YouTube	**Chad Hurley:** USA. He graduated from Twin Valley High School, Elverson, PA in 1995.[49]	**Chad Hurley:** Not covered.	**Chad Hurley:** Hurley was the fifteenth employee of Internet payment company, PayPal. His role was to design PayPal's logo and its user interface.[51]
	Steve Chen: Originally from Taiwan.[50]	**Steve Chen:** Not covered.	**Steve Chen:** He studied computing at university (see 'Universities involved' section in exhibit A7.3). Chen was also an early employee at PayPal.[52]

Notes:

1 www.wordiq.com/definition/Jeff_Bezos: accessed 26 July 2006.
2 www.wordiq.com/definition/Jeff_Bezos: accessed 26 July 2006.
3 *Business Week*, 31 May 1999, Issue 3631: 137–40.
4 www.wordiq.com/definition/Jeff_Bezos: accessed 26 July 2006.
5 www.achievement.org/autodoc/printmember/bez0int-1: accessed 26 July 2006.

6 www.achievement.org/autodoc/printmember/bez0int-1: accessed 26 July 2006.

7 *Fast Company*, February 2001, issue 43: 80–2.

8 www.achievement.org/autodoc/printmember/bez0int-1: accessed 26 July 2006.

9 *Independent* (London), 12 May 1998.

10 *Advertising Age*, 14 July 1997, 68 (28): ps2–s2.

11 *Observer*, 11 February 2001.

12 *Advertising Age*, 14 July 1997, 68 (28): ps2–s2; *Observer*, 11 February 2001.

13 *Guardian* (London), final edition, 8 December 2005.

14 http://ir.baidu.com/phoenix.zhtml?c=188488&p=irol-govBio&ID=138201: accessed 3 July 2006.

15 www.venturetdf.com/china/baidu_mar10-05.php: accessed 3 July 2006; http://en.wikipedia.org/wiki/Robin_Li: accessed 3 July 2006.

16 www.venturetdf.com/china/baidu_mar10-05.php: accessed 3 July 2006.

17 http://64.233.183.104/search?q=cache:aX9c8ooBjzcJ:www.baidu.com/about/en/mt_eric.html+eric+Xu&hl=en&gl=uk&ct=clnk&cd=1: accessed 3 July 2006.

18 www.achievement.org/autodoc/page/omi0pro-1: accessed 10 July 2006.

19 www.achievement.org/autodoc/page/omi0pro-1: accessed 10 July 2006.

20 www.multilingualchildren.org/press/celebs.html: accessed 12 July 2006.

21 www.achievement.org/autodoc/page/omi0pro-1: accessed 10 July 2006.

22 www.persianmirror.com/culture/famous/bios/omidyar.cfm: accessed 17 July 2006.

23 http://en.wikipedia.org/wiki/Pierre_Omidyar: accessed 13 June 2006.

24 www.achievement.org/autodoc/page/omi0pro-1: accessed 10 July 2006.

25 www.achievement.org/autodoc/page/omi0pro-1: accessed 10 July 2006; www.persianmirror.com/culture/famous/bios/omidyar.cfm: accessed 17 July 2006.

26 www.achievement.org/autodoc/page/omi0pro-1: accessed 10 July 2006.

27 www.nndb.com/people/830/000044698/; http://en.wikipedia.org/wiki/Lawrence_E._Page.

28 www.nndb.com/people/826/000044694/: accessed 11 April 2006; http://en.wikipedia.org/wiki/Sergey_Brin; www.imdb.com/name/nm1962236/: accessed 11 April 2006.

29 *Daily Telegraph* (London), 1 May 2004: Article B.

Notes for Exhibit A7.2. (*cont.*)

[30] http://en.wikipedia.org/wiki/Lawrence_E._Page.
[31] *Sunday Telegraph* (London), 1 August 2004.
[32] *Financial Times*, 25 October 2003.
[33] FT.com site, 29 April 2004: Article A.
[34] *Daily Telegraph* (London), 19 April 2001.
[35] *Daily Telegraph* (London), 19 April 2001.
[36] http://en.wikipedia.org/wiki/Sergey_Brin.
[37] http://en.wikipedia.org/wiki/Sergey_Brin.
[38] *Sunday Times* (London), 27 November 2005.
[39] *Sunday Times* (London), 27 November 2005.
[40] *Sunday Times* (London), 27 November 2005.
[41] www.skype.com/company/founders.html: accessed 6 March 2006.
[42] www.skype.com/company/founders.html: accessed 6 March 2006.
[43] www.skype.com/company/founders.html: accessed 6 March 2006.
[44] www.bookrags.com/sciences/computerscience/yahoos-david-filo-csci-04.html.
[45] http://en.wikipedia.org/wiki/Jerry_Yang: accessed 2 May 2006.
[46] www.notablebiographies.com/news/Ow-Sh/Semel-Terry.html.
[47] http://en.wikipedia.org/wiki/Jerry_Yang: accessed 2 May 2006.
[48] http://en.wikipedia.org/wiki/Jerry_Yang: accessed 2 May 2006.
[49] http://en.wikipedia.org/wiki/Chad_Hurley: accessed 11 October 2006.
[50] http://en.wikipedia.org/wiki/Steve_Chen_%28Youtube%29: accessed 11 October 2006.
[51] *Financial Times*, 9 October 2006: Article A.
[52] *Financial Times*, 9 October 2006: Article A.

Source: From individual company profiles by Ian Duff, JETS.

observations, universities in the Silicon Valley area – already a hothouse in semiconductors and software – were particularly significant. Exhibit A7.3 provides information on the universities attended by the ICAP entrepreneurs.

The founders of Google and Yahoo! were at Stanford University. Significantly, the founders of the two non-US ICAPs in our sample also studied at American universities. Robin Li of Baidu, after doing a bachelor's degree in information management at Beijing University, went on to do a masters in computer science at the State University of New York in Buffalo. His partner in Baidu, Eric Xu Yong, after studying biology at Beijing University did his doctorate at Texas A&M University and then did postgraduate studies at the University of California, Berkeley. Niklas Zennström, one of the two founders of Skype, did an MSc in Engineering Physics and Computer Science at Uppsala University in Sweden, spending part of his final year as an exchange student at the University of Michigan, Ann Arbor.

The Internet began in the USA and began its mass diffusion there. The atmosphere that it created emerged first in parts of the USA and, within this context, the first entrepreneurial start-up ICAPs. However, Skype is particularly important because it shows that the facilitating atmosphere that contributed to the emergence and growth of the ICAPs was not solely an American phenomenon. Although the Internet and its mass diffusion began in the USA it soon spread to other parts of the world. Scandinavia was one of those that rapidly adopted first computers and then the Internet. Internet applications were also in the atmosphere in Sweden; indeed, Zennström, who with Janus Friis founded Skype, worked with the ISP business of Tele2, a new entrant telecoms company that competed with the Swedish incumbent, Telia. Before Friis joined Tele2 he had worked with CyberCity, one of Denmark's first ISPs.

Skype is very important because it highlights that Internet content and applications provision is not necessarily an American preserve. The global ubiquity of the Internet means that non-US start-ups, provided they get in early enough, can become highly successful. The implications for Europe, Asia and parts of Latin America are highly significant. Having said this, however, it remains the case that for Skype as for our other non-US ICAP, Baidu, American venture capital played a crucial role.

Exhibit A7.3. ICAP entrepreneurs: universities involved and source of start-up capital

Company	Universities involved	Source of start-up capital
Amazon	Degree from Princeton University (1986) in Electrical Engineering and Computer Science. Graduated *summa cum laude*.[1] While at Princeton Bezos was accepted into the Phi Beta Kappa Society.[2]	Borrowed $300,000 from his parents in 1994 (their retirement fund).[3] In 1995 around $1million of funding was secured from 22 'angel' investors.[4] In 1996 Kleiner Perkins Caufield & Byers invested around $10million.[5]
Baidu	**Robin Li:** Li studied at Peking University, completing a Bachelor of Science Degree in Information Management. He then continued his studies in the USA (from 1991),[6] receiving a Master of Science Degree in Computer Science from The State University of New York at Buffalo.[7] **Eric Xu Yong:** After completing a graduate degree in biology from Peking University, Xu Yong continued his studies in the USA, completing a doctorate at the A&M University in Texas. This was funded by a scholarship from the America Rockefeller Foundation.	In 2002 Baidu raised about $10million from Draper Fisher Jurvetson ePlanet Ventures, a California-based specialist private equity group.[9] In the course of 2004 the company conducted a further round of fund raising (its Series C round) which saw it sell around 10 per cent of its equity to a group of eight investors led by Google.[10] Other investors by this stage included IDG, Peninsula Capital and Integrity Partners, as well as early investor Draper Fisher Jurvetson.[11] For its part Google took 749,625 of the company's shares which amounted to an investment of $5million.[12] As for the collaborative relationship between Baidu and Google this came to an end in mid-2006 when Google sold its 2.3 per cent stake.[13] The price it achieved was said to be around $60 million (£33 million),[14] no bad return on its original $5 million investment.

After completing his doctorate Xu Yong continued with a post-doctorate programme at the University of California, Berkeley.[8]

e-Bay

Omidyar graduated from Tufts University in 1988 with a degree in computer science.[15] His grade point average was only 3.01 and he readily admits that he was not a very good student.[16]

Additional involvement:

Later he made a $100 million gift to endow the Omidyar–Tufts Microfinance Fund (to be administered by the Board of Trustees of Tufts University).[17] At the time this was the largest gift in the history of Tufts University, in addition to being the most significant private allocation of capital to a microfinance initiative by any individual or family.[18]

eBay quickly proved to be a cash generator, alleviating the need for immediate venture capital involvement.[19]

In the course of 1997 Benchmark Capital agreed to make an initial investment of $6.7 million in eBay.[20]

Google

Larry Page: He completed a BSE in Computer Engineering at the University of Michigan Ann Arbor in 1995.[21]

The initial investment came in 1998 when the research project needed more computer power than they could borrow on campus. This led the students to invest in a terabyte (a million megabytes) of disks with which they set about constructing their own computer housings in

Exhibit A7.3. (*cont.*)

Company	Universities involved	Source of start-up capital
	Thereafter he started a PhD programme at the Computer Science Department, Stanford University.	Page's dorm room.[27] This development seemed to be a key transition from Google as a research idea to Google as a potential business.
	At Stanford he was to take leave of absence from the PhD programme in 1998 having already gained his Masters degree.[22]	In buying the new equipment the pair invested $15,000, spread across three of their credit cards.[28]
	Sergey Brin: His BS degree was from the University of Maryland with High honours in Mathematics and honours in Computer Science (1993).[23]	Later in 1998 Andy Bechtolsheim, one of the founders of Sun Microsystems, wrote the two students a cheque for $100,000. Since this was made out to Google it was a serious incentive to register the company (done on 7 September 1998). In the process of officially launching the company they also secured an additional $900,000 from 'angel' investors including 'family, friends, and acquaintances', giving them initial seed capital of $1 million.[29]
	He arrived at Stanford University in September 1993 and completed a Masters (ahead of schedule) in August 1995.[24]	One of these early 'angel' investors was Junglee founder Ram Shriram.[30] His investment was large enough to secure him a seat on the new company's board.[31]
	His PhD within the computer science department was 'expected' in June 1997,[25] but was not completed since he took leave of absence to concentrate on Google during 1998.	Later it was reported that Google had also secured an investment from a venture capital firm which was itself called Angel Investors. This was set up in 1998 by Ron Conway with the purpose of investing in Internet start-ups such as Google. Its financial vehicles, known as Angel-1 and Angel-2, attracted some high-profile investors including Tiger Woods, Shaquille O'Neal, Arnold Schwarzenegger and Henry Kissinger.[32]
	Additional involvement: In 1997 the Google technology had been put to the test as the search engine for Stanford's own Web pages.[26]	

Stanford also had an interest in the company's equity (see facing column).

Another early shareholder in the business, although of a different kind, was Stanford University. As with the company's famous 'angel' investors this shareholding came to light when the company held its IPO in 2004.[33]

Later two prominent venture capital firms took a major interest in Google. These were Sequoia Capital and Kleiner Perkins Caufield & Byers.[34] Together they invested a further $25million into Google, with the new funding being announced on 7 June 1999. This gave both firms a 10 per cent stake in the company.[35]

Skype Niklas Zennström: The bulk of his education took place within his home town, firstly at the Katedralskolan school and then at the town's university.[36] Uppsala is the oldest university in the Nordic countries, founded in 1477.[37]

Despite its long tradition the university prides itself on the 'Active collaboration' which it encourages with the outside world, including the world of business.[38] He obtained a dual degree, with business supplementing his MSc in Engineering Physics and computer science.[39] For the final year of his studies Zennström was

Key among the financial backers was Tim Draper, the US technology investor, best known for his original backing of Hot Mail.[42] His venture capital company Draper Fisher Jurvetson gave the new venture some much needed credibility (not least on the US business scene). It also contributed around $10million to the new venture from around 2003.[43]

Other venture capital groups to take an interest included Index Ventures, Bessemer Venture Partners and Mangrove Capital Partners.[44] Between them they contributed a further $10million to Skype's early funding needs.[45] Another early investor in Skype was Morten Lund, the CEO of anti-virus company Bullguard.com[46] (a company which Janus Friis was involved in setting up[47]).

Exhibit A7.3. (*cont.*)

Company	Universities involved	Source of start-up capital
	an exchange student in the USA, with the host institution being the University of Michigan, Ann Arbor.[40] **Janus Friis:** Left school at 16.[41]	
Yahoo!	**David Filo:** Bachelor's degree (computer engineering), Tulane University, New Orleans;[48] MSc in electrical engineering, Stanford University, then on to PhD programme in electrical engineering. **Jerry Yang:** Entered Stanford in 1990 and within four years he received both his BS and MS degrees in electrical engineering.[49] In 1994 he enrolled in Stanford's electrical engineering PhD programme.[50]	In early 1995 Yahoo! received some practical help (mainly in the form of premises) from Netscape.[51] In the spring of 1995 Filo and Yang started meeting with numerous Silicon Valley venture capitalists. In the end they teamed up with Sequoia Capital, a well-known firm whose most notable investments included Apple Computers, Atari, Oracle and Cisco Systems.[52] The man at Sequoia most associated with the deal was Mike Moritz. The deal was signed in April 1995, with Sequoia agreeing to invest almost $2 million in the new company.[53] The second round of capital-raising took place in the latter part of 1995. This involved Reuters (taking a 2.5 per cent share[54]) and Softbank who invested $65.8 million in return for a 37 per cent stake in Yahoo!.[55]
YouTube	**Chad Hurley:** He received his BA in Fine Art from Indiana University of Pennsylvania.[56] The *FT*'s version suggests that he trained as a graphic designer at Indiana University.[57]	Following the take-over of PayPal by eBay in 2002 early employee Roelof Botha became a partner at Sequoia Capital (backers of Google, Yahoo! and PayPal itself).[61] With this strong personal connection with the YouTube founders, Sequoia became the company's only venture capital backer, with Botha sitting on the company board following the first round of funding in November 2005.[62]

Steve Chen: Chen attended the Illinois Math & Science Academy and the University of Illinois at Urbana–Champaign.[58] He studied computer science.[59] It was while doing this course that he met fellow computer science student Jawed Karim (also a future PayPal employee and co-founder of YouTube.

Karim finished his computer science course in 2004 and went on to become a graduate student in computer science at Stanford University[60]).

This initial funding amounted to $3.5 million. Subsequently, in April 2006, Sequoia put an additional $8 million into the new company, which had experienced a surge of popularity in its first few months.[63]

Notes:

[1] www.fastcompany.com/magazine/85/bezos_1_Printer_Friendly. html: Issue 85: August 2004: accessed 26 July 2006.

[2] *The Independent* (London), 12 May 1998.

[3] www.achievement.org/autodoc/printmember/bez0int-1: accessed 26 July 2006.

[4] *Inc.*, April 2004, 26 (4): 148–50.

[5] *Independent* (London), 12 May 1998.

[6] *Guardian* (London), final edition, 8 December 2005.

[7] http://ir.baidu.com/phoenix.zhtml?c=188488&p=irol-govBio&ID=138201: accessed 3 July 2006.

[8] http://64.233.183.104/search?q=cache:aX9c8ooBjzcJ:www.baidu.com/about/en/mt_eric.html+eric+Xu&hl=en&gl=uk&ct=clnk&cd=1: accessed 3 July 2006.

[9] FT.com site, 31 January 2005.

[10] www.venturetdf.com/china/baidu_mar10-05.php: accessed 3 July 2006.

[11] www.venturetdf.com/china/baidu_mar10-05.php: accessed 3 July 2006.

[12] www.venturetdf.com/china/cn_baidu_5aug05_2.php: accessed 3 July 2006.

Notes for Exhibit A7.3. (*cont.*)

13 *Financial Times*, 24 June 2006, elsewhere, the size of the stake was put at 2.6 per cent, e.g. *Independent* (London), 6 August 2005.

14 *The Times* (London), 24 June 2006.

15 www.persianmirror.com/culture/famous/bios/omidyar.cfm: accessed 17 July 2006.

16 www.achievement.org/autodoc/page/omi0pro-1: accessed 10 July 2006.

17 www.achievement.org/autodoc/page/omi0pro-1: accessed 10 July 2006.

18 www.achievement.org/autodoc/page/omi0pro-1: accessed 10 July 2006.

19 eBay IPO Prospectus, 25 September 1998, www.sec.gov/Archives/edgar/data/1065088/0001012870-98-002475.txt: accessed 14 June 2006.

20 Quoted on www.amazon.co.uk/gp/product/1587991357/026-4460789-3426822?v=glance&n=266239: accessed 18 July 2006.

21 www.nndb.com/people/830/000044698/.

22 www.google.com/corporate/execs.html#larry.

23 www-db.stanford.edu/~sergey/resume.html.

24 http://en.wikipedia.org/wiki/Sergey_Brin.

25 www-db.stanford.edu/~sergey/resume.html.

26 *Siliconindia*, September 2000, 4 (9): 92.

27 www.google.com/intl/en/corporate/history.html.

28 *Technology Review*, November – December 2000, 103 (6): 108.

29 www.google.com/intl/en/corporate/history.html; *Siliconindia*, September 2000, 4 (9): 92.

30 *Siliconindia*, September 2000, 4 (9): 92.

31 www.google.com/intl/en/corporate/history.html.

32 *Independent* (London), 26 April 2004.

33 *Independent* (London), 26 April 2004.

34 www.google.com/intl/en/corporate/history.html.

35 www.google.com/intl/en/corporate/history.html.

36 *Sunday Times* (London), 27 November 2005.

37 http://info.uu.se/fakta.nsf/sidor/about.uu.idE1.html: accessed 7 March 2006.

38 http://info.uu.se/fakta.nsf/sidor/cooperation.idFE.html: accessed 7 March 2006.

39 www.skype.com/company/founders.html: accessed 6 March 2006.

40 www.skype.com/company/founders.html: accessed 6 March 2006.

41 *Sunday Times* (London), 27 November 2005.

42 *Daily Telegraph* (London), 8 January 2005.

43 *Economist*, 17 September 2005, 376 (8444): 69–71.

44 www.skype.com/company/founders.html: accessed 6 March 2006.

45 *Daily Telegraph* (London), 8 January 2005.

46 *Fortune* (Europe), 9 February 2004, 149 (2): 38–46.

47 www.skype.com/company/founders.html: accessed 6 March 2006.

48 www.notablebiographies.com/news/Ow-Sh/Semel-Terry.html.

49 http://en.wikipedia.org/wiki/Jerry_Yang: accessed 2 May 2006; www.akamarketing.com/yahoo-feature1.html1: accessed 2 May 2006.

50 www.akamarketing.com/yahoo-feature1.html1: accessed 2 May 2006.

51 *Newsweek*, 20 March 1995, 125 (12): 44.

52 http://docs.yahoo.com/info/misc/history.html: accessed 2 May 2006.

53 http://docs.yahoo.com/info/misc/history.html: accessed 2 May 2006.

54 *Editor & Publisher*, 16 December 1995, 128 (50): 33.

55 *Editor & Publisher*, 18 May 1996, 129 (20): 35.

56 http://en.wikipedia.org/wiki/Chad_Hurley: accessed 11 October 2006.

57 *Financial Times*, 9 October 2006: Article A.

58 http://en.wikipedia.org/wiki/Steve_Chen_%28Youtube%29: accessed 11 October 2006.

59 http://en.wikipedia.org/wiki/Youtube: accessed 11 October 2006.

60 http://en.wikipedia.org/wiki/Jawed_Karim: accessed 11 October 2006.

61 *Financial Times*, 9 October 2006: Article A.

62 *Financial Times*, 9 October 2006: Article A; http://en.wikipedia.org/wiki/Youtube: accessed 11 October 2006.

63 http://en.wikipedia.org/wiki/Youtube: accessed 11 October 2006.

Source: From individual company profiles by Ian Duff, JETS.

Capital, contacts and connections: the role of US venture capital

Exhibit A7.3 also provides information on the sources of venture capital for the start-up ICAPs. One of the key financial backers of Skype was the US technology investor, Tim Draper, well known for his original backing of Hotmail (founded by Sabeer Bhatia and Jack Smith in 1995 and sold in December 1997 to Microsoft). His venture capital company, Draper Fisher Jurvetson, provided important early funding for Skype, and significant venture capital funding for Baidu.

After borrowing his initial $300,000 from his parents and getting the next $1 million from twenty-two 'angel' investors, Jeff Bezos of Amazon obtained $10 million from Kleiner Perkins Caufield & Byers in 1996 which was also a major investor in Google. Sequoia Capital also supplied venture capital to Google, Yahoo! and YouTube.

US venture capital firms, however, supplied far more than capital on conducive terms. Equally importantly, they also provided contacts and connections, helping their start-ups to develop crucial cooperative relationships with other companies and knowledgeable people. As this brief account of the ICAPs reveals, US venture capital has been particularly important not only for the US players but also for the two non-US actors. This raises important questions regarding the role of venture capital in non-US innovation systems (which, however, will not be further explored here).

Conclusions

In this appendix we have examined the factors explaining the dominance of US Internet content and applications companies in the global new ICT ecosystem. The explanation hinges on two determinants. The first is a set of effects, summarised as dynamic increasing returns, that include low marginal costs, network externalities, 'atmosphere' determinants and financial effects. The second set includes several key institutions that have shaped the growth of this sub-sector, such as universities and venture capital.

Crucially, the study in this appendix has shown that although the main globally dominant Internet companies in layer 3 of the ICT ecosystem are from the USA, this is not inevitably the case. Skype and Baidu are examples of non-US firms successfully entering this space. The challenge for both firms and policy-makers in Europe and Asia is to identify where further inroads can be made by non-US companies into **layer 3**.

Appendix 8: How did East Asia (Japan, Korea, Taiwan and China) become so strong in layer 1?

One of the key features of the global new ICT ecosystem is the prominent position enjoyed in layer 1 – the networked elements layer – by leading companies from four East Asian countries: Japan, Korea, Taiwan and China. But how did these countries and companies come to achieve international competitiveness in layer 1 in areas that were hitherto dominated by US and European rivals? This question is dealt with in this appendix.

East Asian global competitiveness in the new ICT ecosystem

Exhibit A8.1 demonstrates East Asian global competitiveness in the new ICT ecosystem.[1] It contrasts four areas of considerable strength, all in layer 1 (telecoms equipment, semiconductors, computers and consumer electronics), with the medium strength of selected East Asian companies in layer 3.

As can be seen from exhibit A8.1, Japan is very strong in terms of global competitiveness in telecoms equipment, semiconductors (particularly memories) and consumer electronics. Furthermore, it is strong in computers. In the upper layers, however, Japan is of medium strength (NTT DoCoMo's i-mode mobile Internet service, which is very strong, being an example of a significant exception).

Korea is very strong in semiconductors (including memories and displays) and consumer electronics. However, despite major government initiatives in the 1980s, Korea has not been able to establish a significant competitive advantage in computers (although more recently companies like Samsung have begun once again to contest

---

[1] These qualitative indications of competitiveness represent the author's estimates based on his knowledge of data sources such as market share by company and country. A larger and more detailed study than the present one would collect and analyse this data in a more comprehensive way. Exhibit A8.1 is simply intended as a summary.

Exhibit A8.1. *East Asian global competitiveness in the new ICT ecosystem, 2006*

Country	Telecoms equipment	Semi-conductors	Computers	Consumer electronics	Upper layers
Japan	***[1]	***	**	***	*
	e.g. NEC, Fujitsu	e.g. NEC, Toshiba, Hitachi, Fujitsu	e.g. Fujitsu, NEC, Toshiba, Hitachi	e.g. Sony, Matsushita, Sharp, Sanyo	e.g. NTT DoCoMo (i-mode)
Korea	*	***		***	*
	e.g. Samsung, LG	e.g. Samsung, LG		e.g. Samsung, LG	e.g. SK Telecom (Cyworld)
Taiwan		***	***	**	
		e.g. TSMC, UMC	e.g. Acer, Peripherals manufacturers	e.g. OEM producers	
China	**		**	*	*
	e.g. Huawei, ZTE, Datang		e.g. Lenovo, China Great Wall	e.g. OEM producers	e.g. Baidu

Note: [1] Global competitiveness: *** = very strong, ** = strong, * = medium.
Source: M. Fransman.

the small computer market). In telecoms equipment, despite some exceptions (e.g. Samsung's wireless broadband, WiBro, products), Korea is not particularly strong. In the upper layers there are some examples of Korean international competitiveness (such as SK Telecom's Cyworld that is similar to the US virtual reality website, Second Life) although in general the country's competitiveness here is medium.

The big success stories in Taiwan have been in computers (mainly computer peripherals such as monitors, keyboards, mice and motherboards, although companies such as Acer have overall strengths in computers) and in semiconductors (dominated by two large companies, TSMC and UMC, but with many medium-sized companies involved in semiconductor design activities). In consumer electronics Taiwanese companies are strong but not as strong as their Japanese and Korean counterparts. As in computers they tend to specialise in consumer electronic sub-systems. However, in the upper layers there is little evident Taiwanese strength.

China is strong (and has growing strengths) in telecoms equipment and computers. In the former area the outstanding success story is Huawei that is currently making a significant impact on global telecoms equipment markets. Other companies in this field include ZTE and Datang as well as Ningbo Bird in mobile phones. In computers the success story is Lenovo, which has acquired IBM's PC subsidiary. China is rapidly becoming stronger in consumer electronics, partly as a result of the migration to China of production in this area from Japan, Korea and Taiwan. A number of local medium-sized firms have emerged and are battling to find market niches in China and accumulate the competencies and innovativeness that will allow them to compete in the Chinese market with more sophisticated East Asian and Western companies.

However, while it is relatively easy to *describe* East Asian international competitiveness in the ICT ecosystem, it is far more difficult to *explain* why and how this competitiveness has emerged. This is attempted in the following section.

Explaining East Asian competitiveness in the ICT ecosystem

Very different development trajectories in ICT have been followed by the four East Asian countries examined here. In some cases these differing trajectories have resulted in international competitiveness in the same sectors; in other cases the trajectories have conferred distinctive strengths and weaknesses on the countries concerned. These trajectories are summarised in exhibit A8.2. Similarly, industrial structures are also very different in the four countries, as we shall shortly see. In the following sub-sections the different trajectories and development patterns in the four East Asian countries are analysed.

Japan[2]

The birth of the Japanese ICT sector can be traced back to the nineteenth-century communications sub-sector, beginning with the telegraph and later the telephone. It was the powerful Ministry of Communications (*Teishinsho*) that assumed responsibility for the provision of this (and other) important infrastructure. However, from the very beginning the Ministry decided that while government would play the role of network operator (it was only after the Second World War that responsibility for the telecoms network was allocated to a spun-off state-owned company, NTT), the necessary equipment would be provided by the private sector. Moreover, it was decided that several companies – rather than one – should manufacture this equipment.

In this way, the so-called 'Den Den Family' was born. At the head of this family was the Ministry of Communications (and later, NTT). Its role was to take the lead in defining, standardising and designing the equipment that was needed, in procuring it, in constructing the networks and in delivering services over them to final customers. The other family members would cooperate with the Ministry in the definition, standardisation and design of the equipment but would assume sole responsibility for manufacture and supply.

From the Ministry's point of view, a number of important advantages followed from this form of industrial organisation. First, there was a degree of competition between the equipment-supplying companies (what the present author has called 'controlled competition'). This provided an incentive for the companies to make innovative improvements. (Significantly, in the USA AT&T vertically integrated its major equipment supplier, Western Electric, which was fully owned. This meant the absence of the degree of competition that existed in Japan.) Secondly, the large market provided by the Ministry

[2] This section draws on Fransman (1995a).

Exhibit A8.2. ICT trajectories in East Asian countries, 2006

Country	Trajectory
Japan	*Evolving from communications infrastructure* • Late nineteenth century: telegraph and telephone • Ministry of Communications (*Teishinsho*) + Japanese universities (e.g. Imperial University of Tokyo) • Indigenous equipment suppliers: e.g. NEC (Western Electric), Fujitsu (Siemens), Hitachi, Toshiba (GE) • Post-war entry into semiconductors and computers (with assistance from MITI) • Distinct consumer electronics companies, e.g. Matsushita, Sony, Sharp, Sanyo
Korea	*'Bottom-up' learning from consumer electronics* • Korean companies begin assembling simple consumer products such as radios and black and white TVs, e.g. LG, Samsung, Daewoo, Hyundai (1950s and 1960s) • Industrial structure: conglomerates (*chaebol*) • Strong state: pre-1960s protection of infant-industry learning; from 1960s emphasising exports and incentives and government research institutes (e.g. ETRI, KAIST) • Suited to consumer electronics and semiconductors (especially memories) but not to computers or software; relatively weak in telecoms equipment • Early 2000s: highly dynamic Korean ICT industry, e.g. greatest broadband penetration in the world facilitating equipment innovation (e.g. Samsung's WiBro broadband wireless); dynamic services market, e.g. SK Telecom's Cyworld
Taiwan	*'Bottom-up' learning from consumer electronics* • Taiwanese companies begin as low-cost assemblers for US and Japanese firms (1950s and 1960s) • Government plays key role: pre-1960s protecting infant-industry learning; after 1960s incentivising exports, helping to insert Taiwanese firms into global production chains, particularly in computers (peripherals) and semiconductors; creating supportive R&D institutes (e.g. ITRI, ERSO and III) • Industrial structure: flexible networked SMEs inserted into global production chains but increasing their capabilities (e.g. in design) and in some cases own-brand design and manufacture (e.g. Acer in PCs) (from 1980s) • Post-1990s: increasing integration into mainland China

Exhibit A8.2. (*cont.*)

Country	Trajectory
China	*'Top-down' learning from government strategic scientific research institutes* • Chinese companies in computers and telecoms equipment evolve from government scientific research institutes (e.g. under Chinese Academy of Sciences) established after 1949 • Based on dynamic Chinese market some achieve international competitiveness (e.g. Lenovo in PCs and Huawei and ZTE in telecoms equipment) (largely from 1990s) • Many less prominent Chinese firms emerge contesting the domestic market in areas such as consumer electronics (e.g. DVDs) and mobile phones (e.g. Ningbo Bird) • China developing its ICT firms under a more liberal trade regime than the other East Asian countries due to World Trade Organisation (WTO) membership; but large dynamic domestic market gives additional policy tool • In telecoms services four state-owned Chinese companies create dynamic infrastructure and services (i.e. China Telecom, China Mobile, China Netcom, China Unicom) • The big question: How can Chinese companies become more innovative (creating internal capabilities) and achieve international competitiveness?

Source: M. Fransman.

provided a further incentive for the companies to give of their best. Thirdly, close coordination and standardisation was facilitated by this arrangement.

In order to provide further incentives while cementing the basis for cooperation the Ministry (and later NTT) tacitly agreed that the Den Den Family would be closed to outsiders. While this eliminated the threat of competition from new entrants it provided an incentive for the equipment suppliers to make high sunk-cost investments. Since the Ministry/NTT controlled the purse strings it was in command and used its position of considerable strength to insist on innovation, quality, cooperation and timely delivery. As the author's book, *Japan's Computer and Communications Industry* (Fransman 1995a) shows in detail (in areas such as switching, computing and optical fibre), this mode of industrial organisation allowed Japan to catch up rapidly with the USA and Europe and make some important innovations.

The four equipment suppliers in the Den Den Family were NEC, Fujitsu, Hitachi and Oki. With the exception of Hitachi, the other firms established close links with prominent Western counterparts that facilitated an effective mode of technology transfer and learning. NEC, which quickly became the strongest of the suppliers, was established in 1899 by Iwadare, a Japanese businessman who entered into a joint venture with AT&T's Western Electric. In the early 1900s, Fujitsu was established as a joint venture between its parent, Fuji Electric, and Siemens, which was the main German telecoms equipment supplier (as well as being a major producer of electrical equipment).

However, the Japanese companies were not simply passive consumers of technology supplied by their far stronger Western partners. Rather they actively learned, using every opportunity to increase their own technological and innovative capabilities. The fact that they had majority ownership and control of their companies created the incentive. Their goal was to stand on their own two feet as soon as possible and to reap the financial rewards of so doing.

But apart from government procurement, which was crucial, they were also helped by the Japanese state in other ways. One example was the high-quality engineers they were able to employ who had been trained by some of the centres of excellence that had been established in Japanese universities, such as the Imperial University of Tokyo (later Tokyo University). Since the Meiji Restoration from 1868 Japan had given high priority to the establishment of high-quality engineering faculties, originally with Western staffing and training, and they provided the skills base for these and other Japanese companies. Another example was government protection and nurturing of infant industry learning through the imposition of quotas and tariffs and other protective instruments.

Apart from the Den Den equipment suppliers – NEC, Fujitsu, Hitachi and Oki – a number of other companies also became prominent. Foremost among these was Toshiba which established a partnership with General Electric in the USA and became a major electrical equipment supplier. Toshiba was established in 1939 through the merger of two companies – one established in 1875 that was one of the first manufacturers of telegraph equipment and the second set up in 1890 as a producer of incandescent electrical lamps. Another example was Mitsubishi Electric which was spun-off in 1921 from the Mitsubishi

Group's shipbuilding company (now called Mitsubishi Heavy Industries) in order to focus on ship-related electrical products.

There were also smaller telecoms equipment suppliers, a sort of second-tier membership of the Den Den Family, including Sumitomo Electric, Furukawa and Fujikura. Non-telecoms companies established in the pre-war period that would go on to become important players in the ICT sector included Canon, established in 1933 by Goro Yoshida and his brother-in-law Saburo Uchida. The original aim was to develop camera technology and in 1934 the company patented its first camera.

Significantly, the consumer electronic companies evolved in an entirely different context. Here the leading company was Matsushita (producing the National and Panasonic brands). The company was founded by Konosuke Matsushita in 1918, his first product being a light socket. In 1927 the company produced its first real success, a bicycle lamp, sold under the National brand name. Another consumer electronics company was Sharp, founded in 1912 by Tokuji Hayakawa. Its first major product was the mechanical pencil invented by its founder. When the factory was destroyed by the Kanto earthquake in 1923 it was relocated to Osaka and began producing the first Japanese radio sets.

It was around the time of the Second World War that the ICT sector proper emerged, totally transforming all the companies discussed here. This was the result of two radical and increasingly interconnected innovations: computers and semiconductors. Although these innovations originated in the USA and Europe, the indigenous capabilities of these companies made them fertile ground for the adoption and mastery of these innovations, their efforts being greatly assisted by the supportive efforts of the Japanese state.

In the field of telecommunications NTT continued the work of the pre-war Ministry of Communications. In the fields of computers and semiconductors the Ministry of International Trade and Industry (MITI) played a key role in providing trade protection, subsidised credit, assistance from government-funded research institutes (such as its Electro-Technical Laboratory, ETL), inter-firm coordination (where this was not precluded by strong inter-firm competitive rivalries) and help in entering foreign markets (through JETRO, the Japan External Trade Organisation).

Under the stimulus of post-war reconstruction and a rapidly – growing domestic economy (particularly after the 1960s), the new opportunities created by the waves of Schumpeterian change in ICT and other areas and a growing international competitiveness enabled these companies to forge ahead. After 1945 they were joined by a number of new companies, particularly in the consumer electronics area.

One of these was Sony. Sony was started in 1945 when Masaru Ibuka began a radio repair shop in a Tokyo that had been destroyed by war-time bombing. The following year he was joined by Akio Morita, and one of their first successful products was an electrical rice cooker. But both men had good backgrounds in electrical engineering, skills that they had enhanced in carrying out their war-time army duties. These skills were in evidence when, in the early 1950s, they visited AT&T's Bell Laboratories, eventually managing to persuade the company to licence use of the transistor (invented in the Bell Labs by Shockley and his associates in 1948). While the Bell Labs researchers were sceptical that the transistor – invented as an outcome of an attempt to improve telecommunications transmission technologies – would have useful applications in the field of consumer goods, Sony went on to develop the first commercially successful transistorised radios.

Another post-war consumer electronics company was Sanyo, which was founded in 1947 by Toshio Iue, the brother-in-law of Konosuke Matsushita and a former employee of the Matsushita Corporation. Sanyo followed the same path as Matsushita, beginning as a bicycle lamp manufacturer and in the 1950s diversifing its product range into plastic radios and washing machines.

With this corporate structure in place and with the capabilities that had been accumulated in these companies Japan was excellently positioned to take advantage of the new opportunities that would unfold in the ICT ecosystem from the 1960s to the present day.

Korea

Korean economic development also owes a great deal to the ICT sector. In both consumer electronics and semiconductors (largely memories and displays) Korea is among the top countries in the world. However, the evolutionary path that Korea followed was in many respects very different from that taken in Japan. In ICT there have been three undisputed Korean corporate leaders: Samsung Electronics, LG Electronics and Hynix (originally Hyundai Electronics). The rise to global prominence of Samsung in particular has been both rapid and remarkable.

Among the ICT companies included in the *Financial Times Top 500* Global Companies in 2006, Samsung came sixth after Microsoft, Cisco, IBM, Vodafone and Intel and ahead of any Japanese company. Samsung's market capitalisation (the basis on which the *Top 500* are ranked) was $107 billion, compared to $114 billion for Intel and $133 billion for Cisco. Although outperformed by Samsung, LG-Electronics has also been a major success story in areas such as displays, memory semiconductors and mobile phones. In semiconductors (mainly memories) Hynix is the second Korean company, after Samsung, in the world's top twenty. How was this remarkable performance achieved? To answer this question it is necessary to begin with the companies that have been the engine of growth.

Samsung was founded in 1938 by Byung-Chull Lee in Taegu, Korea, as an export business selling dried Korean fish, fruit and veg to Manchuria and Beijing. But it was only from the 1950s, after the Second World War (when Japan was forced to end its colonial occupation of Korea) and after the Korean War, that Samsung was able to start growing rapidly through diversification. Early diversification included sugar manufacturing, flour milling, confectionery machinery and insurance. By the time the Samsung Corporation (established in 1951) entered the ICT field in 1969 it was already an established rapidly growing conglomerate. In 1969 Samsung established Samsung Electronics, originally as a joint venture with the Japanese company Sanyo.

LG was originally established by Koo Inhoe in 1947. The company, named Lucky Chemical Industrial Corp., originally produced a cosmetic called Lucky Cream. During the Korean War the company entered the plastics field, originally producing plastic lids for cosmetic bottles. Soon the product range was extended to include items such as combs, soap containers, toothbrushes and tableware, later, toothpaste was added to the list. In 1958 the company diversified into radios establishing Goldstar (later LG Electronics) which produced Korea's first radio in 1959, exactly ten years before Samsung Electronics started.

The processes by which Samsung and LG entered the ICT sector are relevant.[3] For LG the story is one of a creative entrepreneurial decision to begin producing locally a product – Korea's first vacuum tube AM radio – that was in growing demand. But how does a company

---

[3] This account draws on Kim (1997). I am indebted to the late Professor Kim for many discussions over the years about the process of Korea's economic development.

involved in the areas just outlined diversify into the completely new field of radios? Two events clinched the entry. The first was the decision to employ an experienced German engineer in order to broaden and deepen LG's technological capabilities. At around the same time the company's president arranged to visit several leading electronics firms in Japan, Europe and the USA. These two events led to the decision to enter this field. A Japanese AM radio served as a model, and was reverse-engineered.

While these Korean companies constituted the engine of the emerging ICT sector it was the Korean state that created the supportive environment that made their efforts both feasible and profitable. Determined that the country should pull itself up by its own bootstraps Korean government officials developed industrial policies designed to facilitate the process. Until the mid-1960s Korean industrial policy relied largely on import substitution aimed at providing a protected local market for Korean companies. Strict controls were enforced, limiting the ability of foreign companies to compete in these markets. In some sectors – including cars, steel, shipbuilding and agriculture – high effective rates of protection (i.e. protection on value added) led to rapid industrialisation. In electronics, however, progress was slower until the late 1960s.

From the mid-1960s the Korean government (along with the Taiwanese government) began increasingly to incentivise exports. Crucially, however, a high rate of protection on the prioritised sectors was maintained. This policy of 'walking on two legs' – emphasising both export orientation and at the same time import substitution – allowed the government to create high-powered incentives for Korean companies to accumulate the necessary capabilities in the protected domestic market while at the same time honing their international competitiveness in international export markets. An additional raft of measures added to these incentives, including the granting by state-owned financial institutions of subsidised credit at below market rates to companies that performed well in export markets, tax concessions and foreign loan guarantees. These incentives in effect forced Korean firms to become internationally competitive while they enjoyed protection in local markets.[4]

---

[4] It is worth noting that for a long time influential organisations such as the World Bank failed to understand the true significance of Korea's industrial policy, choosing instead to focus exclusively on the export-orientation side of government policy while ignoring the protection that went with it.

The Korean government was also quick to realise that the ICT sector had particularly important potential for the country's development. In 1969 the government passed the Electronics Industry Promotion Act, accompanying this with the Long-term Electronics Industry Promotion Plan and the Electronics Industry Promotion Fund, which gave preferential funding at subsidised rates to electronics companies. It was within this context that the Samsung Corporation made its decision to enter the ICT sector with the establishment in 1969 of Samsung Electronics. Subsequently, Hyundai and Daewoo, two other large Korean conglomerates, also entered.

In the mid-1960s the Korean ICT companies began to produce black and white TV sets, often relying initially on Japanese and US technology. Later they moved on to colour TV, microwave ovens, semiconductors and displays. As they became an increasing competitive threat to their erstwhile technology suppliers so the Korean companies were forced to turn to alternative sources of technology such as smaller US high-tech companies and Korean engineers living in the USA. At the same time they accumulated their own R&D capabilities, building increasingly sophisticated R&D organisations.

Over the succeeding years a number of important government research institutes were created that worked closely with Korean ICT companies, encouraging them to cooperate where possible (although fierce rivalry between the companies often limited cooperation) and offering them both technology and trained person-power. These institutes included the Korea Institute of Science and Technology (KIST), the Korea Institute of Electronic Technology (KIET), the Electronics and Telecommunications Research Institute (ETRI) and the Korea Advanced Institute of Science and Technology (KAIST). These institutes played an important role from the 1970s to the early 1990s, although thereafter, with significantly increasing R&D capabilities in both Korea and abroad, the large Korean ICT companies came to rely less and less on R&D from government institutes.

By the early 1990s Korea had become the fourth largest producer of electronic products in the world and was second in consumer electronics after Japan. However, this success did not extend to all parts of the ICT ecosystem. While the large Korean conglomerates (*chaebol*) proved adept in becoming internationally competitive in areas such as consumer electronics, memory semiconductors, displays and, later, mobile phones, they found it more difficult to make their mark globally in fields such as computers and software. Nevertheless, their areas of strength in ICT were sufficient to make Korea a major global power in this industry.

Taiwan[5]

Taiwan's main ICT success has been in the area of computer hardware. By the mid-1990s Taiwan produced 72 per cent of the world's computer mice, 65 per cent of keyboards, 65 per cent of computer motherboards, 64 per cent of scanners, 57 per cent of computer monitors and 27 per cent of notebook PCs (the largest market share in the world). How was this remarkable position achieved?

In the 1950s, as in Korea, a number of small Taiwanese firms began to produce simple electronic products such as radios. However, it was from the 1960s that substantial production of these kinds of products took off. The initial stimulus was foreign companies – largely big Japanese electronics companies, including Matsushita and Sanyo – sourcing assembly and some component production in low-cost Taiwan. US companies such as Texas Instruments and General Instruments also became involved in Taiwan at this time.

From the late 1970s a few Taiwanese firms began assembling imported PC kits. However, it was in the 1980s – after the world PC market began growing rapidly following the launch in 1981 of the IBM PC and the emergence of IBM-clones – that the production of computer components became a substantial business in Taiwan. Again, the driving force was foreign multinational corporations (MNCs) searching for a low-cost production base. It was these foreign companies that became the engine of growth, unlike in Japan and Korea where large indigenous firms played that role.

Small and medium-sized Taiwanese entrepreneurs (SMEs) responded enthusiastically to these new business opportunities. They set up as suppliers and sub-contractors to the MNCs. Many of them – like Stan Shih, the founder of Acer, which would become Taiwan's largest computer company – had received engineering training in Taiwanese universities and had already engaged in the production of simple electronic products. (Shih had developed Taiwan's first electronic desk-top calculator and designed a watch pen.) Others furthered their training in

---

[5] This section draws on Dedrick and Kraemer (1998).

the MNCs operating in Taiwan and then left to establish firms to supply their former employers.

Although this response from Taiwanese SMEs was entrepreneurially driven, the Taiwanese government played a crucial supportive role. From as early as the 1960s, sensing that an important new area of economic activity was emerging, the government created incentives for the infant suppliers. These included subsidised credit from government financial institutions as well as benefits provided in export processing zones (EPZs).

From the late 1970s a powerful new government impetus was provided by K.T. Li, who had been Minister of Finance and was now Minister of Economic Affairs. He prioritised both the computer and semiconductor sectors, recognising their potential as engines of Taiwan's growth. With his support several well-funded government programmes were launched aimed at supporting the Taiwanese SMEs involved in these sectors. In addition, he cemented ties with foreign MNCs, persuading some of their leading executives to join his advisory panel. This helped to ensure that Taiwan would become an even more suitable base for these multinationals.[6]

A further crucial role played by the Taiwanese government involved government R&D institutes. Of these, the most prominent was a remarkable institution, the Industrial Technology Research Institute (ITRI). Government-owned and funded, the role of ITRI is to support the technical and innovative capabilities of Taiwanese SMEs, not only in the ICT area but also in other fields such as computer numerically controlled (CNC) machine tools (where the institute played a crucial role in facilitating Taiwanese international competitiveness[7]).

ITRI evolved in order to overcome a significant weakness in Taiwan's industrial structure, which stemmed from the small and medium size of most Taiwanese firms in the high-tech sector that prevented these firms from developing substantial R&D organisations

[6] Years later, a senior executive in one of Japan's best-known ICT companies told me how the company had been 'invited' by the Taiwanese government to establish a new R&D organisation in the country. Asked how the Japanese company had responded the executive replied that since they were heavily involved in the production of electronic products in Taiwan they had little choice but to comply, even though they had no particular desire to do R&D in the country.

[7] For further details about the role of ITRI in the development of CNC machine tools in Taiwan, see Fransman (1986).

and capabilities. The importance of SMEs was and is the main feature distinguishing Taiwan's industrial structure in the ICT sector from those in Japan and Korea where large companies dominated. ITRI's large number of well-qualified engineers[8] would develop internationally competitive prototypes in selected areas that could then be transferred (at a subsidised price) to numbers of Taiwanese SMEs, thus allowing the institute to benefit from economies of scale. Close interaction with these 'customers' ensured that ITRI's products were competitiveness-enhancing (although on occasion there were some complaints that their prototypes tended to be overdesigned and engineered, reflecting the institute's research interests).[9]

An important example is in the field of computers. Here ITRI's subsidiary, the Electronics Research and Services Organisation (ERSO), reverse-engineered IBM's BIOS (basic input–output system, the built-in software that determines what a computer can do without accessing programs from a disk) thus allowing Taiwanese IBM-clone manufacturers to enter the market without paying royalties to IBM. This reduced an important entry barrier. Another significant ITRI subsidiary is the Computer and Communication Research Laboratory (CCL). However, a similar subsidiary – the Institute for Information Industries (III) – established with the support of several MNCs and aimed at developing software capabilities in Taiwan, has been less successful. As we shall see shortly, ITRI also made a huge impact on the Taiwanese semiconductor industry through its fabrication facilities, its prototypes and, most significantly, through the spin-off of what would become some of the largest semiconductor companies in the world, Taiwan Semiconductor Manufacturing Corporation (TSMC) and United Microelectronics Company (UMC) (two of Taiwan's three largest R&D performers).

Out of this context emerged Taiwan's unique industrial organisational structure, consisting of a layered network of Taiwanese firms

---

[8] Many of these Taiwanese engineers came from outstanding US R&D laboratories, such as Bell Labs and IBM's laboratories, both of which laid off many researchers in the 1990s.

[9] But why did Taiwanese SMEs not rapidly consolidate and grow in size through MAs? When I asked this question in Taiwan I was often given by way of reply the Chinese proverb: 'Better the head of a chicken than the tail of a cow' – i.e. Taiwanese entrepreneurs tended to want to remain their own bosses. This constrains the growth of large companies.

which itself was inserted into the global production chains that dominated the world of computer producing firms. At the head of these chains are the main computer companies such as Dell, IBM, Hewlett Packard, Apple, NEC, Toshiba and Fujitsu. Within Taiwan itself there were three layers of firms: the first consisted of a handful of large companies; secondly a larger number of medium-sized firms; and finally many small firms producing relatively simple components.

The strength of this industrial organisational structure lay in the high-powered market incentives that it created, the competencies that it required participating firms to acquire and the flexibility that the network as a whole thrived on. These three characteristics resulted in high quality together with low price, which in turn guaranteed Taiwan a prominent place in the international division of labour in the computer sector. They also facilitated a formidable process of learning that enabled Taiwanese firms to constantly upgrade their capabilities, moving from original equipment manufacture (OEM) to own-design manufacture.

Flexibility was a particularly important characteristic given the rapid changes that occur in both the design and technology of computer and consumer goods components. The Taiwanese network proved to be particularly adept at adapting rapidly to the required changes. The large number of potential suppliers of any particular component, together with market selection by players further up the global production chain, created an effective evolutionary process that selected the fittest who were able to produce what was required and gave them the resources they needed. Those that were insufficiently fit dropped out. The proof of this pudding lies in the Taiwanese market shares referred to at the start of this sub-section.

Further proof is provided by the relative failure of the large Korean conglomerates to make much headway in the computer industry until the most successful, like Samsung, re-entered this market in the early 2000s, making use of synergies with their other consumer products. The in-house production of components including semiconductors gave the Korean companies a significant international competitiveness in areas such as TVs, memories, displays, microwave ovens, digital cameras and mobile phones. Further advantage came from their R&D laboratories, from intra-conglomerate financing and from their global marketing prowess strengthened by the increasing recognition of their brands. They were also able to benefit from economies of scale. But in the area of computers Taiwan was the better performer, and flexibility was one of the major reasons why.

Taiwan's increasing design capabilities in semiconductors were particularly important giving the country a key role in both the design and fabrication of the chips that powered not only computers but also the new mass-produced ICT products such as mobile phones, MP3 players, digital cameras and digital TVs. As mentioned earlier, Taiwan's two major semiconductor companies are TSMC and UMC. These are also Taiwan's main R&D performers. UMC was established in 1979 as a spin-off from ITRI's ERSO, created as a commercial semiconductor company to generate profit from the organisation's research. In 1983 UMC began very large-scale integrated circuit (VLSI) production in partnership with the Silicon Valley company, Vitelic, that had been established by overseas Chinese. TSMC, now far larger than UMC, was set up in 1985 as another spin-off from ERSO. The Taiwanese government provided almost half of the capital, with Philips giving just over a quarter. In 2005 TSMC ranked eighth in the world in terms of revenue, ahead of Japanese semiconductor companies such as NEC, Sony, Matsushita and Sharp.[10] UMC was eighteenth. The second-ranking company was Samsung, which had just over twice TSMC's revenue. First came Intel, by far the largest semiconductor company in the world.

Acer, Taiwan's largest computer company, was founded in 1976 by Stan Shih and four partners. Shih had previously cut his technical teeth in simple electronic consumer products, producing a desk-top calculator and watch pen in Taiwan. Graduating from the National Chiao Tung University in Taiwan, Shih had obtained a BSc and MSc in Electrical Engineering. At first Acer provided consulting services but in 1981, the year the IBM PC was launched, the company sold a PC self-assembly kit. The following year assembly of IBM-compatible PCs began. These used the IBM BIOS that had been reverse-engineered in ERSO. In the 1980s Acer grew rapidly, allowing it in the following

[10] A key role in the development of TSMC was played by Morris Chang, who had been vice-president of Texas Instruments and president of General Instrument. He became director of ITRI and later chairman of TSMC. This example, together with the role played by Taiwanese researchers who had previously worked for distinguished US R&D laboratories such as Bell Labs and IBM's laboratories, highlights the significant contribution that US corporations and institutions played in the development of Taiwan's ICT industry.

decade to acquire several US computer companies. Joint ventures were also important, such as Acer's venture with Texas Instruments in the area of dynamic random access memories (DRAMs). In 2005 Acer was ranked eighth in the world desk-top computer market and fifth in the world computer market, ahead of such companies as NEC, Sony and Apple.

Hon Hai Precision is another world-leading player in the ICT industry and the third-largest R&D performer in Taiwan. Hon Hai is one of the largest contract electronics manufacturers in the world, holding third spot after leaders Solectron and Flextronics. Its customers include Dell, Cisco, Apple and Sony. The company was founded by Terry Gou in 1974 to make plastic switches for televisions.

In 1981 the company began producing the product that would fuel its early growth, the connector sockets that allowed memory modules to be added to PCs. With revenue from connectors and assistance from the Taiwanese government in the form of tax incentives and credit subsidies Hon Hai began to make other components for computers, going on to specialise in the manufacture of computers, consumer electronics and communications products. In 1994 Hon Hai established R&D centres in the USA and Japan and during the following two years the company invested heavily in production facilities in Scotland, Ireland and the USA. In 2001 Hon Hai became Taiwan's largest manufacturing company and was also a substantial manufacturer and exporter in China. Moving up the components value chain Hon Hai has become a significant original design manufacturer and it also offers design engineering and manufacturing services.

China

The Chinese development trajectory in the ICT sector has been fundamentally different from the three other East Asian countries examined here. Characterising the key difference, one Chinese scholar, the late Qiwen Lu, has labelled the Chinese trajectory a 'top-down process'.[11]

What does Qiwen Lu mean by 'top-down'? Lu argues that in both Korea and Taiwan the trajectory of development in the ICT sector was 'bottom-up' in the sense that activity began with the low-skill, low-tech activities of assembly of consumer electronic products such

---

[11] Lu (2003). The present section draws on Lu's work.

as radios and black and white TVs. The next step up the learning ladder involved the local production of basic components (including items such as simple devices, plastic casings, etc.). Only much later, after a good deal of learning, technology mastering and technology capability acquisition, were Korean and Taiwanese ICT companies able to design their own products and compete with them in international markets. Own-brand production had to wait even longer.

In China, by contrast, internationally competitive activity in key parts of the ICT sector emerged from the relatively sophisticated science and technology institutions that had already been created during the pre-reform Communist period, principally under the auspices of the Chinese Academy of Science (CAS). In this sense the process was top-down, beginning with science and technology and moving on to design, manufacturing, distribution and marketing.

The key example is computers. Not surprisingly, after the pioneering progress made in the area of computers in the decade after the Second World War, China was quick to identify this field as a national priority. Indeed, China's first long-term development plan for science and technology, introduced in 1955, prioritised computers as one of six key areas. The first home-grown Chinese computer was developed in 1958, modelled on a Soviet computer. Significantly, it was developed by the Institute of Computing Technology, the Chinese Academy of Science's premier computer research institute.

However, by the time China's major post-Mao economic reforms were introduced after 1978 it was already clear that the 'Chinese System' was not working effectively in the computer field. A major part of the problem was organisational. Specifically, research institutes were organised vertically under the Chinese Academy of Science or different ministries (such as the Ministry of Electronic Industries). They acted as fragmented silos, having little to do with one another. Even more importantly, they had little interaction with the enterprises charged with manufacturing computers (that themselves were separated from the commercial enterprises that had responsibility for marketing and distribution). Reinforcing this insulation and fragmentation were disincentives that minimised interactions. Researchers had little incentive to find out about the ways in which their knowledge could be put to commercial use by the enterprises, which in turn had few incentives to innovate. While this organisational arrangement may have yielded reasonable results in the case of an unchanging product – standard working-class housing, where China like the Soviet Union did relatively well in a short period, is an example – it was totally ineffective in the fast-moving area of computers.

Responding to the lack of progress, a major reform of the Chinese science and technology system was introduced in 1985. One immediate effect of this reform was to cut significantly the budgets of research institutes while allowing them to experiment with the establishment of a new breed of enterprises that could generate a replacing income. These were called science and technology enterprises (*keji qiye*). At a stroke this created the incentives for the marrying of R&D, manufacturing, marketing and distribution functionalities. Although in many cases funding for these enterprises was provided by the research institute (but not by national or local government budgets) which formally owned all or some of the enterprises, the managements of the enterprises were given full autonomy in running the business. This autonomy extended to key decisions in areas such as innovation, diversification, joint ventures, funding and employment.

Like children encouraged to stand on their own feet and find their own way in the world the new science and technology enterprises at first still enjoyed the protection of their erstwhile parents. Accordingly, they were able to get funding from the parent research institute and draw on its scientific and technological expertise (including employing part-time or full-time key experts from the institute). In this way China gave birth to a new kind of enterprise, one that was neither state-owned and controlled nor privately owned and controlled but which, nonetheless, was able to function efficiently, to innovate and to grow rapidly. This is how three of China's four main computer companies evolved; Legend (that later became Lenovo, in 2005 acquiring IBM's iconic PC subsidiary), Stone and Founder. The fourth company, China Great Wall, was a more conventional state-owned enterprise (SOE) under the guidance of the Ministry of Electronic Industries.

The state also attempted to assist the fledgling computer industry in other ways. One of these was through import-substituting protection. In the 1980s higher tariffs were imposed on imported computers than were placed on imported knocked-down assembly kits, the aim being to encourage economic activity based on the latter. However, this attempt at creating import-substituting industrialisation in the area of computers was not particularly successful.

Exhibit A8.3. *Global PC market share, 2006*

Company	Global market share (%)
HP	16.3
Dell	16.1
Lenovo	7.5
Acer	5.9

Source: *Wall Street Journal*, 10–12 November 2006.

One important obstacle was the lack of Chinese-language processing facilities in the computers of the day. It was in overcoming this obstacle through sophisticated indigenous innovation that the four companies referred to were able to get their break, in the process setting themselves on the path that would allow them to compete effectively with the world's major computer companies and become major players in their own right. Significantly, the Chinese-language processing expertise that was used by the companies came from the scientific research institutes. With these capabilities and the Chinese-language applications that they facilitated the four Chinese computer companies were able to grow rapidly.

Lenovo emerged as China's main success story in computers. Its success was underlined when it embarked on a bold strategy of globalisation and in 2005 acquired IBM PC, the company that gave birth to both the era of mass PC-based computing and the Wintel standard that assured Microsoft and Intel a privileged place in this new industry. Lenovo's global PC market share in 2006 is shown in exhibit A8.3.

Conclusion

These brief analyses of the four East Asian countries have focused on the earliest period when the necessary conditions were put in place that would later lead to a sustainable learning-based growth trajectory. It was this trajectory that led ultimately to these countries becoming major players in layer 1 of the global new ICT ecosystem.

Appendix 9: China's telecoms service providers in layer 2

Inevitably – because of its size, its rapid growth and its strategic positioning in the global economy – China will come to play an important role in the global new ICT ecosystem. In appendix 8, China's position in layer 1, the networked elements layer, was considered. In this appendix some tentative comments are offered regarding the Chinese approach in layer 2, the network operation layer.

Is there a distinctive Chinese model for telecoms services in layer 2?

History of the Chinese telecoms services industry

A brief history of the Chinese telecoms services industry is provided in exhibit A9.1.

Competition in the Chinese telecoms services industry

On the face of it, there is little competition in the Chinese telecoms services industry. In the fixed area, the two major companies – China Telecom and China Netcom – are separated geographically and have limited competitive relationships with one another. Furthermore, although China Unicom is the only operator to be licensed to deliver both fixed and mobile services (both CDMA and GSM, though it concentrates on the former), its competition in fixed services with the two main fixed operators is limited in extent. However, this account is misleading since it ignores the extent of competitive forces in the Chinese telecoms services industry.

To begin with, there is competition in mobile between China Mobile and China Unicom. However, there is significantly more competition than just this. First, there is competition between *services*, to be distinguished from competition between *companies*. Services competition

Exhibit A9.1. *A brief history of the Chinese telecoms services industry*

Date	Events
Until 1994	1. Until 1994 the **Ministry of Posts and Telecommunications (MPT)** provided telecoms services through its monopoly, **China Telecom.**
	2. In 1994, due to pressure from other ministries and customers, the Chinese government introduced a competitor to China Telecom, namely **China Unicom** (which gained responsibility both for fixed and mobile services).
1998–2002	1. In 1998, in a reorganisation of ministries, MPT was replaced by the new **Ministry of Information Industry (MII)** that took responsibility for the entire ICT sector. As one of its responsibilities MII was charged with telecoms regulation.
	2. In 1999, China Telecom was split into three: the new **China Telecom**; **China Mobile** (with responsibility for mobile); and **China Satcom** (responsible for satellite communications).
	3. In 2002, China Telecom was split again. The newest **China Telecom**, with about 70 per cent of the old company's resources, covered the populous south and the west, including Shanghai and Guangzhou (Canton). **China Netcom (CNC)**, with 30 per cent of the resources, was given responsibility for the north, including Beijing.
	4. **China Railcom**, with a network based on the rail network, was the final and by far the smallest network operator.
Post-2001	1. 11 December 2001: China joined the **WTO.**
	2. Under WTO rules, China has allowed a small degree of foreign ownership of the state-owned Chinese network operators.
	3. As part of its WTO commitments China is reportedly examining the possibility of a new telecoms regulator independent from MII.
Conclusion	Since 1994 the Chinese telecoms services industry has changed from a **state-run monopolistic industry** to a **state-run oligopolistic industry.**

Source: M. Fransman.

takes a number of forms. There is competition between fixed and
mobile services with substitutability between these two putting significant pressure on the two fixed operators, China Telecom and
China Netcom.

But in addition, China Telecom and China Netcom also compete
with China Mobile through an adapted low-cost Chinese mobile
service called *Xiaolingtong*. This service is based on the Personal
Access System (PAS) and the Personal Handy Phone System (PHS).
(PHS had a brief period of popularity in Japan before it was replaced
by more expensive cellular mobile services, although it continues to be
used largely for data communications.) Essentially, *Xiaolingtong* consists of a wireless local loop which gives the consumer access to the
fixed-line network. Although, therefore, it provides mobility, it is
primarily a fixed-line service thus giving both China Telecom and
China Netcom the opportunity to compete in mobile services with
China Mobile and China Unicom. *Xiaolingtong* is cheaper than the
mobile services offered by the latter two companies and has proved
well suited to dense urban populations. Currently there are well over
50 million users of this service.

At the time of writing significant uncertainty still hangs over the
future of mobile 3G in China. The delay is an indication of how
complex bureaucratic decision-making can be in the Chinese telecoms
system where everything – companies, bureaucrats and regulators – is
in the state sector. However, having said this, China is pressing on with
its own standard for 3G mobile communications, TD-SCDMA.[1]
Although foreign companies such as Siemens have played a role in
the development of this standard, it is the state-owned Chinese telecoms equipment company, Datang, that has been given responsibility
for the development of TD-SCDMA equipment.

China has a telecoms equipment market characterised by intense
competitive rivalry between foreign companies, between foreign and
Chinese companies and between Chinese companies themselves. All
the main global telecoms equipment producers are heavily involved in
the Chinese market where they compete with major Chinese players
such as Huawei, ZTE (Zhongxing Telecommunications Equipment)
and Datang and, in the area of mobile handsets, companies such as
Ningbo Bird, Amoi, Konka and Keijan.

[1] TD-SCDMA stands for Time Division-Synchronous Code Division Multiple Access.

Controlled competition in the Chinese telecoms services industry

Currently, one of the distinguishing features of the Chinese telecoms services industry, at least in comparison to its Western counterparts and countries in Asia such as Japan and Korea, is the constrained role that the Chinese authorities seem to see for competition. Underlining this feature, in March 2007 a deal was struck between China Telecom and China Netcom to limit the competition between them, leaving them in firmer control of their core markets. Both companies, as we saw above, are faced with severe competition from the mobile services of China Mobile. According to China Netcom, the agreement 'is aimed at reducing malignant competition'.[2]

The reason for this approach to competition is straightforward. China needs huge amounts of investment if its infrastructure is to keep up with that in the advanced countries while being extended to the poorer and more remote rural areas. Strong competition reduces profitability which reduces the ability of network operators to invest in their networks, thus necessitating state or foreign investment or borrowing if the required network investment is to be made. According to the *Financial Times*, 'many government and company officials [in China] have long been concerned that overly fierce competition and duplicated infrastructure construction limits profits and wastes state resources'.[3]

On the other hand, the absence of strong competition means that Chinese consumers to some extent pay the price and fund the investment. However, the extent to which they do pay is limited by the existing competition that has been outlined in the previous subsection. In short, China has established its own balance in the trade-off between competition and investment.

A distinctive Chinese model?

It is too soon to tell whether these are characteristics of a specifically Chinese model or whether they are features of a transition model that will be abandoned in favour of the more pro-competition Western/Japanese

---

[2] *Financial Times*, 1 March 2007.
[3] *Financial Times*, 1 March 2007.

and Korean models once the Chinese telecoms infrastructure has been modernised. Clearly, after China has introduced its Next-Generation Network (NGN) it, like other countries, will be confronted by the need to deal with the next NGN, courtesy of rapid technical change. By that time, more information will have accumulated to answer the question posed in the heading to this sub-section.

Appendix 10: Companies in our database, by layer

Exhibit A10.1 lists the database companies in layer 1, exhibit A10.2 those in layer 2 and exhibit A10.3 those in layer 3.

Exhibit A10.1. *Database companies in layer 1*

Company	Area	Sector
3Com	US	Telecoms Equipment
Acer	US	IT
Akamai Technologies	US	IT
Alcatel/Lucent	EU	Telecoms Equipment
AMD Technologies	US	IT
Apple	US	IT
Avaya	US	Telecoms Equipment
Business Objects SA	EU	IT
Cisco Systems	US	Telecoms Equipment
Computer Associates	US	IT
Computer Sciences Corporation	US	IT
Dell	US	IT
Electronic Data System Corp.	US	IT
Ericsson	EU	Telecoms Equipment
Fujitsu	Asia	Telecoms Equipment
Safran-Sagem[1]	EU	Telecoms Equipment
HP	US	IT
IBM[1]	US	IT
Intel Corp.	US	IT
Juniper Networks	US	Telecoms Equipment
Kyocera Corp	Asia	IT
LG Electronics	Asia	IT
Logitech International SA	EU	IT
Lucent Technologies	US	Telecoms Equipment
Matsushita	Asia	IT

Exhibit A10.1. (*cont.*)

Company	Area	Sector
Microsoft[1]	US	IT
Motorola	US	Telecoms Equipment
NEC	Asia	Telecoms Equipment
Nintendo	Asia	IT
Nokia	EU	Telecoms Equipment
Nortel	US	Telecoms Equipment
Palm Inc.	US	IT
Philips	EU	IT
Qualcomm Inc.	US	Telecoms Equipment
Samsung	Asia	IT
Sharp Corporation	Asia	IT
Siemens[1]	EU	Telecoms Equipment
Sony	Asia	IT
ST Microelectronics	EU	IT
Sumitomo (electronic indus.)[1]	Asia	IT
Sun Microsystems	US	IT
Symantec Corp	US	IT
Tellabs	US	Telecoms Equipment
Texas	US	IT
Thomson (ex. TMM)	EU	IT
Tomtom NV	EU	IT
Toshiba	Asia	IT
UTStarcom	US	Telecoms Equipment
Wincor Nixdorf AG	EU	IT
ZTE	Asia	Telecoms Equipment

Note: [1] Only for the part of their business in layer 1.

Exhibit A10.2. *Database companies in layer 2*

Company	Area	Sector
AT&T/SBC	US	Telecom services
AT&T histo.	US	Telecom services
Belgacom	EU	Telecom services
Bell Canada	US	Telecom services
Bellsouth	US	Telecom services
BskyB	EU	Cable/Sat. services
BT	EU	Telecom services
Cable & Wireless	Asia	Telecom services
Cablevision	US	Cable/Sat. services
China Mobile	Asia	Telecom services
China Telecom	Asia	Telecom services
China Unicom	Asia	Telecom services
COLT Telecom Group	EU	Telecom services
Comcast	US	Cable/Sat. services
Cox	US	Cable/Sat. services
DirectTV	US	Cable/Sat. services
DT	EU	Telecom services
Echostar Com. Corp.	US	Cable/Sat. services
Eutelia	EU	Telecom services
Fastweb	EU	Telecom services
Freenet AG	EU	Telecom services
FT	EU	Telecom services
Iliad	EU	Telecom services
Jupiter Telecom. Co Ltd	Asia	Cable/Sat. services
KDDI	Asia	Telecom services
KPN	EU	Telecom services
KT	Asia	Telecom services
Level 3 Com. Inc.	US	Telecom services
Mobile Telesystems	EU	Telecom services
NeufCegetel	EU	Telecom services
Nextel	US	Telecom services
NTT	Asia	Telecom services
Portugal Telecom	EU	Telecom services
Qwest Com.	US	Telecom services
Rogers Com. Inc	Can.	Telecom services
SKT	Asia	Telecom services
Sogecable	EU	Cable/Sat. services
SprintNextel	US	Telecom services

Exhibit A10.2. (*cont.*)

Company	Area	Sector
Swisscom	EU	Telecom services
Tele2	EU	Telecom services
Telecom Italia	EU	Telecom services
Telefonica	EU	Telecom services
TeliaSonera	EU	Telecom services
Telstra Corp.Ltd	Austr.	Telecom services
Tiscali SpA	EU	Telecom services
Verizon	US	Telecom services
Viacom	US	Cable/Sat. services
Vivendi (SFR)[1]	EU	Telecom services
Vodafone	EU	Telecom services

Note: [1] Only for the part of its business in layer 2.

Exhibit A10.3. *Database companies in layer 3*

Company	Area	Sector
Akamai Technologies	US	Software & services
Amazon	US	Internet & e-commerce
Antena 3 SA	EU	Content
Atos	EU	Software & services
Boursorama	EU	Internet & e-commerce
Canal+	EU	Content
Cap Gemini	EU	Software & services
CBS Corporation	US	Content
Clear Channel Com. Inc.	US	Content
Comdirect bank AG	EU	Internet & e-commerce
Computer Associates	US	Software & services
Dassault System	EU	Software & services
E*Trade Financial Corp.	US	Internet & e-commerce
Ebay-Skype	US	Internet & e-commerce
Electronic Arts	US	Content
EMI	EU	Content
Endemol NV	EU	Content
Expedia	US	Internet & e-commerce
Fuji TV	Asia	Content

Exhibit A10.3. (*cont.*)

Company	Area	Sector
Gestevision Telecinco SA	EU	Content
Google	US	Internet & e-commerce
IAC	US	Internet & e-commerce
IBM[1]	US	Software & services
IG Group Holdings PLC	EU	Internet & e-commerce
ITV PLC	EU	Content
Lagardère[1]	EU	Content
Liberty Media Corp.	US	Content
M6	EU	Content
Mediaset	EU	Content
Microsoft[1]	US	Internet & e-commerce
Monster	US	Internet & e-commerce
News Corp.	US	Content
NHK	Asia	Content
Oracle	US	Software & services
Partygaming PLC	EU	Internet & e-commerce
Pearson PLC	EU	Content
Premiere	EU	Content
Priceline	US	Internet & e-commerce
Rakuten	Asia	Internet & e-commerce
RTL Group	EU	Content
Salesforce Com, Inc.	US	Internet & e-commerce
SAP	EU	Software & services
Telecom Italia Media	EU	Content
TF1	EU	Content
Thomson Corp.	US	Content
Time Warner	US	Content
Ubisoft	EU	Software & services
United Internet AG	EU	Internet & e-commerce
Verisign Inc.	US	Software & services
Vivendi	EU	Content
Walt Disney	US	Content
Yahoo!	US	Internet & e-commerce
Yahoo! BB Japan	Asia	Internet & e-commerce

Note: [1] Only for the part of their business in layer 3.

Bibliography

Abbate, J., 1999. *Inventing the Internet*. Cambridge, MA: MIT Press

Aghion, P. and Howitt, P., 2006. 'Joseph Schumpeter Lecture: Appropriate Growth Policy. A Unifying Framework'. *Journal of the European Economic Association*, 4, 2–3: 269–314

Ake, B.Å., 1988. *Innovation as an Interactive Process: From User-Producer Interaction to the National System of Innovation*. London: Pinter

Alleman, J. and Rappoport, P., 2005. 'Regulatory Failure: Time for a New Policy Paradigm'. *Communications & Strategies*, 60, 4: 105–21

Antonelli, C., 1999. *The Microdynamics of Technological Change*. London: Routledge

2001. *The Microeconomics of Technological Systems*. Oxford: Oxford University Press

2002. *The Economics of Innovation, New Technologies and Structural Change*. London: Routledge

(ed.) 2006. *New Frontiers in the Economics of Innovation and New Technology: Essays in Honour of Paul A. David*. Cheltenham: Edward Elgar

Battelle, J., 2005. *The Search: How Google and its Rivals Rewrote the Rules of Business and Transformed Our Culture*. Boston, MA: Nicholas Brealey

Booth, P., 2006. 'Processes and Institutions: New Perspectives on Policy Making and Regulatory Authorities', in E. Richards, R. Foster and T. Kiedrowski (eds.), *Communications: The Next Decade. A Collection of Essays Prepared for the UK Office of Communications*. London: Ofcom

Brock, G. W., 1994. *Telecommunication Policy for the Information Age: From Monopoly to Competition*. Cambridge, MA: Harvard University Press

Buigues, P. A. and Rey, P. (eds.), 2004. *The Economics of Antitrust and Regulation in Telecommunications: Perspectives for the New European Regulatory Framework*. Cheltenham: Edward Elgar

Cantner, U. and Malerba, F. (eds.), 2007. *Innovation, Industrial Dynamics and Structural Transformation: Schumpeterian Legacies.* Berlin: Springer

Cave, M., 1997. 'The Evolution of Telecommunications Regulation in the UK'. *European Economic Review*, 41: 691–9

Cave, M. *et al.* (eds.), 2005. *Handbook of Telecommunications Economics: Vol. 1. Structure, Regulation and Competition.* Amsterdam: Elsevier

Cerf, V., 1989. The Internet Activities Board, Internet Engineering Task Force (IETF), Network Working Group, Request for Comments, RFC 1120

1993. 'How the Internet Came to Be', in B. Aboba (ed.), *The Online User's Encyclopedia.* Reading, MA: Addison-Wesley

Chapuis, R. J. and Joel, A. E., 1990. *100 Years of Telephone Switching, II.: Electronics, Computers and Telephone Switching. A Book of Technological History, 1960–1985.* Amsterdam: North-Holland

Commission Guidelines (2002). 'Commission Guidelines on Market Analysis and the Assessment of Significant Market Power Under the Community Regulatory Framework for Electronic Communications Networks and Services', 11 July 2002. 2002/C 165/03

Conceicao, P., Heitor, M. V. and Lundval, B.-Å., 2003. *Innovation, Competence Building, and Social Cohesion in Europe: Towards a Learning Society.* Cheltenham: Edward Elgar

Cowan, R. and Foray, D., 1997. 'The Economics of Codification and the Diffusion of Knowledge'. *Industrial and Corporate Change*, 6, 3: 595–622

Crandall, R. W., 2005. *Competition and Chaos: US Telecommunications Since the 1996 Telecom Act.* Washington, DC: Brookings Institution Press

Crandall, R. W. and Alleman, J. H., 2002. *Broadband: Should we Regulate High-Speed Internet Access?* Washington, DC: AEI – Brookings Joint Center for Regulatory Studies

Crandall, R. W. and Waverman, L., 1996. *Talk is Cheap: Declining Costs, New Competition and Regulatory Reform in Telecommunications.* Washington, DC: Brookings Institution Press

David, P. A. and Steinmueller, W. E., 1994. 'Economics of Compatibility Standards and Competition in Telecommunications Networks'. *Information Economics and Policy*, 6: 217–42

Dedrick, J. and Kraemer, K. L., 1998. *Asia's Computer Challenge.* Oxford: Oxford University Press

Desai, A., 2006. *India's Telecommunications Industry.* London: Sage

De Sola Pool, I. and Noam, E. M. (eds.), 1990. *Technologies without Boundaries: On Telecommunications in a Global Age.* Cambridge, MA: Harvard University Press

Directive 2002/19/EC (2002). 'Directive 2002/19/EC of the European Parliament and of the Council of 7 March 2002 on Access to, and Interconnection of, Electronic Communications Networks and Associated Facilities (Access Directive)'. Official Journal of the European Communities, L 108/7

Directive 2002/20/EC (2002). 'Directive 2002/20/EC of the European Parliament and of the Council of 7 March 2002 on the Authorisation of Electronic Communications Networks and Services (Authorisation Directive)'. Official Journal of the European Communities, L 108/21

Directive 2002/21/EC (2002). 'Directive 2002/21/EC of the European Parliament and of the Council on a Common Regulatory Framework for Electronic Communications Networks and Services (Framework Directive)', 7 March 2002. Official Journal of the European Communities, L 108/33

Dosi, G. and Nelson, R. R., 1998. 'Evolutionary Theories', in R. Arena and C. Longhi (eds.), *Markets and Organization*. Berlin: Springer: 205–34

Dosi, G., Teece, D. J. and Chytry, J. (eds.), 1998. *Technology Organization, and Competitiveness: Perspectives on Industrial and Corporate Change*. New York: Oxford University Press

The Economist, 2007. Special Report. 10 February

Edquist, C., 2004. 'The Fixed Internet and Mobile Telecommunications Sectoral System of Innovation: Equipment Production, Access Provision and Content Provision', in F. Malerba (ed.), *Sectoral Systems of Innovation: Concepts, Issues and Analyses of Six Major Sectors in Europe*. Cambridge: Cambridge University Press

  2005. 'Systems of Innovation: Perspectives and Challenges', in J. Fagerberg, D. C. Mowery and R. R. Nelson (eds.), *The Oxford Handbook of Innovation*. Oxford: Oxford University Press

Edquist, C. and McKelvey, M., 2000. *Systems of Innovation: Growth, Competitiveness and Employment: Vol. II*. Cheltenham: Edward Elgar

Eisenmann, T. R., Parwer, G. and Van Alstyne, M. 2008. '*Opening Platforms: How, When and Why?*', Harvard Business School Working Paper, 09–030

European Commission, 1999. '*Towards a New Framework for Electronic Communications Infrastructure and Associated Services: The 1999 Communications Review*'. COM (1999), 539

  2000. '*The Results of the Public Consultation on the 1999 Communications Review and Orientations for the New Regulatory Framework*'. COM (2000), 239 final

Fagerberg, J., Mowery, D. C. and Nelson, R. R. (eds.), 2005. *The Oxford Handbook of Innovation*. Oxford: Oxford University Press

Foray, D., 2004. *Economics of Knowledge*. Cambridge, MA: MIT Press

Fransman, M., 1986. 'International Competitiveness, International Diffusion of Technology and the State: A Case Study from Taiwan and Japan'. *World Development*, 14, 12: 1375–96

   1988. 'The Japanese System and the Acquisition, Assimilation and Further Development of Technological Knowledge: Organizational Form, Markets and Government', in B. Elliott (ed.), *Technology and Social Process*. Edinburgh: Edinburgh University Press

   1990. *The Market and Beyond: Information Technology in Japan*. Cambridge: Cambridge University Press

   1991. 'What We Know About the Japanese Innovation System and What We Need to Know', in H. Inose *et al.* (eds.), *Science and Technology Policy Research*. Tokyo: MITA: 445–64

   1993. *The Market and Beyond: Information Technology in Japan*. Cambridge: Cambridge University Press (awarded the 1991 Masayoshi Ohira Memorial Prize)

   1994a. 'The Japanese Innovation System: How it Works', in M. Dodgson and R. Rothwell (eds.), *The Handbook of Industrial Innovation*. Aldershot: Edward Elgar

   1994b. 'Information, Knowledge, Vision and Theories of the Firm'. *Industrial and Corporate Change*, 3, 2: 1–45, reprinted in G. Dosi, D. J. Teece and J. Chytry (eds.), *Technology, Organization, and Competitiveness: Perspectives on Industrial and Corporate Change*. New York: Oxford University Press, 1998

   1994c. 'AT&T, BT and NTT: A Comparison of Vision, Strategy and Competence'. *Telecommunications Policy*, 18, 2: 137–53

   1994d. 'AT&T, BT and NTT: The Role of R&D'. *Telecommunications Policy*, 18, 4: 295–305

   1995a. *Japan's Computer and Communications Industry: The Evolution of Industrial Grants and Global Competitiveness*. Oxford: Oxford University Press

   1995b. 'Is National Technology Policy Obsolete in a Globalised World?: The Japanese Response'. *Cambridge Journal of Economics*, 19: 95–119

   1996. 'The Future of Japanese Telecommunications'. *Telecommunications Policy*, 20, 2: 83–8

   1997. 'Towards a New Agenda for Japanese Telecommunications'. *Telecommunications Policy*, 21, 2: 185–94

   1999a. *Viscous of Innovation: The Firm and Japan*. Oxford: Oxford University Press

   1999b. 'Where Are the Japanese? Japanese Information and Communications Firms in an Internetworked World'. *Telecommunications Policy*, 23: 317–33

2001. 'Evolution of the Telecommunications Industry into the Internet Age'. *Communications & Strategies*, 43, 3: 57–113

2002a. *Telecoms in the Internet Age: From Boom to Bust to ...?* Oxford: Oxford University Press (awarded the 2003 Wadsworth Prize)

2002b. 'Mapping the Evolving Telecoms Industry: The Uses and Shortcomings of the Layer Model'. *Telecommunications Policy*, 26, 9/10: 473–84

2003. 'Evolution of the Telecommunications Industry', in G. Madden (ed.), *The International Handbook of Telecommunications Economics: Vol. III*. Aldershot: Edward Elgar: 15–38

2004. 'The Telecoms Boom and Bust 1996–2003 and the Role of Financial Markets'. *Journal of Evolutionary Economics*, 14, 4: 369–406

(ed.) 2006. *Global Broadband Battles: Why the US and Europe Lag While Asia Leads*. Palo Alto, CA: Stanford University Press

2007a. 'Innovation in the New ICT Ecosystem'. *Communications and Strategies*, 68, 4: 1–22

2007b. *The New ICT Ecosystem – Implications for Europe*. Edinburgh: Koroko (awarded the 2008–9 Joseph Schumpeter Price)

2009. *How Innovation Happens and What Should be Done to Encourage It*, paper prepared for the OECD Innovation Strategy. Paris: OECD

Fransman, M. and Krafft, J., 2002. 'Telecommunications Industry', in W. Lazonick (ed.), *The Handbook of Economics: International Encyclopedia of Business and Management*. London: Thomson

Freeman, C., 1987. *Technology Policy and Economic Performance: Lessons from Japan*. London: Pinter

Freeman, C. and Louca, F., 2002. *As Time Goes By: From the Industrial Revolutions to the Information Revolution*. Oxford: Oxford University Press

Freidman, T., 2006. *The World is Flat: The Globalized World in the 21st Century*. London: Penguin

Gawer, A. (ed.), 2009. *Platforms, Markets and Innovation*. Cheltenham, UK and Northampton, MA: Edward Elgar

Gawer, A. and Cusumano, M., 2006. *Platform Leadership*. Boston, MA: Harvard Business School Press

Gruber, H., 2005. *The Economics of Mobile Telecommunications*. Cambridge: Cambridge University Press

Haddon, L., 2005. *Everyday Innovators: Researching the Role of Users in Shaping ICTs*. Dordrecht: Springer

Hayek, F. A., 1945. 'The Use of Knowledge in Society'. *American Economic Review*, 35, 4: 519–30

Humphreys, P. and Simpson, S., 2005. *Globalisation, Convergence and European Telecommunications Regulation*. Cheltenham: Edward Elgar

International Standards Organisation (ISO), 1994. *Information Technology – Open Systems Interconnection – Basic Reference Model: The Basic Model.* Geneva: ISO

Johnson, C., 1982. *MITI and the Japanese Miracle.* Stanford, CA: Stanford University Press

Kahin, B. and Foray, D. (eds.), 2006. *Advancing Knowledge and the Knowledge Economy.* Cambridge, MA: MIT Press

Katz, J. E. (ed.), 2003. *Machines that Become Us: The Social Context of Personal Communication Technology.* New Brunswick, NJ: Transaction Publishers

Kelly, K., 2003. *Out of Control: The New Biology of Machines, Social Systems and the Economic World.* Reading, MA: Addison-Wesley

Keynes, J. M., 1936. *The General Theory of Employment, Interest and Money.* London: Macmillan

Kim, L., 1997. *Imitation to Innovation: The Dynamics of Korea's Technological Learning.* Boston, MA: Harvard Business School Press

Komiya, R., Okuno, M. and Suzumura, K. (eds.), 1988. *Industrial Policy of Japan.* San Diego: Academic Press

Laffont, J.-J., Rey, P. and Tirole, J. 1997. 'Competition between Telecommuni-cations Operators'. *European Economic Review,* 41: 701–11

1998. 'Network Competition: I. Overview and Non-Discriminatory Pricing', *RAND Journal of Economics,* 29: 1–37

Laffont, J.-J. and Tirole, J., 1994. *Creating Competition through Interconnection: Theory and Practice.* Toulouse: IDEI

2000. *Competition in Telecommunications.* Cambridge, MA: MIT Press

Levine, R., Locke, C., Searls, D. and Weinberger, D., 2000. *The Cluetrain Manifesto. The End of Business Usual.* New York: Perseus Books

Levy, B. and Spiller, P. T., 1994. 'The Institutional Foundations of Regulatory Commitment: A Comparative Analysis of Telecommunications Regulation'. *Journal of Law, Economics and Organization,* 10: 201–46

Lo, Andrew W., 2004. 'The Adaptive Markets Hypothesis: Market Efficiency from an Evolutionary Perspective'. *Journal of Portfolio Management, 30th Anniversary Issue 2004:* 15–299

Loasby, B., 2001. 'Organisations as Interpretative Systems'. *Revue d'Économie Industrielle,* 97, 4: 17–34

2003. 'The Innovative Mind', paper presented at the DRUID Summer Conference 2003 on Creating, Sharing and Transferring Knowledge, Copenhagen, 12–14 June

Lu, Q., 2003. *China's Leap into the Information Age: Innovation and Organization in the Computer Industry.* Oxford: Oxford University Press

Lundval, B.-Å., 1988. 'Innovation as an Interactive Process: From User–Producer Interaction to the National System of Innovation', in G. Dosi,

. C. Freeman and R. Nelson (eds.), *Technical Change and Economic Theory*. London: Pinter: 349–69

1992. *National Systems of Innovation: Towards a Theory of Innovation and Interactive Learning*. London: Pinter

2002. *Innovation, Growth and Social Cohesion: The Danish Model*. Cheltenham: Edward Elgar

Lundval, B.-Å., *et al.* 2002. *The New Knowledge Economy in Europe: A Strategy for International Competitiveness and Social Cohesion*. Cheltenham: Edward Elgar

Majumdar, S. K., M. Care and I. Vogelsang (eds.), 2005. *Handbook of Telecommunications Economics: Vol. 2. Technology Evolution and the Internet*. Amsterdam: Elsevier North-Holland

Malerba, F., 1995. 'Schumpeterian Patterns of Innovation'. *Cambridge Journal of Economics*, 19, 1: 47–66

2002. 'Sectoral Systems of Innovation and Production'. *Research Policy*, 31: 247–64

(ed.), 2004. *Sectoral Systems of Innovation: Concepts, Issues and Analyses of Six Major Sectors in Europe*. Cambridge: Cambridge University Press

2005. 'Sectoral Systems: How and Why Innovation Differs across Sectors', in J. Fagerberg, D. C. Mowery and R. R. Nelson (eds.), *The Oxford Handbook of Innovation*. Oxford: Oxford University Press

Malerba, F. and Orsenigo, L., 1990. 'Technological Regimes and Patterns of Innovation: A Theoretical and Empirical Investigation of the Italian Case', in A. Heertje (ed.), *Evolving Industries and Market Structures*. Ann Arbor, MI: University of Michigan Press

Malthus, T., 1798. *An Essay on the Principle of Population*, eds. D. Winch and P. James. Cambridge University Press, 1992

Mansell, R., 1994. *The New Telecommunications: A Political Economy of Network Evolution*. London: Sage

(ed.), 2007. *The Oxford Handbook of Information and Communication Technologies*. Oxford: Oxford University Press

Mansell, R. and Steinmueller, E., 2000. *Mobilizing the Information Society: Strategies for Growth and Opportunity*. New York: Oxford University Press

Margulis, L. and Sagan, D., 1988. *Microcosmos: Four Billion Years of Evolution from Our Microbial Ancestors*. New York: Summit Books

Marshall, A. 1885. *The Present Position of Economics*. London: Macmillan & Co. 1889. 'Co-operation', in *Memorials of Alfred Marshall*, A.C. Pigou (ed.). London: Macmillan & Co., 1925: 227–55

1890. *Principles of Economics*, 8th edn. London: Macmillan 1962

1920a. *Principles of Economics*, ed. With annotations by C. W. Guillebaud, 2 vols. London: Macmillan & Co., 1961

1920b. *Industry and Trade: A Study of Industrial Technique and Business Organization; and of Their Influences on the Conditions of Various Classes and Nations.* London: Macmillan & Co.

Metcalfe, J. S., 1995. 'Technology Systems and Technology Policy in an Evolutionary Framework'. *Cambridge Journal of Economics*, 19, 1: 25–46

1998. *Evolutionary Economics and Creative Destruction: The Graz Schumpeter Lectures.* London: Routledge

2002. 'Knowledge of Growth and the Growth of Knowledge'. *Journal of Evolutionary Economics*, 12, 1–2: 3–16

2004. 'The Entrepreneur and the Style of Modern Economics'. *Journal of Evolutionary Economics*, 14, 2: 157–76

Meurling, J., 1985. *A Switch in Time.* Chicago: Telephony Publishing Co

Millman, S. (ed.), 1984. *A History of Engineering and Science in the Bell System: Communications Sciences (1925–1980).* Murray Hill, NJ: AT&T Bell Laboratories

Mindel, J. L. and Sicker, D. C., 2006. 'Leveraging the EU Regulatory Framework to Improve a Layered Policy Model for US Telecommunications Markets'. *Telecommunications Policy*, 30, 2: 136–48

Ministry of Internal Affairs and Communications (MIC), 2007. '2007 White Paper: Information and Communications in Japan. Progress of Ubiquitous Economy and Global Business Development'. Tokyo, July

Morton, J. A., 1971. *Organizing for Innovation: A Systems Approach to Technical Management.* New York: McGraw-Hill

Mowery, D. C. and Nelson, R. R. (eds.), 1999. *Sources of Industrial Leadership: Studies of Seven Industries.* Cambridge: Cambridge University Press

Nelson, R. R., 1998. 'The Co-evolution of Technology Industrial Structure and Supporting Institutions', in G. Dosi, D. J. Teece and J. Chytry (eds.), *Technology Organization and Competitiveness: Perspectives on Industrial and Corporate Change.* New York: Oxford University Press

2002. 'Bringing Institutions into Evolutionary Growth Theory'. *Journal of Evolutionary Economics*, 12, 1–2: 17–28

(ed.), 1993. *National Innovation Systems: A Comparative Analysis.* New York: Oxford University Press

2005. *The Limits of Market Organization.* New York: Russell Sage

Nelson, R. R. and Winter, S. G., 1982. *An Evolutionary Theory of Economic Change.* Cambridge MA: Harvard University Press

Nihoul, P. and Rodford, P., 2004. *EU Electronic Communications Law: Competition and Regulation in the European Telecommunications Market.* Oxford: Oxford University Press

Noam, E. M., 1994. 'Beyond Liberalization: From the Network of Networks to the System of Systems'. *Telecommunications Policy*, 18: 286–94

North, D., 1990. *Institutions, Institutional Change and Economic Performance*. Cambridge: Cambridge University Press

Nuechterlien, J. E. and Weiser, P. J., 2005. *American Telecommunications Policy in the Internet Age*. Cambridge, MA: MIT Press

Ofcom, 2006. *Communications–The Next Decade: A Collection of Essays Prepared for the UK Office of Communications*, eds. E. Richards, R. Foster and T. Kiedrowski. London: Ofcom

Organisation for Economic Cooperation and Development (OECD), 2007. Various dates. *Science, Technology and Industry Scoreboard*. Paris: OECD

O'Reilly, T., 2007. 'What is Web 2.0. Design Patterns and Business Models for the Next Generation of Software'. *Communications & Strategies*, 65: 17–37

Pavitt, K., 1999. *Technology, Management and Systems of Innovation*. Cheltenham: Edward Elgar

Petit, P. and Soete, L. (eds.), 2001. *Technology and the Future of European Employment*. Northampton, MA: Edward Elgar

Reich, L. S., 1985. *The Making of American Industrial Research: Science and Business at GE and Bell, 1876–1926*. Cambridge: Cambridge University Press

Rosenberg, N., 1982. *Inside the Black Box: Technology and Economics*. Cambridge: Cambridge University Press

Schumpeter, J. A., 1934. *The Theory of Economic Development: An Inquiry into Profits, Capital, Credit, Interest and the Business Cycle*. New York: Oxford University Press

  1943. *Capitalism, Socialism and Democracy*. London: Unwin

  1954. *History of Economic Analysis*. New York: Oxford University Press

  1961. *Theory of Economic Development*. New York: Oxford University Press

Shapiro, C. and Varian, H. R., 1999. *Information Rules: A Strategic Guide to the Network Economy*. Boston, MA: Harvard Business School Press

Shelanski, H. A., 2005. 'Inter-Modal Competition and Telecommunications Policy in the United States'. *Communications & Strategies*, 60: 15–37

Silverstone, R. (ed.), 2005. *Media, Technology and Everyday Life in Europe: From Information to Communication*. Aldershot: Ashgate

Smith, A., 1776. *The Wealth of Nations*. London and New York: J. M. Dent, 1912

Soete, L. and Ter Weel, B., 2005. *The Economics of the Digital Society*. Cheltenham: Edward Elgar

Steinmueller, W. E., 2000. 'Will New Information and Communication Technologies Improve the "Codification" of Knowledge?'. *Industrial and Corporate Change*, 9, 2: 361–76

Sterling, C., Bernt, P. W. and Weiss, M. H., 2006. *Shaping American Telecommunications: A History of Technology, Policy and Economics.* New Jersey: Lawrence Erlbaum

Tapscott, D. and Williams, A. D., 2006. *How mass collaboration Changes Everything.* New York: Portfolio

Thomke, S. and von Hippel, E., 2002. 'Customers as Innovators: A New Way to Create Value'. *Harvard Business Review*, 1 April

UBS, 2007. *Global Equity Strategy.* UBS Investment Research, 7 February

Van Ark, B., Inklar, R. and McGuckin, R., 2002. 'Changing Gear: Productivity, ICT and Services: Europe and the United States'. GGDC Working Papers, GD 60

Varian, H. R., Farrell, J. and Shapiro, C., 2004. *The Economics of Information Technology: An Introduction.* Cambridge: Cambridge University Press

Vogelsang, I., 2002. 'Incentive Regulation and Competition in Public Utility Markets: A 20-year Perspective'. *Journal of Regulatory Economics*, 22, 1: 5–27

Von Hippel, E., 1988. *The Source of Innovation.* Oxford: Oxford University Press

1998. 'Economics of Product Development by Users: The Impact of "Sticky" Local Information'. *Management Science*, 44, 5: 629–44

Walden, I. and Angel, J. (eds.), 2005. *Telecommunications Law and Regulation.* Oxford: Oxford University Press

Waverman, L. and Sirel, E., 1997. 'European Telecommunications Markets on the Verge of Full Liberalization'. *Journal of Economic Perspectives*, 11, 4: 113–26

Wessner, C. W., 2006. *The Telecommunications Challenge: Changing Technologies and Evolving Policies. Measuring and Sustaining the New Economy.* Washington, DC: The National Academies Press

Witt, U., 2001. 'Economic Growth – What Happens on the Demand Side?'. *Journal of Evolutionary Economics*, 11, 1: 1–6

Index

238

companies, role in ICT ecosystem
(cont.)
importance of profitability 59: global
differences in 67–70
and investment 59
competition 46
East Asian prominence in networked
elements 197
EU telecoms regulation 142–3, 156:
harmonisation between member
states 144; and innovation 157
future trends in 82, 83
incumbent advantage 158–9
and innovation 163
and international performance 103
key determinant of performance
80, 81
and social welfare maximisation 81
in telecoms sector
and innovation process 17, 18:
causal relationship 18
liberalisation of operator sector
117–18
long-distance markets 118–19
and pricing 119
and regulation 16, 17: in Britain 160;
limitations to 160–2; theory of
perfect competition 159
and technological development 110
see also Access Directive; Dominant
position concept; price theory;
significant market power (SMP)
concept
Computer and Communication
Research Laboratory (CCL) 211
computer industry 113
and ELM 23: networked element in
layer xi–xii, 25
invention of microprocessor
114–15
consumer electronics companies
contribution to E. Asian NIE–IS 86
domination of Asian companies 1
and ELM 23: networked element
in layer xi–xii, 25
consumers
and ICT ecosystem 8, 9, 10
influence of 50
and Internet 51
containerisation, effect on transport 26

content
definition in layer 5 of ELM 30
definition of use in internet
systems 170
contestable markets, theory of 161
controlled competition, in Japanese
telecoms 111
Conway, Ron, investment in Google 190
cooperation, and innovative
capability 15
Corning glass company, and optical
fibre 132
creative destruction, *see* Schumpeter,
Joseph
culture, effect of Internet and media 7
Cusumano, M., platforms xviii, xx

Daewoo
and consumer electronics 201
entry to ICT sector 208
Daini Den Den 118
Darwin, Charles
and Schumpeterian Evolutionary
Economics Paradigm (SEEP) 20
survival of species xiv
theory of evolution xiv, 165: and new
ICT ecosystem 35
Datang 198, 199
and TD-SCDMA 220
Davies, Donald, British National
Physical Laboratories, and packet
switching 116
DDI, and NTT 16, 74
Dedrick, J., Asian computer industry 209
Dell, relationships with ICAPs 45
demand-side substitution, and
competition 149
Den Den Family 200
equipment suppliers 110–11, 203
government assistance for 203
innovation incentives 203
investment incentives 202
dense wave division multiplexing
(DWDM) 122
Deutsche Telekom
investment incentives for
Next-Generation Network (NGN)
78: and regulation 135
and T-Online 27–8
Digital Equipment (DEC) 114

Grove, Andy, and Intel 114
Grubman, Jack, financial scandal 123
GSM 1

Hanaro 67
Hayek, Friedrich, knowledge and
    society 98
Hellström, Kurt, Ericsson mobile
    systems 126
High Level Communications Group 144
Hitachi
    and communications infrastructure
        201–2
    and Den Den Family 203
    global competitiveness of 198
Hoff, Ted, and Intel 114
Hon Hai Precision, and ICT industry 214
Howitt, P.
    product–market competition 18
    theory of growth policy 163
Huawei 198, 199, 202
Hundt, Reed, investment in Next-
    Generation facilities 83
Hurley, Chad, and YouTube 175, 184
    role of university 192
Hynix (formerly Hyundai) 205, 206
hypothetical monopolist test 150
Hyundai
    and consumer electronics 201
    entry to ICT sector 208
    see also Hynix

IBM 73, 206
    domination of computer industry 113
    effect of technological development 113
    and internet service provision 170–2
    microcomputers and outsourcing
        decision 114
    Taiwanese cloning of BIOS 211, 213
ICT ecosystem 8
    and benchmarking 103
    coordination problems 105–6
    and innovation 1, 102, 103
    layers of 102
    and platforms xix: global change in xx
    and regulation 2
    symbiotic relationships in 37–8,
        47, 53–4: between ICAPs and
        final customers 43, 44;
        between operators and final

customers 43; between operators
    and suppliers 41–2; between
    operators and suppliers and
    ICAPs 45; dimensions of 37;
    influences on 46–7; with other
    ecosystems 47; within firms
    see also international competition;
    Internet; new ICT ecosystem;
    telecoms regulation
ICT sector
    classification of 21–2
    competition and innovation in 103
    convergence of prior technologies 108
    description in ELM 25
    importance of 3, 102
    and Internet 108–9
    performance of xiii
    productivity gap between Europe
        and USA and Japan 6, 7
    role of new technologies xi–xii
    transformation to new ICT
        ecosystem 3
    see also ICT ecosystem; Internet
    technologies
Ida, Takanori, Japanese broadband 92
IDG, investment in Baidu 188
Index Ventures, investment in Skype 191
Industrial Technology Research
    Institute (ITRI) 210–11
    work in computers 211
information flows, and innovation
    process 40
information technology, and ICT sector
    classification 22
Inklar, Robert, ICT productivity 19
innovation 34
    consumers' role 50
    and DRPT 77, 78–9: assumption of
        exogeneity 79–80; competition
        as central determinant of 18, 19,
        81, 85; failure to deal with
        endogenous innovation 80;
        international competition
    evolutionary process 34
    and firm in evolutionary economics 166
    forms of 35
    and institutions 166
    and Internet 51
    and investment 19, 42–3: in Japanese
        NIE-IS 92

Printed in the United States
by Baker & Taylor Publisher Services